NO SURRENDER

NO SURRENDER

The story of William E. Johns, DSM,
Chief Ordnance Artificer
and how he survived after the
eventual sinking of
HMS *Exeter* in the Java Sea
in March 1942

by

W. E. JOHNS and R. A. KELLY

With a Foreword by
ADMIRAL SIR FRANK TWISS
KCB., KCVO, DSC

W H ALLEN

TO THE MEN OF HMS *EXETER*

First published in Great Britain in 1969
by George G. Harrap & Co Ltd.

This edition published in 1989 by
W. H. Allen & Co Plc,
Sekforde House,
175–179 St John Street, London EC1V 4LL

Printed and bound in Great Britain by
Mackays of Chatham PLC, Chatham, Kent

ISBN 1 85227 151 5

This is not merely my story, but the story of a gallant ship and her two wartime crews, serving, fighting, and dying in two different theatres of war. I remember with humility, but my heart thumps with pride for having been granted the privilege of serving with them.

W. E. JOHNS

ACKNOWLEDGMENTS

The authors wish to thank the men of *Exeter* and the Celebes who have helped and encouraged the completion of this book, and particularly to thank for their reminiscing: Mr Roy Ruse, ex CERA, HMS *Exeter*; Mr Herbert Diggle, ex-Chief Gunner's Mate, HMS *Exeter*; Lieutenant-Commander Arthur Carne, RN (retd), ex-HMS *Exeter*; Dr A. J. P. Borstlap, ARS, Dutch Army; Mr Tom ('Daisy') Adams, ex-CPO, HMS *Exeter*; Mr Cyril ('Putty') Churchward, ex-PO, Painter, HMS *Exeter*; Mr John ('Geordie') Wilkinson, ex-Stoker 1st Class, HMS *Exeter*; Mr Sam Langford, ex-Boy, HMS *Exeter*; Surgeon Commander R. W. G. Lancashire, DSC, RN, ex-HMS *Exeter*.

Mr B. ('Shorty') Howell, Leading Seaman on the *Exeter's* first commission, kindly permitted the use of his photographs of damage to *Exeter* in the Plate action.

Mr Reginald Lumley, naval historian, advised and checked details, particularly of ship classes and dispositions in the Far East sea battles.

Sir Eugen Millington-Drake, KCMG, kindly provided additional material on the Montevideo story.

The report on conditions at Pamalla is included by kind permission of Major John H. McCahon, RM.

For this edition the author wishes to thank sincerely these senior officers and friends of many years for their kind contributions to a story of ships, men and bravery during the Second World War:

Admiral Sir Desmond Dreyer, GCB, CBE, DSC, HMS *Ajax*, Gunnery Officer; Captain John Mott, LVO, Royal Navy, Damage Control Officer, HMS *Exeter*; Commander R. B. Jennings, DSO, DSC and bar, Royal Navy, Gunnery Officer and First Lieutenant, HMS *Exeter*; Commander G. C. H. W. Fowler, Royal Navy, Observer and Signals Officer, HMS *Exeter*; Lieutenant Charles Rendle, MBE, DSC, Royal Navy, Shipwright Officer, HMS *Exeter*; Mr Robert Olausen, who was a boy aboard HM New Zealand Ship (HMNZS) *Achilles*, and is now Hon. Sec. of the HMNZS *Achilles* River Plate Veteran's Association (New Zealand).

Note to 1989 Edition
Since the first edition was published, in 1969, most of the people mentioned in the narrative have either retired or died.

W.E.J.

FOREWORD
by Admiral Sir Frank Twiss, KCB, KCVO, DSC

IT IS A great compliment to be invited to write a foreword to a book. It is even more so in this case for the narrator and many of the characters in the book are old Shipmates and respected friends.

The story here recounted will revive memories for many men who were made prisoners of war when the Japanese overran South East Asia. The story too will appeal to a great many others for it tells of a fine ship and a fine spirit.

The ship—HMS *Exeter*—had the tables turned on her in a cruel and dramatic way. Having played a leading part in the historic action which drove the German battleship *Graf Spee* into Montevideo for repairs and respite, the *Exeter* found herself in a somewhat similar situation less than two and a half years later and on the other side of the world in Sourabaya.

The books recounts the circumstances of this poignant turn of events and what followed. As you read the tale, the spirit of the men who manned HMS *Exeter* emerges clearly in the telling; a spirit and a comradeship which could not be quenched by danger or difficulty, by hardship or oppression. I know from my experience that this is typical of the sailor and the Navy.

It is small wonder therefore that I accepted with gratitude the offer of writing a foreword to this story of a friend who served HMS *Exeter* throughout the 1939–45 war and who continues to serve his Shipmates to this day.

CONTENTS

NO SURRENDER

PRELUDE

'THERE IS blood, and I see a fence or wall. It is insurmountable.'
The fortune-teller fell silent for a moment as she shifted the cards
nervously in her hands. 'Also I see pain and cruelty for a long while,
and — something which is difficult for me to understand . . .' She
stopped once more, a puzzled look on her face. In the silence we
could hear the continual croaking of the bullfrogs from the nearby
lake.

The evening was warm; the party a friendly one; the place a
delightful house in the millionaire's paradise of Miami; but the
Southern tones of that voice had struck a macabre note I had not
expected. Cards and tea-leaves were all right for a lark, but to have
the fortune-teller cover her face with her hands after the first sight
of the cards — this took some accepting. Our host spent a long time
persuading her to continue.

'I do not see death — but a living hell.' Then, without another
word, she gathered in the cards and hurriedly left the room.

I remember feeling strangely uneasy, yet puzzled why I should.
After all, it was a private party, and a fortune-teller was always good
for some harmless fun. There we were, a little bunch of Chief Petty
Officers enjoying a run ashore, nearly at the end of a ship's commission which had been anything but hell. From our quiet and
peaceful base at Bermuda we had steamed out on exercises or to
show the flag, enjoying the carefree atmosphere of countries whose
people were warm, friendly and charming. Rio, Buenos Aires, Montevideo, Valparaiso, South Georgia, Trinidad, Barbados — the list of

places we had visited was as long as your arm and read like the brochure of a luxury cruise.

Now it was June 1939, and we sat sipping our iced drinks in the warmth of a Miami evening, hoping that it would not be long before we were supping our beer back in Plymouth.

Blood, death, and hell? For nearly three years we had basked in sunshine, had played football, cricket, sailed and splashed away at water-polo. We had worked, certainly—extensive torpedo and gunnery exercises, combined-operations practice, and long cruises to show the flag in the vast ocean territory accorded to us. Sometimes these duties had been strenuous, and the weather had not always been perfect; but we felt that we had been lucky with our station.

There had been a murky side. We had left England in foul weather, the subsequent sunshine throwing into violent relief the dirty, driving rain that had formed puddles on the dockside. 31 December 1936. HMS *Exeter* leaving Devonport on another commission. Eight thousand tons of lightly armoured cruiser bound on a peace-time spell of duty operating between South America and the West Indies.

I could clearly recall that morning on the jetty—the Mayor of Exeter, handsomely robed, the Marines band at full blast, and we members of the new crew doled up in our 'number ones' manning the port side to greet the procession. Much was said about the ties between ship and city, but we were eventually piped to dinner, thankful to be out of the rain and back to our thoughts of the Caribbean warmth that awaited us. For many youngsters this was a first voyage, and they were keen for the adventure to begin.

Sitting drinking an iced highball in that pleasantly furnished house in Miami, I found it difficult to think of any incident that had disturbed the routine of those palmy days. The words of the fortune-teller seemed so irrelevant. There had been problems, dark shadows perhaps, and certainly rumblings beneath the surface in more ways than one—but, blood and hell?

There were the riots in Trinidad, which broke out soon after we had arrived at our base in Bermuda. We had just set off on the first nine-month cruise, with Panama as our first port of call, when this was interrupted by reports on 20 June that there was rioting in the oilfields and that the Governor had called for a warship. HMS *Ajax*, then at Nassau, made full speed for the area, but the situation worsened after a native corporal of police had been burnt. We were called to join *Ajax*, and steamed at thirty knots for Trinidad, arriving on the 23rd after a passage of 1400 miles in under forty-eight hours. Three platoons of seamen, stokers, and Marines were landed and posted in the Port of Spain area, while a Marines detachment was sent to the sugar estate in the Couva area.

Perhaps this could have provided the ingredients for blood and hell, but it turned out to be an anticlimax. At no time were we in contact with the strikers, and by Monday 5 July, there was a general return to work and patrols were back on board by 1615 that day.

There were other instances of proximity to disaster. Our first visit to Valparaiso, in September 1937, had been like finding an oasis in that dusty, dirty Chilean coast, seeing the city—the place of everlasting whoopee—rise in terraced slopes around the bay, against the regal background of the snow-capped Cordillera. On our second visit, 24 January 1939, it was no oasis. The atmosphere was hot and sticky, there was not a breath of air, and as we dropped anchor we noticed an ominous tranquillity in the harbour.

I had gone ashore with my shore-going pal, Engine Room Artificer Reg Bolling, relieved to be away from the smell of hot oil that emanated from *Exeter*. Many of us had complained of headaches and lassitude, and aspirins had provided no relief. Perhaps iced beer would do the trick, which was why we steered slowly towards the city and the German bar owned by Willie Muller. This was a focal point for the ship's company, and as we sat at one of the tables outside the bar we were joined by a Chief Petty Officer from the ship. Chiefy, a widower, was very much of a lone wolf, usually wandering ashore by himself, rarely joining any of the usual groups, and then only for a brief intermission before he was away again. So it was this particular evening. He sat with us as we silently sipped our beer in the brief twilight, watching the lights go on and the girls come out. Then we were aware that he was no longer with us.

The night life of Valparaiso had begun. The casinos, cabarets, and theatres were filling, and the dark-eyed girls began to disappear from their positions at the windows overlooking the street. We sat there with our drinks, still conscious of the oppressive atmosphere.

Then we heard a strange rumbling, and the ground began to shake beneath our feet. There were cries of terror as people began to stream out of the houses, rushing to the centre of the road. We moved on to the street with them, curious to know what was happening. I remember Willie Muller's fat wife running past us, mouth open in a long scream, carrying in her arms the huge cash register.

We too were now in the middle of the street, amid the shouting inhabitants, many of them clutching frightened children hurriedly plucked from their beds.

The road shook violently again, and cracks began to appear in the walls of the buildings across the way. Some walls seemed to be on the point of collapse, and we became conscious of the word *terremoto* shouted again and again. Many people lay in terror on the road; others knelt and prayed—and we stood among them clutching our mugs of beer.

Suddenly there was a change in the shouting, and I noticed someone pointing excitedly across the street. I turned to see, framed in the cracking doorway of a house opposite Muller's bar, a portly figure clad only in a vest. It was Chiefy, his clothes, hurriedly retrieved, clutched tightly to his chest. Amid the cheers of shipmates he staggered across to our group and managed to clamber into his uniform, but in the rush he had lost his cap and left shoe.

For others this was no night of humour. The full tragedy of the earthquake was centred on the town of Concepción, where many thousands died and countless more were injured and rendered homeless. *Exeter*, joined by *Ajax* two days later, called at the port of Talcahuano to render what assistance she could, but there was not much that our relatively small numbers could do in such a dreadfully devastated area. There was little doubt, however, that our presence proved a morale-booster, and we returned to Valparaiso with some 350 refugees.

One teenage girl had lost her husband and all her possessions apart from the baby she carried in her arms, a baby that was a few days old. Mother was consigned rapidly to a bed in the sick-bay while her baby was carefully bathed by the Chief and dressed in one of his own vests and a shirt. Later a fund was raised by the ship's company—about thirty pounds—to help them.

The First Lieutenant of *Exeter*, Lieutenant-Commander Jennings, became involved in a stubborn argument with one refugee—an organ-grinder complete with his monkey. 'Jimmy' was adamant, repeating firmly 'No monk!' while the poor organ-grinder groaned his distress at being parted from his business associate. Eventually someone interceded on behalf of the monkey, and the two were allowed to remain aboard, conditional upon the 'act' being deloused.

Valparaiso—earthquake and death, indeed; but surely for us nothing more than another incident in a pleasant cruise. Blood was shed in a less grim warfare which became known as the 'anti-cocker' campaign. Lieutenant-Commander Jennings had opened this very necessary campaign to reduce the complement of cockroaches aboard *Exeter*, and the Marines and seamen who made up the gun crews were as smartly trained in anti-cocker techniques as they were in laying and training the guns.

One Royal Marine, ashore in a San Francisco night club, was enjoying a cool drink while listening to a crooner of somewhat limited and dubious technique. Idly gazing at the floor, he noticed, to his intense horror, a cockroach making passage past his feet. With the instinctive reaction of a cocker-trained rating he drew his walking-cane, brandished it and thumped down upon the cockroach, which meanwhile had taken rapid evasive action. A second thump and more evasive action as the Royal Marine pursued the insect across the floor in a furore of thwacks.

The crooner tried his best, but the clientele were already climbing on to their chairs to watch the new floor show. With rapt concentration the Royal Marine thwacked his way to eventual crushing victory and was met with great applause.

The anti-cocker campaign involved of all things a strange example of cannibalism. When *Exeter* was at Rio the select Country Club at Copocabana invited the Royal Marines band to play for dancing, and there was no doubt that the lads felt this to be the chance of a lifetime. Instrument cases were carefully loaded into the coach to take them to the club, and when they arrived they crossed the dance floor to the band rostrum with supreme aplomb.

The band was a sensation. As the lads unpacked their instruments the naval complement of cockroaches disembarked at speed and spread out over the floor. In a mad, stamping dance the band tried to exterminate them, but help was already on the way—from the hidden recesses of the Club came the native cockers, fiercely and swiftly consuming the invaders.

It had been a huge joke—but so should the fortune-telling have been. I always classed it with the fun we had had when my old pal 'Bunker' Hill used to do his conjuring tricks. Plump, good-natured and full of fun, 'Bunker' would appear dressed as a Chinese mandarin, and his act was known at parties up and down the coast of South America. He often stored his conjuring gear in my workshop on board *Exeter* under the Walrus catapult, where I sometimes found him before supper preparing his routine for the next concert, or giving his silks and garments an ironing.

Perhaps the concert would be at 'Monte'. Of all the wonderful places we had visited, whether in Chile, Brazil, Bolivia, Argentina or the colourful islands of the Indies, our hearts went out to Montevideo. We adopted it as our home port, because in some ways it was like a bit of Britain in a far-off land. We made new friends there and joined the Sunday services in the English church. We found ourselves a reasonable football practice pitch to get our team into training; but in other ways it provided the delights of a foreign capital: cabarets and dance-halls of all kinds, the *asados*—barbecue picnics—and carnivals. There were beautiful beaches and haunts such as Maxim's, Tabaris and Chanticleer. Our only regret was that the beer was not strong enough.

Only one other event had interrupted our tranquil commission. During our stay at Punta del Este, where we were carrying our gunnery and torpedo trials with *Ajax*, we were concerned at the news from Europe, although it seemed very remote and unreal to many of us. Then at 2200 on Sunday, 25 September 1938, we suddenly heard the bugles sound 'Darken Ship', followed almost immediately by 'Side and cable parties muster on the forecastle; special sea duty men to their stations.' A few minutes later we were at sea, darkened completely and heading we knew not where. Early next morning we were out in the Atlantic clear of the Plate, heading north, with gun hoists loaded and crews closed up.

We steamed north for two days, avoiding contact with all shipping during daylight hours and darkening ships at sunset. On the 28th we anchored in Rio de Janeiro and provisioned; but that same evening we were at sea again, continuing our northward progress.

Home Fleet? Gib? The buzzes flew. Then on 4 October we turned south once more, and by the 7th came news that the great fuss was over.

Then there was news of a return home. The strange unease aroused by that Miami fortune-teller dispersed in thoughts of Devon. On 11 July we returned to our base at Bermuda, and on 9 August, with paying-off pennants streaming, we left for England, arriving at Devonport on 17 August 1939. It was good to be home again. We had been away for two years and eight months—a long separation.

Chapter 1

RETURN TO
SOUTH AMERICA

OUR FOREIGN leave was all too short. We were recalled to *Exeter* at Devonport on 23 August, to find that we were to return to South American waters, but this time in an atmosphere of considerable tension. There was a terrible inevitability about events during late August, and we had no illusions about the difficulty of operating in those distant waters. Although most of the countries along the American seaboard were neutral, the memory of the armed raiders of the First World War still remained, and that stretch of sea had been the scene of violent and significant battles. This was to be no return to the fun and cabarets of our favourite 'Monte'.

With the rearrangement of the zones of command, Vice-Admiral Lyon had been appointed C.-in-C. South Atlantic, and we were to be transferred, with HMS *Ajax*, to this new command. Our old skipper, Commodore Henry Harwood, was in command of the South American division, flying his broad pennant in *Exeter*, whose new skipper was Captain S. F. Bell, previously the commander of HMS *Repulse*. Captain Bell could well have been the most junior captain in the Royal Navy at that time, but, junior or not, we thought him a great chap. Within a very short time we knew that he never used two words where one would do, and never a word when a look or gesture would suffice. His fierce gaze was enough to send officers and men scurrying away at top speed to their allotted tasks.

Captain Bell took over command on 25 August, and we sailed that same evening for the Cape Verde Islands. At 1700 the next day we joined the 11th Cruiser Squadron, *Dauntless* and *Colombo*, as escort for the transport *Dunera*, bound from Ushant to Cape St Vincent. We left the convoy off Cape St Vincent on the 28th and, making passage by way of the Cape Verde Islands, we arrived at Rio de Janeiro on 7 September. During that week at sea events had moved over the brink into war, and *Exeter* was now assuming the active role for which she had been designed.

Sometimes doubts had been expressed about her suitability. Of 8390 tons, she carried a crew of 600, and had a top speed of 32 knots—a speed which compared favourably with many of her sister-ships and, indeed, with the new German battleships. But she had been built during a period of treaty limitation, and instead of an effective armament of eight 8-inch guns she had been fitted with only six, supplemented by four single 4-inch gun mountings, mainly for protection against aircraft. Added to this lack of firepower was the fact that she carried a small fuel load—only 1900 tons—giving her a range of 10,000 miles at 11–14 knots.

Refuelling was to be the biggest headache, a factor which greatly worried Commodore Harwood. The neutral harbours of South America were now virtually closed to us—only one visit every three months—and we were destined to endure long spells at sea, each day filled with exercise action stations and with unbroken, monotonous control stations throughout the night. Our main source of supply was at the Falkland Islands, almost 2000 miles to the south of Rio de Janeiro.

On 8 September *Exeter* left Rio and steamed south to search for the German merchantmen *General Artigas*, *Monte Pascoal*, and *Gloria*, which had been reported off the Patagonian coast and could be menacing the Falklands. At 0700 on the 9th we rendezvoused with *Ajax*, and Commodore Harwood ordered the other cruiser to Port Stanley as guardship. We were to maintain a patrol in the region of the River Plate, where we remained between 10 and 18 September.

It was believed initially that the German merchantmen were to be used as transports, but as it now seemed that they might be used for armed attack, a convoy system was rapidly organized. HMS *Cumberland*—another 8-inch cruiser—was ordered to Rio to organize local convoys in company with the destroyer *Havock*. *Exeter* was to operate convoy protection in the Plate area with the destroyer *Hotspur*.

There were several scares and many alterations of plan during September, and ships of our division were dispersed widely, seldom having the chance to act as a unit. Fuelling problems—particularly acute for *Exeter*—were partly solved at this stage by the stationing of the naval oiler *Olwen* in the mouth of the River Plate. Later she was relieved by *Olynthus*.

On 3 October there was great excitement when we were ordered to join *Ajax* in the Rio area. SS *Clement* had been attacked and sunk on 30 September, 75 miles south-east of Pernambuco, and there began a series of conflicting reports on the operation of armed surface raiders in the South Atlantic. We remained with *Ajax* in the Rio area, while *Hotspur* moved to the Rio-Santos area, and *Havock* took up her patrol position off the Plate. There were plans for reinforcements—*Cumberland*, at present in Freetown, was to join *Exeter* to carry out sweeps north of the Rio-Plate area; the New Zealand cruiser *Achilles* was on her way to join *Ajax* and the destroyers in their patrol of the Rio and Plate areas.

HMS *Cumberland* joined us on 9 October, and we both refuelled from *Olwen* on the 14th in San Borombon Bay. *Achilles* arrived on 26 October, and on the following day Commodore Harwood transferred his pennant to *Ajax*, while we steamed to Port Stanley for minor repairs. We were there until 4 November.

Then back to sea in some filthy weather—first patrolling in the Rio area and then down to the River Plate. All at that time seemed to be quiet, although there were several German merchant ships in port and we had to watch their every move.

Both *Ajax* and *Exeter* were back at the Falklands by 29 November, tasting the 'delights' of Port Stanley. We were certainly beginning to know this desolate spot, which I had first seen back in 1937 when *Exeter* had called there and we had spent three weeks on East Falkland, in the north-east group of islands. The visit had not been one greatly favoured by the ship's company, who had heard tell of the monotony of these barren islands and had been affected by the most dreadful rumour of all—that the pubs closed promptly at ten. But we had also arrived in half a gale, and on many subsequent nights the weather had been so bad that the liberty boats were not able to get ashore. On the occasions we were able to land we found a wild moorland with rocky outcrops and a soft, spongy soil. For the

Scots among us it suggested home; it also struck chords—however dissonant—in those of us who had spent any time at Scapa Flow.

But all this was before we got to know the kindly people of the Falklands and before we had tasted their hospitality. There was the occasional dance, the bi-weekly cinema show, and a concert given by the ship's concert party which the local inhabitants greatly appreciated—all in the little Town Hall of Port Stanley.

It was while we were there that we were asked to demolish a tall wireless mast—good practice for our demolition lads who 'captured' the post and blew it up with gun-cotton. It took eleven seconds to demolish something which had taken many weeks to erect and which during the First World War had, as an eagerly sought target, drawn the German Fleet to its destruction at the battle of the Falkland Islands.

Now, two years later, we found it a haven of rest once more after grim weeks at sea, and although there was a strong feeling that the Germans might attempt to stage some operation on the anniversary of the battle, nothing happened. Anyway, it would not be long before *Exeter* would depart for a major refit at Simonstown. HMS *Dorsetshire* was to relieve us on 23 December.

On 2 December *Doric Star* was sunk by a German surface raider, and the menace to British shipping in our area became starkly obvious. By 9 December decisions had been taken to concentrate our forces in the area of the River Plate. *Achilles* fuelled at Montevideo on the 8th and left to join *Ajax* off English Bank. We were ready to leave the Falklands. Somewhere—about three thousand miles away—a single enemy warship was reported to be moving possibly towards the coast, perhaps Rio, perhaps the River Plate, even possibly the Falklands. We were now to be positioned in one of those operational areas—but would it be the right one?

Chapter 2

THE BATTLE OF THE RIVER PLATE

'CLEAR LOWER DECK' had been sounded as usual by the Marine bugler, and we fell in on the quarterdeck facing the ship's officers. Commander Graham waited for the master-at-arms to report, then brought the ship's company to attention and turned smartly on his heel to face the Captain.

'Ship's company correct, sir.'

For a moment after giving his salute of acknowledgment Captain Bell was silent, looking meaningfully along the rows of his assembled crew. 'Hooky' Bell—how appropriate a nickname as he perched there on the grating in front of us with that eagle nose and the penetrating gaze.

'I have received orders that we are to rejoin Commodore Harwood aboard HMS *Ajax* off the mouth of the River Plate, along with the New Zealand cruiser *Achilles*.'

We stood, faces nipped by the cold wind driving from the Antarctic; from bearded three-badgers to smooth-faced sprogs there was the one thought—just what was in store for us? So far our patrols had been fruitless; but this could be our first encounter with the reality of war. It was something for which we were now really prepared. Every morning before dawn the bugler would sound the 'Awake'. Men would roll from their hammocks, groping for cigarettes and matches for a quick 'burn' as they lashed up and stowed their hammocks. Within a few minutes the bugle would sound 'Action stations'—always a slightly unnerving call until we heard the single 'G' note blown at the end to indicate practice only.

Practice or not, we jumped to it with a clattering of iron ladders

[13]

and a fierce, purposeful scramble to designated stations in the director, on the bridge, in the gun turrets, and deeper in the engine and boiler rooms. Gangways and spaces were cleared to enable fire and repairs parties to move freely.

Twice a day we moved to those action stations. As the ordnance artificer of 'Y' turret I would move to my after gun position and swing automatically into a routine which by this time I could do in my sleep.

Now as we stood on *Exeter*'s upper deck, our hair blown by the wind, some of us thought of 'Monte'—our 'home port'—and wistfully dreamed we were off to the bars and friendly cabarets. But that would not happen either—it would be another of those abortive trips followed by a return to the Falklands with all their bleakness and biting winds.

At 0700 on Tuesday, 12th December, H.M.S. Exeter *joined H.M.S.* Ajax *and* Achilles *about 250 miles eastward of the River Plate. At noon that day, Commodore Harwood made the following signal*:
'My policy with three cruisers in company versus one pocket battleship. Attack at once by day or night. By day act as two units, 1st Division (*Ajax* and *Achilles*) and *Exeter* diverged to permit flank marking. First Division will concentrate gunfire. By night ships will normally remain in company in open order. Be prepared for the signal ZMM, which is to have the same meaning as MM,[1] except that for Division read Single Ship.'[2]

On the Tuesday night we carried out exercises mainly for flank marking—that is, the two divisions attacking from different directions so that each could observe the other's fall of shot. We passed imaginary signals to each other and gained some useful practice on the gunnery fire-control equipment. Then just before 0500 we went to dawn action stations.

It was going to be a beautiful day. The weather had turned warmer as we steamed north, and now the breeze barely ruffled the

[1] MM. Commanders of divisions are to turn their divisions to course . . . starting with the rear division.
[2] Sir Eugen Millington-Drake, *The Drama of Graf Spee and the Battle of the Plate* (Peter Davies, 1964).

surface of the sea. As we stood down from our stations I looked ahead at the shapes of *Ajax* and *Achilles*. We were steaming in line ahead, without the sign of a ship or a wisp of smoke to mar the clean line of the horizon. Then I went below to my mess, to lie down on the lockers—not to sleep, but to think.

At about 0610 a flag signal broke at *Ajax*'s yard, and our chief yeoman, Tom Remmick, dashed to Captain Bell, who was in his sea cabin on the bridge. There was little need to read the signal, as there was now an obvious blob of smoke on the horizon, and soon after *Exeter* broke formation and steamed in the direction of that smoke.

At 0615 the ship making smoke was identified as a pocket battleship, probably Admiral Scheer. *The units divided in accordance with the Commodore's plan,* Exeter *to the N.W., the other two cruisers to the N.E.*

Suddenly the bugle sounded 'Action stations', and we all listened as usual for the familiar 'G' note, but it did not come. We knew that *Exeter* was going into action for the first time.

There were some who were still sceptical—just another merchant ship; but everyone rushed to action stations collecting gear, opening lockers, donning flash suits. Taut faces revealed the first signs of fear and apprehension. Down below in gangways and spaces the chippies, cooks and stewards, who formed the fire and repair parties, gripped more tightly than usual their saws, hoses and axes, and serious-faced they waited.

'A pocket battleship,' said one who always knew what was going on. '*Admiral Scheer*,' said another. In the welter of speculation the beauty of the day was forgotten, and we were all conscious of the increasing throb of the engines as *Exeter* began to pile on the knots. Two minutes later we were in battle.

At 0617 Graf Spee opened fire on Exeter *at 20,000 yards with her main armament of 11-inch guns.*

Even as I ran aft to my turret, my heart pounding, shells were falling into the sea around the ship, and the range was closing rapidly as the two ships sped towards each other. It was a frightening prospect being in the path of 12,000 tons of armour-plated battleship with superior firepower, but it was still odd that she should have chosen to come in and fight when she could have dictated the entire battle at long range.

The gap narrowed. Water and metal sprayed the ship from near misses even before the enemy had come fully over the horizon, and I began to hear the first screams of pain as men were struck down by the hot flying metal. For all of us—teenage sprogs and professional sailors alike—war had become the ghastly reality that it always is.

'Are we in range yet?' Captain Bell repeatedly asked. Then the fire bells rang followed by the single note, and *Exeter* gave a tremendous heave as her two forward 8-inch gun turrets fired their first rounds in anger.

'Ship is now engaging *Scheer*,'[3] said the detached voice over the loudspeakers. Again the shrapnel cascaded on to the exposed and unprotected high-angle gun and torpedo positions. The range had come down quickly, and our three 8-inch turrets were loading and firing with speed and precision—a great tribute to our period of training. The first two salvoes were short, but by the third our 8-inch shells were straddling the enemy.

My turret came into action just after 0622—about five minutes after what was now known to be the *Graf Spee* had opened fire on us—just as a shell burst close amidships, on starboard side, killing the torpedo-tube crew on deck. Hot metal sliced through to the Chief Stokers' bathroom, killing members of a decontamination party, while metal peppered the catapult area and cut down my mate 'Bunker' Hill only yards away from the little caboose where he kept his conjuring gear.

Then the forecastle was hit and the paint shop set alight. Smoke obscured the bridge as the fire parties fought the flames abreast of the two forward gun turrets. The reverberation of the gunfire all but burst their eardrums as they clung to their swirling hoses. Through the smoke a man would totter, sway, and fall, then in a moment clear of smoke a figure would rush in and drag the inert body back into the billowing whiteness. Suddenly a blinding flash, a terrible rending sound, and the forecastle lay revealed, a mass of twisted metal and burning timbers. Not a living soul among the debris.

[3] It was still thought at this stage that the enemy vessel was the *Admiral Scheer*.

Our first major disaster came with an 11-inch direct hit on 'B' turret, the one manned by the Royal Marines and the turret which I had left only weeks before. The explosion blasted the two gun-barrels apart, where they remained as a 'V' sign of mute defiance. The big, rugger-playing Marines corporal miraculously scrambled clear of the wrecked turret, unaware that another Marine, both legs badly damaged, was clinging around his neck.

'B' turret had been in action for only ten minutes prior to that hit; now, as though to crush the Churchillian gesture, another 11-inch shell tore through the rear of the turret, spraying the superstructure and the bridge with hot metal, wreaking severe damage on the wheelhouse beneath. Most of the bridge staff were killed, and seven telegraphists in the W/T office were scythed down. What tangled steelwork had remained upright after the first explosion was now flattened, mangled corpses littering the deck of that once immaculate turret. The 'bootnecks' I had worked and joked with had been blasted out of existence.

Deeper down in the ship, in the transmitting station, grim-faced Marines bandsmen anxiously watched the gunnery brain panel. Only four lights winked back at them from the indicator board where normally six lights glowed as guns were brought to the ready. Occasionally the 'Royals' would break into a hoarse cheer as *Exeter* fired another four-gun broadside, rearing up as the shells sped from her barrels.

The ship shuddered as shells tore into the hull, sometimes with such force that they screwed through the thin armour-plating and out of the other side of the ship before bursting.

On the wrecked bridge the navigator lay slumped across his compass. The main gyro was out of action and the lower wheelhouse smashed. Below, Petty Officer Green, the Chief Quartermaster, struggled furiously with the jammed steering-gear. With blood gushing from his leg, he called up to the bridge, 'What the hell's going on up there?'

A frightened voice quavered in reply, 'What shall I do? Everybody is dead up here.'

Answering the order to get below, a young boy seaman fell into the PO's arms. Helping one another, they somehow got below decks and stumbled through the mess-decks for the after steering position.

They never made it.

Captain Bell, wounded in the head, had moved aft near the emergency steering position, where in that after compartment the sailmaker and an engine room artificer clung grimly to the huge iron-spoked steering-wheel, turning it now to port, now to starboard, but never away from the enemy. Using a boat's compass snatched from a damaged sea-boat, Captain Bell continued to con his ship in action, passing his orders along a chain of seamen, stokers and Marines to the two men struggling with the great wheel.

Down below, in the gyro-compass room, the young electrical artificer checked his delicate instruments. He felt the ship hit time and time again forward of his compartment, until a terrifying ripping sound ended in an explosion in the compartment above him. His little cubby-hole began to get hot, the air thickened, until he found it increasingly difficult to breathe.

Climbing to the armoured hatch, he sprang the small manhole open and was immediately struck by flames and smoke from above. Quickly he closed the manhole and ran to the phone. He dialled Damage Control HQ, asked for his Chief, and reported, 'There is a fire in the compartment above the gyro-compass room; it is too fierce for me to do anything about it. The compass room is full of smoke, and I am finding it hard to breathe. Can you send a fire party?'

The reply came, 'Wait.'

The young artificer waited, with the fire burning fiercely above, his compartment getting hotter and hotter. For almost an hour he held on, watching the electricity supplies fail and his master gyro compass click erratically to a stop. Then he phoned again to report failure of the gyro compass, but this time the line was dead. In the darkness, scared and alone, with what appeared to be a blazing inferno above him, there was nothing he could do but wait.

In the compartment above, a fire party battled against the flames and eventually brought them under control. When they lifted the hatch the young artificer came out of it like a bat out of hell, continuing at high speed up through the various compartments to the upper deck.

In another part of the ship there was the strange sound of a piano.

The padre, George Groves, had stopped to play before he moved on with his bottle of Scotch with a wee drop for all and sundry.[4]

Within the first fifteen minutes *Exeter* had been hit by at least five 11-inch shells, and her superstructure had been penetrated by thousands of fragments of shrapnel from near-misses. At 0632 her starboard torpedoes were fired in local control at *Graf Spee*. Soon afterwards two more 11-inch shells screamed into her, the first putting 'A' turret out of action, the second striking the most decisive blow yet. This second shell penetrated the light plating amidships, cutting through several bulkheads and exploding in the Chief Petty Officers' flat.

At that moment Petty Officer Green, with the young boy seaman, was passing through the flat on his way aft. They and others in the area received the full impact, and virtually everyone was killed or maimed. Terribly burnt, Jimmie Green was to be unconscious for seventeen days, later to be remembered by Captain Bell as the man who 'was burnt the colour of a baked potato but who refused to die'.

The CPO and ERA messes were now a huge, blackened tomb, a space large enough to take at least a dozen London double-decker buses. Wire jumping-ladders now hung where two hours before strong iron gangways had stood. Kit lockers had been rolled by the explosion into battered drums of steel.

All the control positions, whether gunnery or torpedo, forward or aft, port or starboard, had been wiped out. Captain Bell, steel splinters in both eyes, stood soaked in petrol cascading from the punctured petrol tank of the Walrus aircraft above him, by his side Commander Robert Graham, and around him on all sides twisted ironwork and shrapnel-riddled bodies. It is said that at this stage Captain Bell turned to his Commander and said laconically, 'Well, if things get any worse we shall have to ram her.' Two minutes later Commander Graham slumped to the deck with shrapnel in both his legs.

Inside my turret, after firing only two or three rounds, we would find the ship's head slew away, and our target would be lost to us. To regain we would have to swing around on the other beam before

---

[4] In peace-time when we did a shoot he always played the piano. He did not like the noise.

we could bear again on the enemy. We did not know at that time that this was because two valiant characters were hanging with great concentration to the massive after wheel in a courageous effort to prevent the ship being hit.

'B' turret had gone early in the action. Now 'A' turret had been hit and its crew scattered in all directions. *Exeter*'s forward guns were silent, and all that was left intact were the engines, racing at almost top speed, and the two guns in my turret.

How ironic that, with all the battering and the slaughter above and below decks, the engines kept running, driving us towards our adversary. My pal Roy Ruse said afterwards, 'To us in the engine room it was just another high-speed run, except for a listing to port or starboard when the ship altered course, a violent shudder when the shells struck home. High speed requires extra vigilance to bearing temperatures and auxiliary engines, so we were kept very busy. Normally we should not have known what was taking place on deck, but Commander (E) Sims took an occasional trip above and came back with a not-so-good report. Then we began to take a list to starboard as the compartments on that side became flooded.'

Sub-Lieutenant (E) John Mott RN was the Engineer Officer in charge of damage control in HMS *Exeter*, and he relates his story as follows.

'I was alerted by the bugle call "Action Stations" (there were no electric alarm "rattlers" fitted, as in more modern ships) but by the time I had reached the Damage Control HQ in the Engineers Workshop the ship's side was already being perforated by splinters from near-misses. Eleven-inch HE shells from what we thought was the *Admiral Scheer* were exploding alongside. Splinters also damaged the two Walrus aircraft on the catapults, causing aviation petrol to flood the upper deck, but fortunately another near-miss sent up such a spout of sea water that it washed all the fuel away.

' "A" and "B" turrets were quickly put out of action by direct hits on both, killing many of the crews, and most of those on the bridge except Captain Bell and one midshipman. The captain, having no communications to the engine room or steering position, transferred his control to the after superstructure when a chain of messengers passed orders from man to man to the engine room and steering compartment. It was a little time before it was realized that one member in the "chain" was deafened by gunfire, which tended to delay messages.

'Probably the most devastating damage was caused by an armour-piercing shell which struck the ship fine on the port bow and drove through three bulkheads before exploding over the 4-inch magazine, killing everyone in the Chief and Petty Officers' Flat, and causing extensive damage. The fire-main was ripped apart, which helped automatically to extinguish the fires, but the resultant drop in fire-main pressure caused those in the engine-room to start more pumps, to try to maintain the pressure. The effect of this was to pump water into the ship, which had already taken on a substantial list to starboard.

'Not long after this a young seaman messenger appeared with a message from the captain, "Please, sir, the captain wants to know if we're going to sink." The answer I gave was "No. Tell the captain I will report to him as soon as I can."

'Then I went up to report to the captain. I can still see him standing with his striped pyjamas showing under his uniform, with blood all over his face, but apparently in complete control of the situation. The Gunnery Officer was on top of "Y" turret directing the fire and within shouting distance of the captain. As "Y" turret ceased firing through damage to its electrical supply down below, the captain remarked, "What do we do now? Alter course and ram her?" I did not pass on this last observation to my splendid teams battling below trying to restore order and supplies out of near-chaos. I interpreted it as to have one more go to see if we could fix the trouble.'

Aboard *Graf Spee* Commander Rasenack, the gunnery officer, was asking permission from Captain Langsdorff to bring all guns to bear to finish us off. It was as well that we remained in blissful ignorance of this, and also to our advantage that the German captain, badly concussed by gun-blasts, because he went outside of his armoured position on bridge to watch, had apparently not sufficiently recovered from the effects to give this order.

Shells whistled through the ship like a red-hot tornado, and in the after medical station set up in the wardroom Surgeon Lieutenant Roger Lancashire had a miraculous escape. As he recalls:

'I was sitting on my haunches taking the drugs out of the cupboard when there was a loud crash and a blast of air and I felt something whizz across the top of my cap. I was bowled over backward. Later in the day I found a part of the fuse cap, which had nearly decapitated me, embedded deeply in the fanlight casing.

'My chief assistant throughout the action was SBPO[5] Clifford Scoble. Unfortunately, when we were hurriedly recalled to Devonport after four days leave in August 1939, we had to sail without our LSBA[6] Ellsworth, but when we arrived back off the River Plate and met up with *Ajax*, we discovered that they had recently acquired a young SBA[7] as part of their own complement, and by a generous gesture he was transferred to *Exeter*. We gave him a first-aid kit and a roving commission, and he did excellent work tending the wounded in other parts of the ship. For obvious reasons Scoble and I could not leave our action stations. The splinters from *Graf Spee*'s first salvo severed the ring main, but immediately the secondary circuit was activated; however, we lost the use of our electric sterilizer.

'Casualties arrived in droves, but thanks to our well-trained assistants—including the master-at-arms, Tom King, together with the Royal Marine bandsmen who joined us as soon as they discovered that their transmitting station was no longer functioning—we were able to cope. When I was informed that Captain Bell and Commander Graham had been blown off the bridge and had transferred to the after conning position, and that both had been wounded, I decided that I had better ascend and see what I could do to help. As I poked my head through the hatch cover from the wardroom flat a hand shoved me down again with a yell 'Port Twenty'. I passed the message on to the chain of men for transmission to our perspiring heroes in the emergency steering position, and was then allowed to proceed. Captain Bell was in considerable pain from the steel splinters in his eyes. He was also bleeding badly from both legs. I was able to patch these up, and he promised to contact me later (if and when he could spare the time!) so that I might attend to his eyes.

'Everyone up top appeared to be soaked in the fuel which was

[5] Sick Berth Petty Officer.
[6] Leading Sick Berth Steward
[7] Sick Berth Attendant

streaming from the two Walrus aircraft. I saw the one on the port side heaved overboard, and there was "Guns" (Jennings) standing on the top of "Y" turret shouting out his orders. In the distance I could see *Graf Spee* being harried by *Ajax* and *Achilles*, who appeared to be darting in and out of a smoke-screen. The captain gave me a running commentary about the action, pointing out that all he had left was "Y" turret, which was firing with considerable difficulty to keep the right gun in action.

'Later on I was able to attend to Commander Graham's wounds in his cabin, and round about midnight the captain descended and aided by Joe Watts, our wardroom messman (who held a torch for me) we adjourned to the gun room and I was able to remove the splinters from one eye and bandage it up. The other one had to wait until we arrived at Port Stanley, where he was billeted at Government House and I was able to work under much easier conditions.

'I witnessed so many acts of sheer courage and determination that it is impossible to mention them all. Outstanding was Marine Russell, who had a forearm severed when the turret suffered a direct hit. He had a tourniquet round his upper arm, and toured the ship, cheering everyone on. It was very sad for all of us when he died in hospital some days later. I can never forgot PO Jimmie Green, the Chief Quartermaster, who was literally burned to a cinder. I have never known anyone to survive such burns. It was his courage that kept him going, and it was a humbling experience and a privilege to have him as a patient. It was very sad for me that I could do nothing more than ease the pain for 'Bunker' Hill, and make his passing easier. He was suffering from internal blast injuries. I had got to know and appreciate him enormously, for during the past three years we had both been members of the ship's concert party.

'Captain Bell gave up the use of his day cabin for stretcher cases. I can remember operating on a young paymaster sub-lieutenant, Causton, on the deck of the sleeping cabin, assisted by Scoble. We knocked him out with an intravenous anaesthetic and laboriously stitched up his ankle tendons; otherwise his foot would have to be amputated. (By odd chance I met this young man at Simonstown Naval Base about four years later when I was on my way to Durban, and I was pleased to find him with a reasonably good foot.) The medical team managed to keep going without any sleep for the next three days until we arrived at the Falklands.'

The next development was the order to jettison the aircraft. Both Walrus aircraft were severely damaged, and the RAF crew, who had lovingly nursed the two planes throughout the long commission, were slowly winding the first towards the sea—but allow Lieutenant G.P. Fowler to tell the story:

'This is the record of the most frustrating day of my life, 13 December 1939, as the Observer and Signal Officer on board HMS *Exeter* in the action with the German pocket battleship *Graf Spee* off the River Plate.

'Having been on the Bridge for Dawn Action Stations, I was dozing in my cabin when the Action alarms sounded. I hurriedly dressed up in my flying gear, grabbed my chart board, code-book etc. and made my way to the upper deck. I got stuck in the manhole because the main hatch was closed in the captain's flat, and had to strip off my Mae West to get through.

'When I reached the flight deck I found that the starboard air-craft—which had just finished its short maintenance inspection and was ready for flight at the inboard end of the starboard catapult—had been hit by splinters, as had its catapult. The RAF flight hands were winding this aircraft out by hand to jettison it over the side. This was necessary to enable the port aircraft to be run back on its catapult ready to be flown off. It was splinters from this shell which wrecked my cabin and nearly put paid to Surgeon Lieutenant Roger Lancashire, as he was rigging the wardroom as the after dressing station.

'I had just reached the bridge via the port ladder when I was knocked down by blast and small splinters from the shell which had hit the right gun of "B" turret and had carried on to wreck the bridge. I reported to Captain Bell as he made his way aft from the devastated bridge to the after control position, asking for any special instructions. His laconic reply was "None. Spot."

'I was unable to find the ship's position because the navigator, Lieutenant Commander Bowman-Manifold, was dead and the chart table wrecked. I then realized that I had been hit by a small splinter in my right thigh muscle. A large "rock" had smashed my chart board, and the lead backing of my aircraft code had saved me from further injuries. Apart from the minor paint chips in my eyes, I was serviceable and able to fly.

'I got back to the flight deck at the time that the triatic stay parted and came down across the starboard wing of the port aircraft, rupturing its petrol tank. That aircraft too had to be jettisoned. Escaping petrol saturated everything and everybody.

'I found my pilot, Lieutenant Geoffrey Lamb, and I think the blacksmith, trying to lever the burning starboard 4-inch ammunition lockers over the side. They were unable to move the turnbuckles, and eventually handed this ammunition over the side. Since the cartridges appeared to be burning and not exploding, I did not allow them to use the large foam fire-extinguisher on its trolley, reckoning that at any moment we might have a much more serious petrol fire, should a shell explode in the vicinity.

'At about this time I saw my Chief Petty Officer Telegraphist Newman and his team rigging emergency aerials on the starboard side of the upper deck. Since the forestay and the triatic stay had parted, the masts were whipping about like fishing rods and all the aerial array had gone.

'I then reverted to being the signal officer and went forward to the bridge. I found Chief Yeoman Remick dying, Chief Yeoman Higgenbotham and Signalman Honey dead. Also dead were all in the remote control wireless office, and a dazed Yeoman Harbon on the flag deck. He was trying to get a 10-inch signalling projector off its stand to take to the after control position. The bulbs fitted neatly into the knee pockets of my flying suit, we humped the projector aft and set it up on its mounting, where 'Torps' [Torpedo and Electrical Officer] Lieutenant Commander Smith, saw it. "Cannot spare any amps for that, must keep 'Y' turret going." Fair enough, I thought. As far as we were concerned, getting that aerial rigged was top priority.

'In exposed positions on the fo'castle, on both sides of the bridge, were the short-range 0.5 inch Oerlikon gun mountings and their crews. Quickly the devastating result of the *Graf Spee*'s shrapnel on the exposed crew's positions was known, and the order was passed to them to "take cover". This they did by going through the door behind them, which led into the lower bridge space, from where the immaculately kept bridge ladder led up to the bridge platform and the Commodore's sea cabin. Here they huddled and crouched together, not seeing but hearing the deadly shrapnel crashing against the bridge structure behind which they crouched.

'The crews were inside, taking cover, when the bridge received a direct hit from an 11-inch shell, killing or wounding almost everyone on the bridge. The Oerlikon crews just below the explosion were splattered with debris from pieces ripped off the bridge structure and clouds of flying debris, which penetrated their thin clothing and cut savagely into their eyes and bodies. Amidst the general havoc and frightening uncertainty of every one of them, together at the bottom of the bridge ladder, they saw the head of one of the senior bridge staff come tumbling down the steps of the wrecked bridge ladder to stop only when it landed amid their unmoving feet.

'When I was told of this I remembered very clearly his last "run ashore", which had been with me in Rio de Janeiro. He did not go ashore often, but this evening we had been working late and came into the mess for supper at the same time. We were both surprised to find the mess empty of other messmates. On inquiring of the messman, "Where is everyone?" we were told "They have all gone ashore together." It was something which during our long commission we could not remember ever happening before. On the spur of the moment we decided to go ashore and join them. We did, and he enjoyed himself in his quiet way among his shipmates. I am so glad we went; it could have been an omen.

'Amid the chaos and the wreckage an order came, "Stand by Oerlikon guns, We are going to ram"—but it never happened.

'Again an 11-inch shell fell short, to burst in the sea on the port side of *Exeter*, sending shrapnel into the crews manning the port 4-inch guns and pom-poms, also tearing holes in the Walrus aircraft housed near them.

'Close behind each 4-inch gun mounting was a ready-use locker, filled with shells of fixed ammunition. This meant that the shell and its brass cylinder, filled with cordite, were fixed together. In the cylinder base was its detonator, and in the nose of the shell its fuse. The brass cylinders were stacked horizontally like wine bottles.

'Then someone shouted "Fire." The crews looked behind them and saw the shell ready-use locker burning. The brass cylinders quickly became hot and began to explode. Midshipman Archibald

Cameron, the officer of quarters, and A.B. William Gwilliam, ran to the nearby boatswain's store and returned each with an oilskin. Approaching the locker, they wrapped an oilskin around a hot shell and holding it above their heads, ran with it to the ship's side, throwing the shell into the sea. They continued to do this until all the dangerously hot shells had been removed and the fire extinguished.'

Midshipman Don was awarded a Distinguished Service Cross and Boy Gwilliam a Conspicuous Gallantry Medal.

Lieutenant Commander R.B. Jennings was the gunnery officer of HMS *Exeter*, also the first Lieutenant of the ship. He had just stood the middle watch, 00.01 hours to 04.00. Dawn action stations were ordered about 04.45 — too soon after going off watch to make it worth while turning in, he thought. He shaved. Dawn action stations were sounded off, and it seemed to him to be unduly drawn out. At approximately 05.40 hours they stood down and the ship reverted to third degree of readiness. He went below and turned in.

Outside his cabin was the keyboard, complete with the Royal Marine sentry who had the good sense to shake him when the 'beat to quarters' was sounded, *without the 'G'*. As he crossed the bridge to reach the ladder up to the DCT (Director Control Tower), the captain said to him 'There's the fucking *Scheer*. Open fire on her.' He climbed quickly with the rest of his crew up the iron ladder to the DCT. The director trainer was already in his position, and soon the director had been trained upon the distant pocket battleship. Also in the DCT, waiting anxiously for the enemy vessel to come within range of *Exeter*'s smaller 8-inch guns, was Lieutenant McBarnet and Midshipman Sturdee, the spotting and rate officers, also the headphoned telegraphists. Quietly and carefully keeping the director tower fixed upon the approaching pocket battleship, were the director layer and director trainer, together with the young director sight-setter. High up behind them PO Trueman, the range-taker, was already sending ranges to the transmitting station, the gunnery brain of the ship. (PO Trueman was to lose an eye during the action.)

The approaching ship was already firing at *Exeter* from maximum range, and causing her serious damage.

At last the enemy came into range and Lieutenant Commander Jennings, with the target in his director sight, gently squeezed the director firing pistol.

HMS *Exeter* had fired her first shots in anger.

At first only the four gun-ready lamps of the two forward turrets lit up in the DCT. The two gun-ready lamps of 'Y' turret aft did not light up because on the ship's present course the turret guns could not bear. Then the ship's arcs were widened; this allowed 'Y' turret guns to bear and open fire. Quickly the six guns reloaded, the gun-ready lamps of the three turrets lit up together, and another 8-inch broadside sped towards the enemy.

Early in the action an 11-inch shell from the pocket battleship fell short and burst into a thousand pieces of shrapnel, sweeping through *Exeter*, killing and wounding many and causing widespread damage. Suddenly nothing worked in the director. There was no answering ring as he squeezed the director firing pistol, no lights shone back at him from the gun-ready panel and there was silence from the fall-of-shot hooter. With only reduced peacetime complement, Lieutenant Commander Jennings had to forgo the luxury of a boy or ordinary seaman manning a range and time of flight board in the DCT. He had lost contact with his turrets—the director cables had been cut through by shrapnel.

At this early stage in the action he was not aware of the extent of the damage to the two silent foremost turrets, 'A' and 'B'. They could not be seen from the DCT and dense smoke from the fiercely burning fire in the paint shop hid both the bridge and the forecastle from him. There was no more he could do. After telling his director crew to join in dealing with any damage they came upon, he climbed down from his eyrie, high above the bridge.

Jennings was surprised at finding the bridge and compass platform deserted at not seeing any bodies or wounded. He made his way to the after-control position and stood talking to Lieutenant D.T. Wickham inside it—he had not been relieved by Paymaster Sub-Lieutenant Tyler, who had been killed when running to his after-control position. An alteration of course which 'Guns' had not noticed brought *Graf Spee* into 'Y' turret's arc of fire with deafening results. He has a hurt certificate to support this. He moved aft and climbed on to the roof of my turret to spot fall of shot as we fired another deafening broadside. Then focusing his binoculars on *Graf Spee*, he shouted spotting orders to us through the open centre position. Shrapnel whined about him, at times burying itself in the deck timbers or, deflected from the metal surfaces, hummed away below decks, killing or wounding men in the repair parties. Then the ship took another direct hit, the electrical power to 'Y' turret failed and the last two guns fell silent.

The ship was still under fire when he jumped down from the roof of the turret and went forward along the booms to the starboard 4-inch guns, then down to the Chief Petty Officer's locker flat where a shell with a 65-foot delay burst after entering at the fore end of the PO's mess, causing terrific havoc. He speaks of the well-ordered projectile which plunged through 'B' turret's ammunition embarkation hatch and left through the side of the sick bay unexploded. In its passage it knocked over the sick berth Chief Petty Officer Pope, spilling the medicaments he was arranging on a tray. He remembers this hit being very early on, possibly only seconds before we had opened fire. With the Commander wounded in both legs and now in his bunk, the gunnery officer went forward to ascertain damage to the ship:

'Now aware of the desperate situation we were in, I wiped the sweat and grime from my face, closing my eyes against the sting of the acrid cordite fumes, and muttered, "My God, these bloody guns have got to keep going now." '

Inside 'Y' turret conditions were getting bad. Both guns were being fired as soon as they were loaded, the confined space beginning to fill with cordite fumes, while the breeches through lack of cooling water became fiercely hot.

The water reservoirs for cooling the guns, and the air to clear the fumes from burning cordite residue, had all but gone. The crew cursed, sweated and choked as they cried out to me, 'For God's sake, Chief, give us some air and water.'

How could I tell them, sweating and toiling under such terrible conditions, that the supplies which came from outside the turret had long ago been shot away and there was nothing I could do but eke it out? This had been a gruelling time for us. We had been hit five times in the first fifteen minutes. Commodore Harwood, seeing *Exeter*'s plight, had ordered a torpedo attack—under smoke—to be carried out. This had the desired effect of making *Graf Spee* slew to avoid torpedoes. Many years later in Germany her navigating officer told me that one torpedo missed their stern by only two or three feet. The attack of the two light cruisers also took the full force of the pocket battleship's gunfire away from *Exeter*.

From somewhere forward I heard the crash and shudder of yet another explosion. The lights in the turret flickered, dimmed then went out and the guns fell mute. The sweat on my body ran cold as I realized that, with our last two guns unable to move, we were now at the mercy of the enemy.

I waited helpless in the darkened gun-house, praying hard that it was not the fact that the ship's dynamos had been damaged which had caused the electric power cut. The young midshipman tried to telephone out the situation, but every line was dead. Everything in the turret had been working like clockwork, then suddenly it all stopped. Quickly I went below to the pump space where my large Vickers pump, supplier of the turret's life-blood—oil—stood in its mounting, hot, oily and unmoving.

Now, unable to do anything, I began to think of other things. Strange, my mind went back to the Devonport Gunnery School. I saw clearly the narrow road, skirted on one side by the high railings of the football and cricket pitches. I remembered how the ordnance officers and senior chiefs discussed you, as you walked down that fifty-yard road to the Ordnance Office and workshops.

What would they think when the news of this action reached home? How I had the only two guns left in the ship capable of firing back at the enemy—and they were silent. Never mind the fact that it was impossible for me to move them; they were my guns. I had been trained always to keep my guns firing. Would the true facts ever be known? How I had literally stood on my head, tripping the interlocks to keep both guns in action, until the power failed?—Then a shattering thought hit me. Would I and the ship ever survive this one-sided action?

Never in my wildest dreams had I expected to find myself in such a predicament. The odds were stacked heavily against us.

Down below, the electrical and engine-room staffs shone their torches on the turbine cases, at times lighting up the racing prop-shafts, making their way to the dynamo and circuit boards. There they found that the explosion had shaken off the dynamos, and working feverishly, they had them back on again and the dynamos running. The lights glimmered and power returned to the turret, and we were in action again.

At once we found further trouble. The electrical supplies to the gun pointers were now no longer functioning, and our last link with any other part of the ship had been severed. Quickly, with the help of the local director-layer, we changed over to local control. This meant that we had to obtain for ourselves all the gunnery data that we needed—range, deflection and whether our shells were falling over or short. I never thought to be in this position, but I knew these guns well and that they, like humans, had their own special weaknesses. How I prayed, as I stood on my tool-bag in that fume-filled centre position between the two 8-inch guns, that nothing further would go wrong.

When we opened the centre position hatch bright sunlight streamed in. I could clearly see *Graf Spee* steaming on a course parallel to ours, flying from her foremast the largest flag I had ever seen, with its great swastika. On board the German battleship, Captain Langsdorff asked the officers near him 'Why is it the English never know when they are beaten? All their guns except two are silent and out of action. The ship is on fire and down by the bows, yet they still come for us?'

Then fate hit out again. The right gun developed trouble after loading; a burr preventing the rammer from returning fully back. I shouted for a hand-spike and started forcing the rammer-head back, bit by bit. This did clear it, and allowed us to fire, but now every time we rammed the burr got larger and the rammer more difficult to return, so that it took longer to load the gun. Then we hit *Graf Spee*—slap in the middle of her huge bridge control. As it erupted in a large reddish-yellow flash the young midshipman controlling the firing cried jubilantly, 'We hit her. We hit her.'

At the height of the action, their number tragically depleted, the telegraphists came hauling the temporary aerial along the boat deck, climbing precariously around the damaged mast and clearing away the old aerials.

Silence had come for *Exeter* not only when her last two 8-inch guns ceased firing, but also when her topmast was blown over and the aerials fell, twisting around the red-hot funnels and wrecked bridge.

Communications with Commodore Harwood aboard *Ajax* had been lost for much of the action.

When contact with the Commodore was again restored his first signal to *Exeter* was 'Rejoin battle. Report damage.'

Exeter replied 'Ship is on fire. Have rigged jury aerials. Only one gun in 'Y' turret firing. Have reduced speed. Forward bulkheads severely damaged. Ship three feet down by the bow. Steering from auxiliary position aft.'

Upon getting *Exeter*'s damage report, he made back—'Break off action. Go to Falkland Islands if you can make them.'

Exeter turned south towards the cold Antarctic, as smoke belched from her blackened guts.

Ajax and *Achilles* closed in as the *Graf Spee* altered course to westward. Just as she had been all set to finish us off, the tables had been sensationally turned. But for HMS *Exeter* the blood bath had ended.

Next day *Exeter* 'stopped ship' twice to bury her dead. Sixty-five had died in that action.

Aboard *Exeter* the first men to be called upon to carry out repairs were the shipwrights, men whose primary job—come hell or high water—was to keep their ship afloat. *Graf Spee*'s heavier and longer-range guns had opened fire at extreme range, and many of her opening salvoes fell short. On impact with the sea the shells had burst into thousands of pieces of red-hot shrapnel, which scythed through the ship's thin hull above and below the water-line, causing serious flooding in compartments and flats that housed electrical equipment. These holes below the water-line were the first to be plugged by the shipwrights. Mr Rendle, the warrant shipwright officer, early on found his staff stretched to the limit. He gives his account of his busiest day:

Battle of the River Plate 13 December 1939

1. Time 5–30am. approx. First action stations alarm. All closed up and repair parties reported being in their allocated stations throughout the length of the ship. Fire and repair parties reported to D.C.H.Q. in engineers workshops. (Damage control headquarters.)

2. Second action stations at approx 6am. sounded off and all rushed

to their stations again. There were shells exploding astern of the *Exeter* almost immediately.

3. The enemy was on target and shortly it became difficult to communicate thro' telephones. (Shrapnel damage to the telephone lines.)

4. One could not discern hits on the enemy from our salvoes. (Extreme range for our guns.)

5. Direct hits on both forward turrets. 'B' turret was hit and put out of action. Afterwards 'A' turret met the same fate, this left only 'Y' turret in action. A hole about 7 feet x 6 feet was made in the forecastle deck abaft the breakwater. Both faces of the turret's barbett were shattered but were temporarily repaired with sheet metal by the engineers, to keep the seas out.

6. Attempts were made at this stage to prevent sea water flooding into the after cabin flat and thence down into the gyro room hatch.

7. The gallant efforts of the fire and repair party to work aft, were made impossible by the continuous firing of 'Y' turret guns overhead at a low angle. It seemed probable the elevating gear of the turret was damaged but in fact the range was so close that the guns had little elevation.

8. There was an enormous explosion within the ship at bulkhead No.90 in the CPO's kit and locker flat. The blast seemed to catch one in the stomach and the damage was about 16 feet x 14 feet in the steel decking. (This shell exploded in the CPO flat.)

9. At this stage the damage control officer gave the order 'On gasmasks' and efforts were made with water hoses to clear the area of dense, black smoke.

10. This 11-inch shell from the *Graf Spee* had entered the port hull at about station 80 and was deflected aft, exploding in the flats.

11. Minutes later we were hit again on the starboard side aft, with much splintering of the ship's hull, through which one could clearly see the *Graf Spee*, enshrouded in a mist of yellow smoke.

12. An 11-inch shell penetrated the sick bay which was below the bridge.

13. An 11-inch channel was cut diagonally through the wrecked bridge and along the deck of the wireless office killing 7 WT

ratings, it continued on to explode over the 4 inch starboard HA guns.

14. The scene on the upper deck was one of utter devastation. The bridge was badly splintered with shrapnell and almost all staff were killed or wounded. The steering gear was damaged beyond repair. The stays of the foretop mast had been shot through and was swinging around in the roll of the ship and the wind. This was a cause of great anxiety as the mast was swinging from side to side uncontrollably. There were suggestions that we put a charge on the mast and blow it down, but there was no way of controlling its descent. It could have fallen on to the sick bay which was full of wounded men. Eventually it was decided that palm trees had to sway a lot in the wind, so jury stays were lashed to the mast and near structures to decrease the strain on the heel of the mast and its fittings. The topmast and main topmast were unrigged at Port Stanley, later, and left behind in the Falklands.

15. Generally, all manner of wedges were bunged into holes in the ship's side to prevent flooding. On one occasion the round legs of a bathroom stool were sawn up and wrapped around with ferenought material. Our best assets were mattresses and hammocks as temporary water stoppers and pinewood shores already cut to different sizes to fit various hatches.

16. The sickbay was full. The wounded were tended in the passage and on the upper deck. Hot Bovril was distributed, and bully beef sandwiches.

During *Exeter*'s last visit to Montevideo two nondescriptly dressed men—each carrying a bundle—had been brought aboard by a member of the British Embassy staff just before the ship sailed. Quickly they had been put down in the cells and a Royal Marine sentry posted. They were two seamen from the New Zealand cruiser, HMNZS *Achilles*, who during the ship's visit to Montevideo—despite the fact they were both under punishment stoppage of leave—had felt the need for cold beers and had broken out of the ship, taking the small 'skimming dish' (outboard motor-boat) ashore, tying it up to the landing stage at the end of Rio's main street, the Rio Branco. When later, their thirsts quenched, they returned to the boat they found to their horror the skimming dish had vanished—and so had their ship. Later, when HMS *Exeter* visited Montevideo, the two were put aboard for handing over to their own ship for punishment.

When for the second time 'Action Stations' sounded off (and this time without the 'G') the Royal Marine sentry shouted 'Bloody hell, chaps! Action Stations' and rushed off to his station. Quickly the two New Zealand ratings followed him out of the cell flat—to where? Punishment, cold beers, their irksome quarters forward in the cell flat all dwarfed into insignificance as they realized the ship they were in, HMS *Exeter*, was in action.

During the battle the two Kiwis were free-lance action stations men, wandering from one dangerous spot to another, pulling wounded men from burning compartments, putting out fires, and helping wherever needed. After a near-miss which cut the halyard and brought down the White Ensign the two men reached it almost before it came to rest on the ship's rail, undraped it amid flying shrapnel and hoisted it to a new position on the top rung of a vertical ladder, from whence it billowed out again.

This was a brave act, as they were completely exposed in an area constantly raked with shrapnel and saturated with petrol from the damaged Walrus aircraft.

This is a vivid account extant from another of *Achilles'* crews, Seaman Boy Olausen:

'In August 1939, when the war clouds were gathering, HMS *Achilles* went into dry dock in Auckland and had a bottom scrape and repaint. She had just returned from an island cruise in the Pacific. After the docking we provisioned ship, took on our full complement of ammunition and sailed on the 28th of August 1939 under sealed orders. At this period the true realization of world happenings did not register too seriously with me, and I believe it was the same for the other youngsters of my age. I had just turned seventeen in the July.

'Our original destination was to have been Balboa; however, when it became known that we were at war with Germany we altered course for Valparaiso, the main port of Chile, arriving there on the 12th of September. Beforehand we had completely obliterated all mention of the ship's name, and painted all the gleaming brass over with grey paint. Imagine, then, our great surprise when on entering

Valparaiso the newspaper headlines read "Welcome H.M.S. Achilles". When we left they read "Farewell to the million dollar sailors of the love ship."

'We refuelled and provisioned ship in Valparaiso and started a lengthy patrol up and down the west coast of South America from the Straits of Magellan to Buenaventura. We saw several German merchant ships, but they were all in internment in South American ports, although in Callao (Peru) we had anchored and shut down the boilers when a signal was picked up from a German ship asking for permission to enter port. Had we been able to get up sufficient steam to get out and intercept her outside the territorial waters of Peru, then we would have claimed our first victim of the war. However, our presence along this coastline kept German merchant shipping in ports.

'On 20 October we passed through the Magellan Straits into the South Atlantic, and after patrolling various areas we arrived in Rio de Janeiro on 10 November, leaving there on the 12th to commence an extensive patrol to the east and south, finally going into Montevideo on the 8th of December. The next day we sailed again and joined up with HMS *Exeter* and *Ajax* in the River Plate area. There Commodore Harwood revealed to the captains of the three cruisers his plan of action should the squadron encounter the German pocket battleship which had been creating havoc with Allied merchantmen in the South Atlantic. Until the battle it was believed to be the *Von Scheer*.

'On the morning of the 13th of December all was as usual on *Achilles*. We had been to Dawn Action Stations, which was an exercise carried out every day at sea. Because of the possible meeting with the enemy I believe we stayed a little longer than normal at action stations. The ship reverted to cruising watch, and those not on duty went below—some to finish off their interrupted sleep and others to read or do a few personal chores. I went down to the port waist, where I and several others hung their hammocks, and lashed up and stowed away my hammock. Still feeling tired, I stretched out on the fire box in the waist and dozed, only to be abruptly wakened by the sound of the alarm rattlers. Now, in practice the bugle is sounded off first and the rattlers after. In the real thing the opposite occurs. In my sleepy state I realized the significance of the alarm, and instantly came to. I got up and put my foot under several hammocks, shouting at the same time to wake up the unconscious. I then ran up to the iron deck and up another ladder to the flag deck. There I saw "Pincher" Martin, a signalman, hoisting a signal in a hurry. "What's up, Pincher?" I asked. His reply was "Get into your bloody turret." I shot along to "B" gun deck and climbed into the turret, but in doing so I glanced astern of us, and there, not too far away, were three great big splashes. Needless to say, I wasted no more time. I quickly took my place on the telephones, which was my action station. I immediately tested all the phones, and it was only seconds later that the order came over the phone "With C.P.B.C. and full charge Load." I shouted this out into the turret, and the banging and clattering of shell hoists and breeches of guns began. Some few seconds later I received another message over the headphones. "Our enemy is the *Scheer*." I made this known to the turret's crew also. I am sure I saw a distinct alteration in the colour of the men's faces: I have no idea what mine looked like. Funnily enough, at this stage I had no sense of fear. I felt more a sense of urgency. I do remember a strong feeling of anger, and felt quite happy that we were pumping shells out at a rapid rate . . . some must be finding their target. All around me cordite cases and brass 1-inch firing tubes were building up, so I got off my seat and started to dispose of the cordite cases through the aperture in the turret door, where most of them went overboard, out of the way.

'The action had been going on for a time, when our right gun started giving trouble. It would recoil, but would not run out to the firing position again unless it was given a push. The ordnance artificer was called, and in no time he remedied the fault.

'We had a delay in "B" turret in getting shells up from the shell room. This was brought about by the "disappearance" of a knife which was used to cut the grommets from the driving band of the shells before they could be put into the shell hoist. In order to keep up the salvoes we began using the shells which were held in brackets around the turret. So it was that we fired, not only armour-piercing, but also H.E. shells and one practice shell, which I understand ended up in a bunk on the *Graf Spee*. If that is correct, then we did get a "Hit". In all the *Achilles* fired some 1,235 shells, 342 of which came from "B" turret.

'During the heat of the battle there was a loud crunch at the front of the turret and a tinkling of metal on metal on the roof. This was obviously caused when a salvo landed close to us and created the damage and casualties we suffered. At that time we were unaware as to what damage had been done. But through the headphones I could hear scraps of conversation coming from the various fighting positions and it prompted me to call up Max Dorset, in the Director, and ask him if he was O.K. He confirmed that he was. During a lull in the action I decided to open up the hatch in the turret roof and have a look around to see what our enemy looked like. In doing so I had an eerie sort of feeling, and can remember thinking, bearing in mind the noise I had heard on the turret roof beforehand, "What if a shell came over now and just skimmed the roof . . . that would be my lot" so I prudently closed the hatch and got back on my seat. I felt a lot safer behind the inch of steel around me. Upon reflection it was a silly thought, because a shell would slice through that turret like a knife through butter.

'When the main action was over and we had reverted to positions for shadowing we were able to go out on deck, and it was there that we had photos taken. The canteen manager brought up chocolate and cigarettes (the latter no one would buy anyway. They were South American and tasted terrible.) The order was given to "Splice the Mainbrace", and we all had a large tot of rum. As a Seaman Boy of seventeen I was not entitled to have a normal rum issue, but this was a special occasion and despite the protest from one Able Seaman that I was issued my tot before the "Good Able Seamen got theirs" I decided to let him see that I was an old campaigner at drinking rum and knocked it back in two gulps. Naval rum is fairly potent, as I found out, I couldn't breathe properly for about two minutes. But I never let him see that. I often wonder if that AB remembers the occasion.

'Before returning to New Zealand the *Achilles* went into Buenos Aires, as the *Ajax* went to Montevideo. We were greeted by the English community of BA and entertained at a park, the name of which eludes me. After a period of time three of us decided this was too tame for us. So against all orders we decided to take a trip into the city. Although the *Graf Spee* crew were interned, they were permitted to roam the streets freely, and two memories of this remain very vivid in my mind. The first was approaching a table on the footpath where four of them were drinking. Three of them got up, saluted us and extended their hands. We did likewise and shook hands with them. The fourth member of that group just sat there grasping his mug of beer and never looked up or said anything. We promptly decided that he was a dedicated Nazi; the others weren't. After leaving them we sauntered along streets and narrow lanes, and finally found that we were walking line-abreast down a narrow street, and coming towards us in similar formation were four Germans. There was no way that we were going to give way to them, and as the street was so narrow someone had to. People on the footpath began to stop to see what would happen when we met. Mind you, they weren't the only ones wondering, but one thing was for sure — we wouldn't be giving way; we decided that as the distance between lessened. Just as we came to within probably ten feet of them they stopped and stepped aside to let us through, and saluted us at the same time. We did likewise and shook hands, and I do believe to this day that the bystanders were really disappointed. We weren't; in fact we were very happy to meet and converse with them, where possible.

'After our visit to BA we went to the Falklands and then set off for New Zealand, arriving back in Auckland to a resounding, never to be forgotten, welcome.'

How did the battle appear from *Ajax*? In the words of her gunnery officer, Lieutenant-Commander D.P. Dreyer, RN:

'The real drama of the Battle of the River Plate started for us in early December when Commodore Harwood reckoned that *Graf Spee* might well decide to head for the River Plate area and he concentrated his three available cruisers there, including his flagship *Ajax*. We met on the 12th and he made the electrifying signal to the three ships — "My policy with three cruisers against one Pocket Battleship is attack at once by day or night." It was just the sort of signal that Nelson (or indeed Admiral Cunningham) would have made. It certainly set the adrenalin flowing. *Graf Spee* had six 11-inch guns, the same guns as those which had sunk one of Beatty's battlecruisers at Jutland. She was a formidable adversary, but we all knew that from time immemorial it has been British naval policy to take the offensive in battle, not to try and shadow, and keep in touch until bigger ships could join us (*Ark Royal* and *Renown* were in fact two thousand miles away), but to attack at once. Heavy casualties were probably inevitable, and our three ships might well be sunk, but faint hearts never won in love or war; the enemy might also be damaged. The rightness of the policy was shown by the outcome of the battle.

'*Ajax* was a good ship and a happy one, and we had a fire captain in Charles Woodhouse. I don't think that we really expected to meet *Graf Spee* the next day, and neither did Commodore Harwood. We did not fly off our aircraft for a reconnaissance. After dawn action stations I retired to my cabin when suddenly the alarm rattlers and the pipe "Pocket Battleship in sight" jerked me sharply into action. It was a perfect day, and we opened fire at almost maximum range. After a short while, as previously planned, we concentrated our fire with *Achilles* until half an hour or more later when the latter suffered damage and casualties to her bridge and gunnery control personnel from an 11-inch near miss. This upset fire from the light cruisers, which was also adversely affected by the Seafox aircraft which we had flown off from *Ajax* and which reported *Achilles*' fall of shot for ours. So our fire was good at the beginning and at the end, though there was a confused period in the middle.

'We were lucky to escape the fire from *Graf Spee* in the early stages when *Exeter* was so heavily engaged; but during that period I remember seeing hits from *Exeter* on the enemy which were probably of critical importance on the ultimate result. Although *Exeter* herself suffered very severe damage and many casualties the indomitable spirit of Captain Bell and his West Country crew ensured that the ship survived to fight another day. But when *Exeter* was eventually forced to withdraw from the action *Graf Spee* shifted her fire to the two light cruisers. Though she had scored eight 11-inch hits on *Exeter* in the first half of the action, in the second half she only scored a near-miss on *Achilles* and one 11-inch hit on *Ajax*. This poor result was partly due to the avoiding action that we took and to the fact that *Graf Spee* was under helm for much of the time. The purpose of this was to make her a difficult target to hit, and this she achieved, but the constant manoeuvring reduced very considerably the effectiveness of her own fire.

'The 11-inch hit on *Ajax* occurred when the range was down to

9,000 yards, the shell passing through the Commodore's cabin and bathroom and through the barbette and working chamber of "X" turret before exploding. "X" turret was virtually destroyed, and four Royal Marines were killed and five wounded in the working chamber. The base of the shell hit the barbette of "Y" turret and severely restricted the training of the turret until after the action, when the damaged part was cut away. Further casualties occurred in "X" turret when a fire started in the hoist. While the gunhouse door was open for a hose to be brought in two Royal Marines were killed by splinters from a near-miss.

'The only other casualty in *Ajax* occurred when the mainmast was brought down by a direct hit from a 5.9 inch shell (their only success). The W/T aerials came down too, and unhappily a splinter from the shell killed an Ordinary Seaman who was one of the crew of an AA gun.

'When action was broken off we shadowed *Graf Spee* which, despite all our firing, was obviously able to proceed at her maximum speed and had all six 11-inch guns in action. However, as the day wore on we were astonished to realize that she was heading for the River Plate. In fact she was much more severely damaged than we could see, and she had lost 36 men killed and 58 wounded.

'It transpired later that Captain Langsdorff had signalled to Berlin "To break out to open sea and shake off these two cruisers is obviously impossible . . . As ship cannot be made seaworthy for breakthrough to the Homeland with means on board I decided to go into River Plate at risk of being shut in there."

'So we had four days of intense anxiety waiting for *Graf Spee* to come out from Montevideo and reopen the battle. We anticipated with considerable apprehension a devastating night action at close range in which we could possibly torpedo her, but could expect heavy damage in return.

'Fortunately, it was not to be. On the evening of the 17th we learned that *Graf Spee* was disembarking some of her crew, and as dusk fell she left harbour. *Ajax, Achilles* and *Cumberland* (which had joined us) closed towards the harbour entrance. *Ajax* flew off her aircraft, which reported that *Graf Spee* had stopped with a boat alongside. Soon after we received the signal "*Graf Spee* has blown herself up."

'The relief was intense. We had been very strung up from the four days of waiting, and now tension was released. Everyone crowded on deck and as *Achilles* came close by we cheered and cheered madly.

'It was an incredible climax to a very great drama.'

Chapter 3

LICKING WOUNDS

LISTING HEAVILY to starboard, her forecastle aflame, her bridge a mass of twisted, useless metal, H.M.S. *Exeter* turned towards the Antarctic ice-fields. In a cloud of smoke and flame she dropped over the southern horizon, to be lost completely to the world. As the Battle of the River Plate moved towards its fantastic denouement[1] *Exeter* struggled at 18 knots on the 1200-mile journey to the Falklands, a seemingly impossible task for a ship of whom *Ajax*'s officer-observer had said, 'I have never seen such a shambles, anyway in a ship which survived. Her mainmast was moving perceptibly as she rolled.'

Captain Bell was indeed perturbed about that mainmast. He described it as whipping like a piece of bamboo, and even considered the possibility of shipping it, but was fearful that further casualties might result. There was enough to worry about in the basic problem of keeping the ship seaworthy and safe from further attack. At one point a telltale sign of smoke on the horizon caused some concern, but we discovered later that it was a merchant ship whose crew in their turn had with trepidation thought we were a potential Nazi raider.

Fortunately the weather was reasonable, although it worsened a little as we moved south and the ship began to roll badly. Three times we stopped to consign our dead to the Antarctic sea, wrapped in their rough canvas shrouds. Then, on the morning of the third day, we made landfall—a return to the Falklands, but with sixty-two officers and men no longer aboard. As we entered the winding

[1] See Appendix 1, p.206.

[43]

channel leading into Port Stanley I looked with horror at the red, decomposing hulk of the old iron steamship *Great Britain*, abandoned and rotting on the mud outside the harbour. Was this to be the plight of *Exeter*?

Back at the mouth of the River Plate the British cruisers had broken off the action, after *Ajax* had received a damaging hit and had limited ammunition left.[2] Captain Langsdorff, after an inspection of his ship, decided that *Graf Spee* was not seaworthy for the North Atlantic and made his decision to enter Montevideo. At 1954 hours on 17 December the *Graf Spee* blew herself up, and on the 19th her captain shot himself.[3]

For us this was in the realm of the unknowable, and there was too much to occupy us for thoughts of the future. Daily we patched and plugged the holes in *Exeter*'s hull, rigged jury aerials, repaired and re-checked equipment. I had plenty to do to bring the guns in 'Y' turret back into full working order, and there was the daily visit we made to our wounded in the hospital ashore, a place so full that many of the patients slept in beds in local dwellings, while the Falklands folk slept on the floor. Daily we buried more of our shipmates.

Captain Bell had the remaining splinters taken from his eye—he had already endured one operation while at sea—and there was the overriding anxiety to keep alive those serious casualties that remained. This was made a more viable task when, about a fortnight later, a special hospital team arrived from Buenos Aires.

There was also the special problem of the two lads from HMNZS *Achilles* awaiting transfer back to their ship.[4] Their names were Ashley Ramond Synnott and Thomas Collins: Collins was drowned when HMS *Neptune* was lost off the coast of Africa on 19 December 1941, while Synnott came through the war and joined the Merchant

---

[2] This was thought to be the case, but Harwood in fact broke off the action so that he could attack, if given the chance, at night.

[3] The story of the Battle of the River Plate, its final phases, and the aftermath are described in some detail in *The Drama of Graf Spee and the Battle of the Plate* (Peter Davies, 1964), by Sir Eugen Millington-Drake, K.C.M.G. A commentary on the aftermath, written later by Sir Eugen, is in Appendix I, pp. 206–212.

[4] See pp. 34–35.

Service, going on to hold a Master's Ticket with the Union Steamship Company of New Zealand.

After the battle they were returned to *Achilles* with a glowing recommendation for their bravery and conduct under fire, which was taken into account when they were brought before their Captain.

After a while rumours began to spread through the ship about what was going to happen to us. Some said we were all going to leave the ship and be split up among other vessels; others reckoned we were all going to South Africa to be drafted from there. Meanwhile the drawling voice of 'Lord Haw Haw' was busily broadcasting to the world that H.M.S. *Exeter* was at the bottom of the sea.

Then Captain Bell had us all up on the quarterdeck to give us the real information, the welcome news that we were to take *Exeter* home to Devonport. For this we were indebted, as we were to learn later, to the view of Winston Churchill. 'I was most anxious,' he wrote later, 'about the *Exeter*, and could not accept the proposals made to me to leave her unrepaired in the Falkland Islands till the end of the war.' The following minute indicates some details of Churchill's thoughts at that time:

FIRST SEA LORD, CONTROLLER AND OTHERS   17.xii.39
This preliminary report of damage to *Exeter* shows the tremendous fire to which she was exposed and the determination with which she was fought. It also reflects high credit on the Constructors' Department that she should have been able to stand up to such a prolonged and severe battering. This story will have to be told as soon as possible, omitting anything undesirable (i.e. what the enemy should not know).
What is proposed about repair? What can be done at the Falklands? I presume she will be patched up sufficiently to come home for a long refit. . . . We ought not readily to accept the non-repair during the war of *Exeter*. She should be strengthened and strutted internally as far as possible. . . .

It was a proud moment when, one afternoon, we saw steaming into the harbour at Port Stanley two 8-inch cruisers, HMS *Dorsetshire* (Captain D.C.C. Martin) and *Shropshire* (Captain A.W.L.T. Bisset). They had come, as one might put it, to take us home.

That afternoon I was walking aft to my turret on the quarterdeck when I heard the shrill sound of the bosun's whistle. At the top of the gangway stood the grey-haired captain of HMS *Shropshire*. He removed his cap smartly and stood stiffly to attention, looking at the young sub-lieutenant and the quartermaster in front of him.

'Gentlemen, may I have the honour to come aboard your gallant ship?'

On a cold morning in late January 1940, with cruel winds lashing from the Antarctic, we steamed out of Port Stanley, regretfully leaving some of our wounded but glad to be on the way home. Later our escort cruisers were replaced by ships of the famous Force H, the aircraft carrier *Ark Royal* and the 32,000-ton battle-cruiser *Renown*. *Ark Royal* left us after a while to chase and report on German merchantmen off Portugal, so *Renown* ploughed on with us towards the Bay of Biscay, where, three days out, we were joined by nine destroyers of the Western Approaches command. They swarmed around us like flies, only leaving us to investigate any 'pings' that came up on their asdic sets—and this was a fairly frequent occurrence, as U-boats were being briefed to prevent us getting back to port.

The proximity of these submarines was tragically indicated one Sunday morning when one of the large Blue Star Line ships, *Sultan Star*, came up over the horizon ahead of us and passed across our bows two miles ahead. All her crew were on deck, excitedly waving their recognition of us. We waved back and returned the cheers; then within minutes we were miles apart, and she was just dipping over the western horizon when the explosion occurred. Huge pillars of smoke and flame soared skyward where the Star boat had been. That pack of U-boats had missed us by a mere ten miles.

Our attendant destroyers made about three or four depth-charge attacks per day until we arrived at Plymouth on 14 February. One U-boat even followed us to within a few miles of the English coast until she was spotted and attacked.

Then Plymouth came into sight, and as we passed the familiar lighthouse the keepers hung over the rails and cheered. The grassy slopes of the Hoe were a solid mass of people, cheering, shouting, and waving to this scrap-heap of a vessel that they had christened only nine years before. Then past Admiralty House, Mount Wise, with a group of VIPs following us upstream in the C.-in-C.'s barge.

Past the ship's birth-place where dockyard workers banged lustily with their hammers, their faces showing the pride in the skill that had built this ship which had refused to go down.

Cranes dipped their jibs in salute, and sirens shrieked a hysterical welcome home to the ship of which Captain Langsdorff had said, 'I knocked out their foremost guns; I smashed their bridge; yet, with only one gun firing, they came at me again. One can only have respect for such a foe as that.'

We moved into our berth, already thronged with more cheering crowds and with waiting newsreel-cameramen and reporters. There in the middle of the crowd stood a man in reefer jacket and yachting-cap waiting to come aboard, a man who was to write later, 'My view prevailed. The *Exeter* reached this country safely. I had the honour to pay my tribute to her brave officers and men from her shattered deck in Plymouth Harbour.'

The wire went taut; the gangway dropped and the portly figure clambered aboard to the strains of *Roll out the Barrel* from the Marines band. Winston Churchill, First Lord of the Admiralty, had come aboard the ship which he had told the world would return.

KNIGHTSBRIDGE 7972.

28, HYDE PARK GATE,

LONDON, S.W. 7.

December, 1959

I send the Veterans' Association of the Survivors of the famous River Plate Battle my warm good wishes and my memories of their gallant and successful action in 1939.

Winston Churchill

Chapter 4

INTERMISSION

EXETER'S SHIP'S company went on leave, and many men went afterwards to other ships, in particular to HMS *Kenya* and HMS *Bonaventure*. I went to 'school' to take examinations for Chief Ordnance Artificer; then we were all caught up in the crisis of Dunkirk. Some of our electrical artificers went as staff to the Maginot Line—an unfortunate waste of talent—while I had a spell in the French super destroyer-leader *Le Triomphant* before she was taken over by the Free French Forces.

Then I was frequently away on mystery refits to damaged ships. With a team of artificers I carried out the refit while the tired and battered crew went on leave. It was on one of these refits that I was travelling to Rosyth and crossing the Forth Bridge, from where, looking down from the train, I could see HMS *Repulse* coming in from sea. When the train arrived at Rosyth we were almost alongside her as she made fast, and it was indeed an enjoyable occasion to meet my old friend and best man, Jock.

When I returned to Plymouth it was to find that German bombers were making attacks on the city and docks, but there was *Exeter*, swarming with dockyardsmen who were replacing the old bridge and funnels and changing the guns in the two foremost turrets. I could see that they were removing the old catapult and fitting a modern twin type, and that the old single 4-inch guns were being replaced by twin high-angle and surface guns. She was certainly getting more than a mere 'face-lift'.

Then my promotion to be Chief Ordnance Artificer came through, and a week later I was called to the Ordnance Lieutenant's office.

[48]

This was obviously for yet another 'draft chit', and I wondered just what was in store for me. Having had one ordeal by fire and a variety of work since, I think I was prepared for anything.

The Ordnance Officer, Lieutenant S. Dobson, RN, came straight to the point. 'You have to go to sea again—in fact, you have a choice.'

I must have looked at him a bit oddly at that moment. In wartime no sailor volunteers for anything—it is a superstition among us—and having a choice seemed very much like volunteering.

'You have the choice of two ships, Bill. You are going as Chief of either the newly built *Charybdis* or your old ship. No hurry. Let me know in the morning.'

Perhaps there *was* an element of choice. HMS *Charybdis*[1] was a brand-new 5.25-inch ship, offering much to a gunnery expert. But I had been watching *Exeter* taking almost new shape and knew in my heart what my decision would be. For better or for worse, I chose to return to *Exeter*—a decision to have more far-reaching implications than I knew at that moment in time. For me the die was now cast.

When I rejoined *Exeter* I found that there were nine of us from the previous commission, mostly Chiefs of various departments—Roy Ruse, Chief Engine Room Artificer; Bill Eddey, Chief Electrical Artificer; Harold Newman, Chief Telegraphist; the Gunner, Mr Dallaway; Leading Seaman John (later Gunner W.O.); Stoker Petty Officer George Crocker; Stoker Petty Officer Osborne from the store; and the 'Tanky', Leading Stoker Jan Cloake. When the day came for recommissioning we found that the majority of the new crew had never been to sea before, and on my staff of ordnance artificers only three out of the eleven had ever heard a gun fire before. Yet, in the tests that lay ahead of them and the personal victories that each of them was to win, they turned into a team of experts to be proud of. No Chief in the Royal Navy ever had a better staff at the back of him.

Exeter had indeed been transformed. The terrible desolation that had been the CPO's flat after the Battle of the Plate was now reorganized and reconstructed, and there was a new mess under the

---

[1] *Charybdis* was later sunk by E-boats on 23 October 1943, with the loss of nearly all her crew. No gunnery ratings survived.

bridge. It was difficult for the nine of us who had come back to believe that she had ever taken such a tremendous battering.

Our new skipper, Captain Beckett, was a stout bulldog type who was everywhere in the ship, asking questions and keeping the ship's company constantly on their toes. This was essential if we were to bring a raw crew up to the standards needed for our next spell of duty. Tragically, on the very day of commissioning, Captain Beckett died on the gangway.

Captain O.L. Gordon took over command of *Exeter* the next day, and the process of storing and provisioning, training and loading with ammunition went on—even though Plymouth became the target of a three-day blitz of great intensity. The young, untried crew received their initial 'battle training' in their home port, and the new barrels of *Exeter*'s guns grew hot from their first action against enemy aircraft.

On 24 March 1941, we left Devonport on the start of the second wartime commission, and as I looked back at the blitzed city of Plymouth enveloped in a pall of smoke it seemed unbelievable that I had stood on that same deck just over twelve months before, on *Exeter*'s triumphant return from the Plate. Now we were prematurely back at sea after steaming out into Plymouth Sound, because we were providing too much of a target for the enemy night bombers. In escaping we were leaving our families and friends to one of the heaviest periods of bombing apart from the London blitz.

Frank Clements looked back at the city with strong emotions. He and his wife of three weeks had been staying at the Strathmore Hotel, not far from the Hoe, and had been in the thick of the bombing. Now, to be separated so abruptly with *Exeter*'s departure was certainly tough.

Then the smoke from Plymouth was gone, the horizon clear, and we were on passage once more, arriving at Scapa Flow on my birthday and in a howling blizzard.

For the next month we operated with the 1st Cruiser Squadron, attempting to weld our new ship's company into a fighting unit. Gunnery, torpedo and action stations kept us busy almost every minute of the day, but the crew were learning fast. Then we went on a lone patrol duty in the Denmark Strait, the channel the German raiders were using to break out into the Atlantic. There were some alarms during the fortnight, but they came to nothing, and our main concern was the news over the BBC of another heavy raid on Plymouth.

At Scapa telegrams began to arrive in the ship, telling many that their wives, mothers or members of their family had been killed. Would they be able to get leave for the funeral? Would they be given a chance to visit close relatives in hospital or to do something about the homes that now lay in ruins? There was in fact nothing any of us could do and not the faintest indication of when we should see Plymouth again.

We were later ordered down to the Clyde, where a large convoy of troopships lay at anchor. We had no idea of our destination, but I remember that boxes and boxes of stores were rushed aboard before we sailed, and when they were opened they revealed large numbers of sun-helmets.

We sailed with the convoy WS 8B on 22 May 1941, together with the 7th Destroyer Flotilla, under the command of Captain Vian (later Admiral of the Fleet Sir Philip Vian) in HMS *Cossack*. Also in company with us was the anti-aircraft cruiser *Cairo* and the Polish destroyer *Piorun*. *Repulse* and *Victorious* were to have been the major force in the convoy, but they had been ordered to sea prior to our sailing. The German battleship *Bismarck* had broken out into the North Atlantic.

After that brief, dramatic encounter between *Bismarck* and battle-cruiser HMS *Hood*, which resulted in the sinking of *Hood* on 24 May, the German battleship made off in a south-westerly direction in an attempt to reach the safety of the French coast. Unknowingly her course now began to converge upon the south-westerly course of our convoy 8B, far out off the west coast of Ireland.

At midnight on 25–26 May *Exeter*, the only warship remaining with the convoy, crossed ahead of *Bismarck*, only about 100 miles to the north-west, no great distance at sea, and our convoy would have been in danger had the German warship altered course to starboard. For a spell the German was lost to our hunting units. *Exeter* had not been detached, as she was guarding a very important troop convoy, and during the night we slowly steamed out of the hunting area. It was at 1030 that same morning, 26 May, that *Bismarck* was at last sighted by a Catalina flying-boat. Now every ship within a thousand miles seemed routed to the kill—everyone, that is, except *Exeter*, who steamed along with her convoy of troops, ironically, as charts later showed, the nearest warship to *Bismarck* that night.

We heard the news of the sinking of *Bismarck* on the morning of 27 May, over the ship's broadcasting system. A message was passed by flag signals to the convoy, no doubt to their immense relief and satisfaction, for by now we were steaming farther south, away from the area of conflict and out of the main U-boat danger zone. Our destroyer unit did not rejoin us, but we continued down to Freetown, accompanied on that leg by several Gibraltar-based destroyers, then around the Cape to Durban, and on the last leg of the journey to Aden.

Our mission accomplished, we parted company with the troop convoy at Aden and returned to Durban. This part of the trip, Aden-Durban, was to be the pattern of convoy duties for the next few months.

At the end of September we moved on to Ceylon and docked at Colombo, where our stay became a little too extended for our liking. There was every indication that we were to move on to the Far East—Japan was on the brink of war, and the C.-in-C. East Indies had spent some time on board *Exeter* watching us put the ship through her paces.

I remember one morning feeling very morose indeed. I felt somehow that I was destined to visit the East and that such a trip would be with evil results. The strange feeling returned that I had had that evening when the fortune-teller strode from the room. Blood there had certainly been, and some pain, but the fence and the cruelty. . . . I looked from my workshop through the wire caging to the electrical workshop where Bill Eddey, the Chief Electrical Artificer, worked. Bill had been with me in *Exeter* at the Plate, and we had often chatted about the Far East, where Bill had spent a commission. He could describe the range of delights and dangers on the China coast, but he would always end his lurid narration with the final comment, 'You know, Johno, if we don't look out it's a cod's head and a tin of rice for us.' Little did he know.

There was not a great deal of time for such speculation—events were moving quickly and *Exeter* was busy on a number of special duties. We visited Male, in the Maldives, and later paid a diplomatic call at Calcutta. October and November were uneasy months, with the Japanese occupying bases in Indo-China and the threat of invasion extending to the British base at Singapore. During early November we were engaged with HMS *Glasgow* in convoy protection in the Bay of Bengal.

On the night of 7 December 1941 *Exeter* was ordered to join forces with two of Britain's mightiest warships, the battleship *Prince of Wales* and the battle-cruiser *Repulse*, both operating from Singapore in the South China Sea searching for Japanese invasion fleets. Pearl Harbor had been attacked early that morning and the invasion of Malaya was beginning.

At that time we were escorting a convoy of slow ships to Rangoon, but we were ordered to leave them to make their own way while we set off to join what was intended to be the nucleus of the Eastern Fleet under Admiral Sir Tom Phillips, who flew his flag aboard *Prince of Wales*. We looked forward to joining the two great ships as they, like *Exeter*, were manned by Devonport ratings—but we did not make it. The two warships, with their escorting destroyers, were already out 'hunting', only to be hounded themselves by waves of Japanese aircraft.

We heard the grim news of their sinking as we were speeding through the Malacca Strait to make contact; but we could not believe that those two ships could have been destroyed by torpedo-bombers. They had been marked vessels from the beginning, easily identified as being in Singapore from the photographs in the world Press which showed them lying at anchor. When they steamed north into the huge bay where they hoped to find and destroy Japanese convoys they were sighted by enemy aircraft and soon attacked by numerous waves of torpedo-bombers which flew in regardless of the heavy fire thrown up by both ships.

After a heavy attack by nine planes the steering-gear of *Repulse* was twisted and useless, and she steamed round in a circle completely out of control. Then further waves of planes released their torpedoes at her and she was soon afire and slowing down. When a further unit of bombers hit her with everything they had she began to heel over quickly. From her sloping deck, even out through portholes, men scrambled from the doomed ship, jumping into the oil-polluted sea, where they choked and gasped for breath, while before their stinging eyes their ship, now upside down, plunged beneath the waves.

Just a mile away, stopped completely and with fire and smoke belching from her, fore and aft, *Prince of Wales* sank lower into the sea while Nippon pilots continued to send torpedo after torpedo into her already ripped and gaping hull. While she was still afloat many men were rescued by the gallantry of a destroyer captain who, regardless of intense enemy attack, tucked the stern in hard against the heeling flagship. Although many men were saved, Admiral Sir Tom Phillips and his Flag-Captain went down with their ship.

We altered course for Singapore and arrived there on the 10th, now the only ship of any size remaining in the area. We immediately made everything ready for the arrival later that day of the survivors from the two Devonport ships. I had many friends aboard both of them—forty of the ordnance artificers were of my own branch, and I had one particular friend aboard *Repulse*—a person whom I had not seen since we last met on the dockside at Rosyth.

Later that night, in utter darkness, the destroyers came in with their load of grim, silent, oil-stained men. I shook the hands of dozens that I knew as they came painfully ashore; then I noticed Jock, ran to him, and clasped him tightly by the shoulders. Like all the others, he oozed oil everywhere; but before anything else—the hot bath and the clean overall suit that I hugged under my arm— there was the tot of rum I had ready. Would that I could have done much more for him, for Jock had been best man at my wedding. I am always reminded of him when I hear his favourite song *Over the Sea to Skye*. He came from Stornoway, and his name was Malcolm McLean.

On Christmas Eve we took a convoy from Singapore back to Colombo, one of the ships carrying many of the valuable cargo of survivors from the two warships. Jock was among them, but he was soon to take to the water again when his new ship HMS *Cornwall* was later sunk off Colombo by the Japanese.

From then on it was the convoy pattern as before, running troops and stores to Singapore. I often wondered whether it was really worth the effort. It was becoming increasingly obvious that our time was running out. Daily there were more and more Japanese aircraft, while we saw few if any of our own. The Japanese planes were flying in neat formation, obviously from established airfields near by, and now as we ran our convoys to Singapore we were easily within their range and could be bombed for long periods of each day.

I remember vividly one occasion when we had been attacked persistently since lunch-time. The Japanese planes had come in, wave after wave, for about four hours at high level, and the Gunnery Officer (later Admiral Sir Frank Twiss, Second Sea Lord) sent for me on the bridge and said, 'Chief, I think we will give them a salvo of 8-inch from "A" turret, but first get this fresh ballistic correction put on the fire-control table.'

I went below and saw the correction put on, then returned quickly to the upper deck to watch the effect of the 8-inch blast. Each gun was loaded with a round of fused, shrapnel-burst shell, and both were elevated to a set, predetermined angle and waited for the next wave of complacent Nippon pilots to make their run in.

We did not have to wait long. They came over in a neat, tight formation, high in the sky, and 'A' turret began to train on them, edging a little more to the right, the guns steady in elevation. Then the fire-gong sounded and a yellow flash shot from both guns. In the sky ahead of the bomber formation two brownish-red bursts appeared as the shells exploded. The planes broke formation before the release buttons could be pressed and darted in all directions, their bombs scattered in the ocean miles from us. After that little exhibition we went to tea.

Our convoy routine continued as more men and supplies were poured into Singapore. We were all very tired—since her move to the Far East Station *Exeter* had spent a considerable time at sea, and with the situation in our area rapidly growing worse there was no prospect of rest in the near future, if, in fact, there was to be a future.

Chapter 5

THE BATTLE
OF THE JAVA SEA

THE FALL OF Singapore on 15 February came as no surprise. We had known for weeks that the blow would fall, and now realized that there remained for our use only the Dutch base in Java, one of the vital ports which the Japanese would obviously attack as swiftly as possible. They landed in Sumatra on the 16th and in Bali on the 19th; the capture of Java would mean more than just another ripe plum falling into Japanese hands—it meant the possibility of an invasion of Australia and an increase in the pressure on India and Ceylon.

The Dutch C-in-C, Admiral Helfrich, in nominal charge of Allied ships in the East Indies area, decided to reinforce the Eastern Striking Force under Rear-Admiral Karel Doorman. He ordered H.M.S. Exeter, *H.M.A.S.* Perth *and the destroyers* Jupiter, Electra *and* Encounter *to make for Sourabaya.*

We were at Tanjong Priok, in Batavia, when orders came and we set sail on 25 February. We steamed in a constant state of first-degree readiness to Sourabaya, arriving off that port in the early afternoon and eventually anchoring at 1600 to a welcome of air-raid sirens and Jap bombers. Senior officers had already been rushed ashore for an emergency conference, and within three hours we weighed anchor and were at sea again.

Now we were part of what Captain Gordon called a 'mixed bag' of ships, British, Dutch, American and Australian, which searched the area for three days looking for enemy transports said to be

[56]

steaming southward between Borneo and Celebes. At dawn on the 27th the Japanese air force found us and we were subjected to bombing for most of the morning, fortunately without loss or real damage.

With many of the ships short of oil, the force returned to Sourabaya with the intention of anchoring within the protective minefield until nightfall, when our patrol would be resumed. We were just on the point of entering harbour, at about 1415, when the flag signal 'Follow me' was made by the Admiral in response to a report that Japanese forces had been seen to the northward. Some of the destroyers had already entered harbour, but the regrouping took only fifteen minutes, and the Allied and Japanese units were, at 1430, only about ninety miles apart.

At 1500 we were piped to tea and had our 'wet' at action stations. By 1530 we had moved to full action stations, second in line with *De Ruyter* ahead of us, and astern of us the USS *Houston*. As Lieutenant-Commander Twiss described it, 'The visibility was extreme, the sea calm, and as we roared through the water everyone was waiting, watching, and wanting like hell to get going.

'Shortly after 4 P.M. the look-out in the crow's nest, a midshipman who had just been sent up or was on his way up at the time, reported masts right ahead. Gazing intently at the horizon, it was soon possible to see a series of small sticks appear, which grew and grew: having no hulls attached to them they seemed to be a veritable forest.'[1]

At 1614 on February 27th the Allied unit was in position 06.28 S., 112.26 E., off the north coast of Java, steaming on a W.N.W. course, and in the following order:

> De Ruyter, Exeter, Houston, Perth, Java, Edwards, Alden, Ford, and Paul Jones, *in the line ahead.*
>
> Electra, Encounter, *and* Jupiter *about five miles to the west of* De Ruyter *on a parallel course.*
>
> Witte de With *and* Kortenaer *some two miles to the west of* Paul Jones *on a parallel course.*

An enemy force was sighted some 14 miles ahead of the Allied ships. (See Appendix 2, p. 213.)

[1] Oliver L. Gordon, *Fight it Out* (Kimber, 1957).

As the superstructures began to appear we realized that this was no convoy of transports, but two units of a Japanese naval force, five four-funnelled *Sendai* 5.5-inch cruisers followed by six large modern destroyers in one unit and eight in the other.

At about 1620 the action began. We straddled the enemy quickly and soon had what looked like a hit on the second cruiser, which threw up a thick column of smoke and was not seen during the rest of the battle.

Japanese destroyers were streaking out from behind the smoke-screen to fire their torpedoes and disappear behind the protective curtain again, the action becoming greatly confused amid the rolling masses of smoke. Ships appeared and disappeared, sometimes friendly, sometimes enemy—we could never be sure. It was also difficult to tell the fall of shot, and gunnery control became very complicated. USS *Houston* could tell her fall of shot because her ammunition had a coloured smoke burst.

Further enemy ships had joined the battle, and were identified as two modern cruisers of the *Myoko* class, *Nachi* and *Haguro*, each with a main armament of twin 8-inch guns. These soon engaged both *Exeter* and *Houston*, and we began to be subjected to fierce salvoes.

We registered a hit on one of these cruisers, clearly visible from the gunnery control tower. As Captain Gordon wrote, 'I was watching the fall of shot through my binoculars and saw the big orange flash of the shell bursting on the cruiser's lower bridge structure, followed by the uprising of a column of yellowish smoke.'[2] The Japanese cruiser turned away under cover of smoke and took no further part in the action.

Our excitement was short-lived. We were at that moment being effectively straddled, and a near-miss threw the ship sideways with considerable force. A few minutes later, at about 1700, an 8-inch shell hit the after starboard 4-inch gun, wiping out the right gun crew, but miraculously sparing the left crew. The shell continued through a boiler-room ventilator, exploding in 'B' boiler room with a terrifying roar, followed by the deafening noise of escaping super-heated steam.

Six of the ship's boilers were now out of action and our speed was

---

[2] *Fight it Out.*

greatly reduced. My pal Roy Ruse, Chief ERA, described what he experienced below decks.

'The shell had passed through the main steam pipe leading from the two port boilers in the forward boiler room. All hands in the after boiler room were killed instantly by the escape of steam, with the exception of one stoker petty officer who must have been very near the outlet air-lock when it occurred.

'The sudden loss of steam from the four boilers in the after boiler room and two port boilers in the forward boiler room naturally caused a panic everywhere. Speed dropped to practically nothing, and lights in the engine room dimmed considerably. Main engine throttles were closed down to conserve steam in the two remaining boilers and auxiliary engines in both engine rooms tripped due to lack of steam pressure.

'I remember someone shouting, "The port main feed pump's stopped", but my main concern was that the main engine oil pumps had stopped and the main engines were trailing. Luckily we were fitted with two electrically operated oil pumps which, after a struggle, I managed to get going, for by this time the dynamo outputs were picking up again. Eventually the two remaining boilers managed to increase their output enough for us to get normal machines working again.'

We fell farther and farther behind, losing touch with the fast-moving Allied line as the engagement was fought at about 27 knots and we could now muster only 15. Our plight was quickly noticed by the Japanese destroyers, who closed in for the kill, torpedoes at the ready. *Jupiter* and *Encounter* promptly counter-attacked and made smoke to hide us, while *Electra* gallantly engaged three large destroyers at 6000 yards until she was silenced.

Exeter was ordered to break off action and return to Sourabaya. As we left the smoke-filled battle area we could see a pall of dark smoke that indicated the last of the destroyer *Kortenaer*, struck amid-ships by an enemy torpedo which cut her in half. Then, just as we thought we were free from trouble, a Japanese 8-inch cruiser closed from the northward, intent on finishing us off. We opened fire at her at a range of about 16,000 yards with all available armament, which apparently so surprised the enemy that she made smoke and disappeared behind its screen.

Meanwhile efforts were being made by the engineers under Lieutenant-Commander (E) Chubb to enter the damaged boiler room,
but they were beaten back by the intense heat. Superheated steam
at a temperature of 500°F. has the effect of peeling off the skin and
leaving the flesh like a soft peeled tomato. It was not until early the
following morning that conditions allowed anyone to penetrate the
boiler room to take out the dead.

The remainder of the journey was without incident. It was dark
when we met up with the Dutch destroyer *De With*, who challenged
us by light signal, then led us through the minefields and into the
relative peace and security of Sourabaya Roads.

Bert Diggle, gunner's mate of my old station, 'Y' turret, told later
how, 'in the first action a near miss put "Y" turret out of action and
threw the turret's crew about. We lost power and communication to
forward control, so we switched to aft director and unexpectedly
found pressure had in the meantime been restored. We followed aft
director and fired one broadside before losing pressure. A local sight-
layer told us later that we had scored a direct hit on one of the
cruisers. Apparently the Jap aircraft had been blown overboard and
there had been some hundred casualties.'

Despite this success, the overall effect on the Allied forces had
been disastrous. *De Ruyter* had been hit during the early stages of
the action, then *Exeter* and *Kortenaer*, soon after 1700. *Electra*, shortly
afterwards hit in the boiler room, was eventually silenced and sunk.
At 1745 the Allied forces regrouped and attacked the enemy, *Perth*
setting fire to *Haguro*. At 2125 *Jupiter* was blown up by an underwater
explosion, leaving one destroyer, *Encounter*, and four Allied cruisers.
The American destroyers had returned to Sourabaya to refuel and
reload.

The remnants were closely shadowed, lit by flares dropped by
enemy aircraft, and battle was rejoined later, when both *Java* and
De Ruyter were sunk as a result of the Japanese torpedo attack.[3]
Houston and *Perth* withdrew from the action and returned to Tanjong
Priok. The following morning both cruisers were sunk in an action
against Admiral Kurita's force of three cruisers and nine destroyers.

[3] The Allies were not at that time aware of the advanced stage of Japanese
armament development, particularly of the torpedo. See Appendix 3, p. 215.

All that remained, locked inside the fortress of islands that made up the East Indies, were *Exeter, Encounter* and USS *Pope.*

Chapter 6

SCUTTLE OR FIGHT?

WE BURIED OUR dead in the European cemetery at Kembang Koen-
ing—a neat resting-place, blessed with a breeze that had the hint of
spice in it. For those who remained aboard to repair the damage
there was the harsh reality of twisted pipes and shattered valves,
and for others, with the time to think, a disturbing feeling of remote-
ness as the Jap conquests increased. Artificers and engine-room staffs
down below worked at speed to restore five boilers to working order,
to provide steam for 20 knots with perhaps more later. All this
against a continuous background of gunfire as the ship's 4-inch HA
guns drove off Japanese air attacks.

During a lull in the raids I sat on an iron locker between the two
starboard guns. It was a hot day, and there was the ever-present
stink of cordite and a feeling that there would be no end to it all.
The engine-room boys were working wonders, but what use would
it be if we could only make 15 knots? We would be a sitting target
in an area where Japanese cruisers and destroyers were as plentiful
as flying fish.

My thoughts went back to the final setting of that action in the
River Plate. *Graf Spee* fully operational yet trapped in Montevideo,
with the small British unit patrolling outside. *Exeter* now trapped in
Sourabaya, but with our boiler room blown up, a ship not fully
ready for sea or for action and with several Japanese units patrolling
the surrounding waters. Ironically Captain Gordon was now faced
with a decision on the future of *Exeter* as Captain Langsdorff had
been brought to the moment of decision with his pocket battleship.

Were we to scuttle as they had done, or put to sea where the Japanese waited for us?

'Buzzes' had it that we were to scuttle in the harbour entrance, but preparations continued—making ready the engines for sea, evening out the 8-inch ammunition from the after turret to the two forward turrets. Bert Diggle, Chief Gunner's Mate, who had been ashore with the funeral party, returned on board to check how the equalizing of the ammunition was proceeding and to ensure that essential gunnery stations were filled, even at the expense of less essential duties. The job was made easier by the Gunnery Officer, Lieutenant-Commander Twiss, who commented tersely, 'You can clear the sick-bay; there are no sick from now on, and that includes the doctors.'

On the evening of 28 February, 1942 HMS Exeter *sailed from Sourabaya in company with the destroyers HMS* Encounter *and USS* Pope.

The skipper and the Navigating officer, Lieutenant-Commander Hudson, had been at a special conference ashore, and soon after we sailed the Captain's voice came over the loudspeakers. He explained that the unit had been ordered to proceed well eastward and north-ward of Bawean Island and thence westward through the Sunda Strait to Colombo. He warned us that we could expect no air support and no surface help other than that of our two escorting destroyers. I do not think that he rated our chances very high, but typically he did not show it. 'We shall just have to rely on our own efforts and determination,' he concluded.

So much for the 'buzzes' about scuttling. Even a feeling of opti-mism developed, and some of the crew began to plan what they would do in Colombo. Others grew more sceptical as the intensely bright moonlight continued and the strain of maintaining first-degree readiness began to tell.

It was so quiet—too quiet. With visibility at ten miles we were almost in the same vulnerable position we would be in when dawn revealed us in the approach to Sunda Strait.

There was one scare at 0400 when two merchantmen and their escort appeared to westward—but we avoided them successfully. At 0750 the look-out in the crow's-nest reported topmasts, but after what seemed to be a turn towards us the enemy force resumed its previous course. This move may well have been made to enable the cruisers to fly off their aircraft.

Bert Diggle, aft in 'Y' turret, knew very well what was to be expected and told his crew that they would very soon be in the middle of it. Then he sent some away for breakfast with the warning, 'First salvo, and back as fast as you can.'

At about 0935 the Allied unit was in contact with the enemy—four heavy 8-inch cruisers, Nachi, Haguro, Myoko *and* Ashigara, *and three destroyers,* Kawakaze, Yamakaze *and* Inadzuma. Exeter *reversed course to the eastward, and* Encounter *and* Pope *conformed, taking up their positions ahead.*

Bert Diggle had just gone himself to breakfast. 'On my way,' he said, 'I gave the upper-deck armament a look over and was amused to see a live duck had been fitted with a lifebelt (an inflated condom) which had been fixed round its neck by Hugo, the Maltese cook. I got to the CPO's mess and then I heard the turrets move. I grabbed a piece of bread and a couple of hard-boiled eggs and rushed back to "Y" turret.'

There was no escape. The route to Sunda was blocked, and we would have to fight it out. We opened fire at between 14,000 and 20,000 yards, hitting hard and fast with all three turrets, but it was a one-sided action from the start, the Japanese cruisers being able to concentrate their fire and possessing also the extra turn of speed.

Fate was also unkind to us from the beginning of that action. Our transmission centre developed a fault and our gunnery brain was virtually paralysed, the running action being fought with the emergency use of a clock and Dumaresq (an outmoded piece of apparatus from which gunnery answers—rate and deflection—were worked out; named after the inventor, Captain Dumaresq RN). Under the protection of smoke we weaved in and out, loosing off broadsides in the brief visual contacts with the Japanese ships. Surprisingly we were now making 25 knots, and steam in a fifth boiler was raised to push *Exeter* to 26 knots. The engineers had worked a miracle, but the enemy still had a few knots more in hand.

Local problems were also cropping up. 'Y' turret's gun crew ran into difficulties with a failure of air blast resulting in a build-up of cordite fumes in the turret. Then a hangfire on the right gun could have caused a disaster similar to the serious explosion in HMS *Devonshire* during a peace-time gunnery exercise, but the situation was saved by the coolness of Able Seaman Jock Lindsay in the loading seat. If he had panicked when he found he could not use his loading levers he could have blown up the turret by opening the breech during a misfire period.

Fire from the ten-gun Japanese cruisers was intense, and spotter aircraft were used by the enemy throughout the action. At about 1120 Exeter *received a direct hit.*

We all felt the shudder as the shell exploded. Again it was a single 8-inch shell, but this time it ended up in 'A' boiler room on the other side of the ship. By another adverse stroke of fate the main steam line was again penetrated, and from it gushed the superheated contents. Fires broke out in the ship. We felt way come off the ship as the engines slowed and one by one the electric breakers 'fell off the board'. Power to the dynamos failed, the turrets stopped moving, and the guns ceased firing.

ERA Alf Carne found that he could not raise the engine room or switchboard on his telephone. 'I knew that the previously damaged "B" boiler room could not feed the dynamos, so I kept my fingers crossed that "A" would soon be on line again. I kept the "gags" on the turbo-generating controls to keep the machines going as long as possible, but it was soon obvious that serious damage had occurred somewhere.'

All turrets were motionless, and we became an easier target as all Japanese destroyers closed in. Shells from the enemy cruisers were first straddling and then hitting us from a long range. Fire broke out over the ship, smoke became an increasing hazard and irritant, and down in the bowels of the ship flames were creeping towards the 4-inch magazine. Strangely, many communication lines were still open, and we were all trying to find other methods of bringing *Exeter* back into action, but to no avail. In the Battle of the Plate she had taken far greater punishment, but her speed had not been impaired; now, in the Java Sea, the punishment had not been as extreme, but it had

struck more completely at her vitals. As we slowed down we realized
that the end could not be far away.

There was nothing our two destroyers could do. They had made
smoke for us, and now *Encounter's* captain, seeing our plight, turned
his ship back to our assistance, to be told firmly to leave us and to
get away if he could. Soon *Encounter* and *Pope* were lost to view in
the smoke.

We waited apprehensively at our silent action stations, powerless
to retaliate against the shells that now fell more often around us.
Then the order came at last, over the broadcast system that was still
working, 'Sink the ship.' Seacocks and valves were opened, charges
exploded below decks to open holes in the ship's bottom, and the
Java Sea flowed in. A few minutes later, about 1135, Captain Gordon
gave the equally terse command, 'Abandon ship.'

My blood ran cold as I heard it. I turned to young Bob Berry
and said, 'Come on, let's go.' Outside the workshop we joined a
crowd from the engine room going up the main ladder on to the
starboard waist, a slow job until someone suggested opening the
main hatch, which made escape an easier matter.

From the upper-deck directors and bridge to the boiler and engine
rooms below, near the deep cordite magazines, the men of *Exeter*
came on deck for the last time. It was every man for himself, yet
there was no panic and no one seemed to be in a great hurry—after
all, there was nowhere to go.

Failure of power meant that boats could not be swung out, but
floats and rafts were cut adrift and thrown over the side. Jumping
nets were rigged, and the wooden planks we used to sit on at church
each Sunday were heaved overboard. As men puffed air into their
lifebelts and kicked off their shoes they even had time to glance at
the choppy sea below and realize that at least the water would be
warm.

Roy Ruse in the engine room received his orders from the Engineer, Commander Drake.

'All the machinery was left running as it was, for as long as the
steam lasted, and we all trooped out of the engine room, quite
orderly, and no panic. I was last to leave the forward engine room
and say goodbye to a ship in which I had three commissions of
happy memories. Looking back over events, I think that with our

full quota of boilers we could have shown the Japs a clean pair of heels.'

Aft, inside the quarterdeck turret, Bert Diggle heard the last order and took the manhole cover off. 'Immediately the turret filled with smoke, on top of the cordite fumes already there; consequently conditions were very bad. With the choking fumes and smoke, I was unable to see more than a few feet. I passed the order to the magazine and shell rooms to open seacocks and abandon ship and report when clear. Petty officer Jan Padden reported, "All men out, and the water rising rapidly." He must have been the last man out of the magazine and shell room.

'The right gun's crew left first, followed by cabinet and left gun, and in spite of the appalling conditions in the turret they did precisely as ordered, with no panic. Lieutenant Kerr, the Officer of the Quarters, on leaving the turret, said that he would do lower quarters. I could not see if the gun house was clear, so I crawled around to ensure that all the men had got away. I could not see the manhole but knew where it was. I found it by falling out of the turret and cracking my head. With the combination of this and the fumes I passed out and came to lying on the quarterdeck.'

ERA Alf Carne, down in the forward dynamo room, prepared to leave. 'Our normal exit was about 30 feet up a vertical steel ladder through the watertight bulkhead door to the locker flat above. This trunking carried on as a natural air vent to the forecastle deck. About a week before the action I had fixed a loose wire ladder to the exit on the forecastle deck and this saved our lives.

'We heard no order to abandon ship and I did not know of it until the screen door 30 feet up opened and a stoker petty officer, in charge of the damage control party in the locker flat above, shouted down, "Alf, can we use your ladder?"

'When I asked him why, he replied, "A and B boiler rooms are on fire" (I thought we were getting rather hot) "and there's a fire in the flour store forward. We're bloody well trapped and it's abandon ship."

'I agreed, but made sure that my lads got up the stretch to the locker flat first and then on to the upper deck. I stayed in the ventilation trunk with my torch until all the damage control party were clear.

'When I reached the deck I remember thinking how fresh the air was and what a nice sight the Nip ships were—line ahead and all guns firing. Then I registered the fact that they were firing at me, and I started moving aft in a hurry. Flames were licking part of the superstructure, but our battle flags were still visible in the smoke and flames. Someone—I do not know who—was running ahead of me when suddenly, with a roar like an express train, a salvo caused me to crash to the deck. A terrific explosion shook me for a few seconds, and when I recovered, the man ahead of me was nothing but a bloodied wreck of two legs—his torso was missing. A great sheet of metal seemed to be floating in the air—it was the lid of "Y" turret. A direct hit had smashed the whole of the after superstructure.

'The time between climbing out of the dynamo room and going over the side was probably only a minute or two, yet at the time it seemed far longer. Strange how one reacts— I took my shoes off and laid them carefully with cap, gloves, and torch just abaft the fan intake and promptly dived 30 feet over the heeling ship's side into the sea. I've never attempted such a high dive before or since.'

The ship's company followed the floats and rafts over the side. Enemy shells straddled and hit more frequently now, but *Exeter* still had way on so that the crew, swimming and clinging to rafts, were strung out in a long line astern. This cleared them a little from the oil that was now leaking from the ship and took them out of the direct line of fire.

Petty Officer Churchward, the ship's painter—better known as 'Putty'—was going aft along the upper deck from his action station. 'Shells were dropping in the water near us as I came down the port ladder from the forecastle to the 4-inch gun deck. Then I heard a shell whistling towards the ship and I fell flat on my face on the iron deck. There was a crash right underneath me, and I felt a terrific blow on the part of my leg which was resting on the hot, iron gun deck.

'I sat up, but my foot remained where it was, at almost right angles to my leg. Somehow I managed to struggle over to the guard rail and hung on there. I remember that the Navigating Officer asked me if I needed a hand to get over the side, but I said I thought I could manage it.

'I set off aft, slowly hauling myself along on one leg, and came at last to the ladder going down to the quarterdeck. Somehow, in terrible pain, I got down its nine steps. Then I looked over the side and saw a little way aft that a jumping ladder was rigged—a kind of large square pole and hanging from it a large wire ladder, like a net. As I made my way down the net I had some difficulty as my broken leg, hanging judas as it were, became caught in the rungs. Then I found myself near the water and, a moment before letting go and splashing into the sea, I looked up towards the blue sky, murmured the words "The sea is His",[1] and fell in.'

Black smoke was pouring out of *Exeter* amidships as she began to list. As I came aft I noticed many rafts still aboard and stopped a young seaman about to jump over the side. I undid the knife dangling at his belt and began to cut loose what rafts I could see. I had just negotiated the ladder to the quarterdeck when a shell hit the superstructure of the officer's cabin flat, just behind me, and the blast threw me to the deck and almost over the side.

I sat up and put my hand back over my shoulder to feel the wet patch. Yes, it was blood, and it was also certainly time that I left. I placed my shoes neatly under the ladder, blew up my lifebelt, lowered myself over the side, and let go.

Exeter still forged ahead at about five knots, listing more now and spawning in her wake a line of rafts, men, and boxes, followed by oil and flotsam. Only one boat was lowered; that was no more than a gesture, for the bottom had already been blown out while it was in the davits.

We floundered uncomfortably in a choppy sea, feeling the shock-waves as the shells exploded in the water around us. Bert Diggle recalls being flung head over heels under the surface by a salvo falling about twenty yards away.

Exeter heeled farther to port, but still moved ahead, smoke and flames rising from her, the turret guns pointing skyward. Then, from starboard, a Japanese destroyer approached at speed to finish her off with torpedoes. The enemy destroyers fired four torpedoes, one of which hit and tore open *Exeter's* hull; I remember noticing that it was just below our mess. For a moment she straightened herself

---

[1] When this part is said in the prayers the sailors usually add under their breath, 'and He can have it!'

defiantly and heeled over to starboard. A few minutes later there was a tremendous upsurge of frothing water and she had gone.

Exeter *sank just before noon on 1 March, 1942.* Encounter *and* Pope *continued to engage the enemy, but were eventually abandoned and sunk after being put out of action by gunfire and continuous dive-bombing.*

Chapter 7

TAKEN FROM THE SEA

I THINK I must have been one of the last to leave the ship because it was not many minutes after that I saw Captain Gordon and some of the officers leave *Exeter* by the starboard side. By this time the survivors were strung out for some distance on a motley collection of rafts, floats, planks, and what have you—almost in a straight line. This probably extended over several miles. The water was warm, but we knew that sharks were plentiful in the area, and wondered more than once if the old yarn was true that explosions in the water tended to drive them away for a time. If it were true, how long would it last?

Now *Exeter* had gone, leaving an expanse of choppy sea and the hot afternoon sun. With her had gone all our personal possessions and what little security we had, and those who survived her now swam or floated helplessly in the middle of the Java Sea. They had kicked off their clothing and were beginning to feel the burning sun on the areas of flesh exposed above the water.

Some of the Japanese ships had begun to close in, their crews lining the guard rails. I remember one destroyer approaching us, the crew running up from below decks and from their gun positions: jubilant little yellow men eager to catch a glimpse of the floundering British. Then in a trice they all returned to their stations, hatches were slammed shut, screws turned, and the destroyer moved off at speed.

At that moment I was sharing a church plank with a young Irish telegraphist. I remember how that infernal plank kept rolling and turning over in the choppy sea. We were still worried about sharks, but much more concerned at being alone with a piece of wood miles from the nearest shore. We could be reasonably certain, too, that there were no other Allied ships in the Java Sea.

Now the *Exeter* was sunk, the main battle was over, and the enemy cruisers soon disappeared with their escort destroyers over the horizon to hunt our two destroyers. Later, two of the Japanese destroyers returned to pick up our scattered survivors. They steamed towards us, stopped engines, and began to drift down towards some of the groups of swimmers.

Bert Diggle said that after he had left *Exeter* he managed to help Millburn—a non-swimmer— to a small float, from where they both watched the ship go down. Later a Japanese destroyer drifted near by, so he paddled Millburn over to it and managed to get him up the ladder and inboard. Bert grabbed the ladder but just did not have the strength to pull himself out of the water. Two of the ship's company got hold of him and yanked him aboard, where he collapsed.

Some men found it very difficult to reach the destroyer, which was drifting quite quickly, and often the distance they had to swim was too great. Our First Lieutenant, Lieutenant-Commander Cooper, had been floating on his back and had watched the destroyer pass at a distance on its first run, then noticed that it had moved upwind and was drifting down a second time. He had been two and a half hours in the water and was feeling almost all-in, when he managed to grasp the rope ladder and pull himself on to the deck of the Japanese ship.

The Irish lad and I clung as best we could to our plank, but I was beginning to feel the wound in my back, which was still bleeding badly, and eventually I was helped into a nearby float. There was a great deal of good comradeship in the Java Sea that afternoon. Men who were able to swam from raft to raft to talk to their friends and to give reassurance where necessary. 'Putty', with his shattered ankle, was being carefully looked after on one of the floats; farther over, the utmost care was being taken of Dally, who had been terribly burnt and was expected to die at any moment.

Alf Carne felt very lonely during his first moments in the water. 'It seemed to me that I was very isolated, but gradually I met up with a few others and we collected a drifting and holed Carley float.

I think about five of us climbed on this raft, including a chief stoker with a splinter through his back and in his lungs. He, poor chap, died within half an hour.

'I found that I had a sliver of steel—like a needle—through the fleshy part of my ankle. I hadn't felt it and had no idea when it hit me. I pinched it out and left the two little holes. Later this was to turn septic, and I feel the effects of it to this day.'

I had been in the water for three hours when I noticed the Japanese destroyer— one of the latest type that had been in the unit that had disposed of *Exeter*. As the ship slowed almost to a stop we wondered what was going to happen next. Would they shoot us out of the water? Were they going to pick us up or not?

Within a few moments ropes were put over the side, and gradually we all swam, paddled or floated towards the ship. Covered in fuel oil and unsure of our reception, we hauled ourselves aboard. The Japanese crew helped no one, and every few minutes the ship turned her screws and moved on. Many of our men, completely exhausted from their efforts to climb, could not hold on when the ship moved, but fell back into the water incapable of making further attempts.

When we reached the upper deck we saluted as is the custom on our own men-of-war. We were met by a squad of Japanese sailors armed with rifles, and a Chief Petty Officer with a long, drooping moustache who asked in English, 'Officer?' We were subjected to a search, but as most of us had very few clothes on this was not a prolonged operation. The Japanese sailors then prodded with their rifles, moving us aft to where quite a gathering of our ship's company began to muster on the quarterdeck.

After I had been aboard for about ten minutes the English-speaking C.P.O. came aft, asking: 'Who number one? Who number one?' I was pointed out as being the senior rating aft, and was led away to one of the Japanese officers who was waiting just clear of the quarterdeck.

'Who else was in harbour when you left? How many ships were there with you today?' asked the Jap C.P.O. interpreting for the officer.

'I don't know,' I replied. 'As an engineer I work below decks and did not see the harbour at all.'

'What were the bird's-nest fittings on top of your masts?'

I made no answer. I felt sure that they knew already that it was
our radar. Instead of replying I put my hand behind me and felt my
shoulder, then showed my blood-covered hand. The officer muttered
something and went away and I was pushed and prodded by the
guards back to the others on the quarter-deck. The interrogation
was over.

Meanwhile men were still hauling themselves aboard from the
sea. The Captain of Marines almost didn't make it—he was swimming hard against the tide and the ship's movement, but when he
eventually and laboriously hauled himself in he was greeted by a
great cheer from the *Exeter* men already aboard the destroyer.

Some men tried to climb aboard aft but were sucked down by the
destroyer's propellers as she moved off, and in the confused situation
it became a point now to search the sea for our friends and to
question those who came aboard whether they had seen a particular
pal.

Then the time came when the Japanese decided that they had
enough of us aboard. Up came the ropes, although many were still
trying to clamber aboard, and behind the ship many still struggled
in the water. The destroyer increased speed, steamed away to the
north, and all we could do was to wave to our shipmates in the
water. Soon it would be dark.

Not long after we had got under way action stations sounded
aboard the Japanese destroyer. The crew ran quietly to their stations,
guns were unlocked, trained, and loaded, while control positions
were manned. We were made to lie flat on the deck, the 5.1-inch
guns pointing over us ready to fire, but nothing came of it. The guns
were trained fore and aft again, crews stood down, and we saw for
the first time the 'Eastern grin'. Later we were to become only too
aware that all was not well when the Japanese grinned in that
manner.

We were given our first meal later that evening, all sitting on the
deck, while little white snowballs were passed round. It seemed to
us that these 'rice balls' were very much the equivalent of our own
'meat balls', and we laughed and joked about this odd diet. It was
as well that we could laugh at that introduction to rice—later men
would consider selling their souls for one of those little 'white
snowballs'.

We washed the rice down with a mixture of condensed milk and water which the Japanese had made up in a couple of 'fannies'. Later we slept, or wrestled with our thoughts and fears, under a starry sky. Many thought of home and when we would be able to return, for as far as we knew we were the first naval prisoners of war to be taken by the Japanese Navy, and it was still an open question where they were likely to take us and what they would do with us there.

The destroyer steamed on through most of the following day until, in the late afternoon, we sighted land and eventually could see a harbour opening up. From the preparations on board we had the feeling that we might be put ashore there. We were somewhat of an embarrassment to the destroyer crew—our numbers were large relative to the Japanese ship's company, and the idea of taking the destroyer over had never been far from our minds. We did indeed disembark, but not ashore. In the harbour, flying the familiar red ball, was the largest oil tanker I had seen—she dwarfed the tankers that were busy refuelling some destroyers near by.

Boats came alongside, and we were pushed down into them and taken off to the large oiler, where we were met by Japanese guards somewhat more aggressive than those aboard the destroyer. With much prodding, we were directed below, and once all were aboard the hatch covers were slammed back and we sat there in the pitch darkness and the dreadful stench between decks. After about two hours we were permitted a spell on deck, arranged in batches, and I shall never forget, when my turn came, leaning with some of the others over the stern, gazing into the clear water. We could see the ship's screws and swimming around them—like two goldfish in a bowl—were two huge sharks. I shuddered when I recalled how we had been so long in the sea.

The sharks dominated conversation that evening. I felt nothing but revulsion, and had someone suggested that I might like to eat a shark steak he would have had a very short answer. Time was to alter that feeling.

We found that the harbour we had entered was Bandjurmasin, in South Borneo, probably the harbour from which the enemy ships had sailed to engage our unit and sink *Exeter*. We spent the next day aboard the oiler, and in the later afternoon we saw signs of other ships arriving. To our surprise, we made out the shape of a small Japanese gunboat escorting in, of all things, a Dutch hospital ship. The Japanese had apparently captured her at sea while she was looking for survivors from the *Java* and *De Ruyter*, and, despite the Red Cross emblem and international agreements, she was now 'in the bag', complete with full medical staff and nurses.

Chapter 8

OP-TEN-NOORT

You CAN imagine our thoughts on being transferred to the Dutch hospital ship—the possibility of friendly attention and treatment for our badly injured men. At that stage we were still partly under the illusion that the Red Cross and the Geneva Convention had some meaning; some of us even had pleasant thoughts of repatriation. But we should have taken more notice of the fact that the hospital ship and its complement were, like us, prisoners, and that the Japanese had little regard for the vessel other than as a means of conveying us to some unknown destination.

For those of us who were wounded the transfer to *Op-ten-Noort* was the first chance of real medical treatment. We were called in turn to the operating theatre, where the Dutch doctors and nurses treated us with skill, and where our Surgeon, Surgeon Lieutenant Wyatt, was able to make sure that we were well attended to. Nine of us needed urgent treatment—the Chief 'Buffer', CPO Acotte, had a broken thigh, and there was 'Putty' Churchward's shattered ankle to be treated.

Down in the operating theatre everything that was done was watched closely by the Japanese guards. It was, in fact, from that quarter that I first heard the voice of the Nip raised in anger, part snarl, part scream. From the recesses of my hospital bed, wrapped in a clean bandage and after a drink of hot milk, I felt it was all too unreal. The Dutch nurse had assured me that my back would be all right and that I should try to get some sleep. Yet, in spite of this, I lay thoughtful and anxious, realizing deep down what a terrible situation we had fallen into. It could all become very, very unpleasant. As I lay there the throbbing of the ship's engines indicated that *Op-ten-Noort* was still steadily under way.

During the second day aboard shouting and screaming Japanese guards rushed into the ward. A rifle was poked at me, and the Dutch nurse said in her broken English, 'You get from the bed out.' Slowly, because my left arm and shoulder were strapped and bandaged, I struggled from the bunk. I was fortunate in being able to stand—others less fortunate were being prodded to get out—and I heard the Dutch doctors protesting that the seriously injured men could not be moved, let alone driven from their beds.

The Japanese guard stood by and watched as I got to my feet, then I was given a shove and barely had time to grab my only personal property, a torn blue overall suit, before I was marched forward to join the rest of the ship's company.

A hatch was opened and I was pushed through into a converted store which now housed my shipmates; an indescribable place, unlit except for a small bulb at one end and having all the appearance of some cave from the Arabian Nights. Jammed together, all sitting with knees up—there was no room for straightening them—were *Exeter's* ship's company. There had been neither the time nor the opportunity for them to wash the fuel oil from their sore skin, and many were completely naked. Some were sick and in need of hospital treatment, particularly those whose tongues were swollen from the effect of salt water and oil. But no treatment was forthcoming; no doctor came down into the hold to see them. How lucky I had been in my temporary luxury, but now I was with the others down in the 'madhouse'.

In my hospital bed I had had no idea of these terrible conditions, but within a few minutes of my arrival I was not only aware of them but was taking my turn in the maddest queue I have ever joined, and one that lasted all day. The men had found some old Bols gin bottles in the store, and groups shared a bottle which they filled with their only real sustenance—water. The supply came grudgingly from a tank with a tap locked and bolted because the ship did not make enough water to supply the sudden influx of prisoners.

From this locked tap came a drip of water which would fill one of the Bols bottles in about half an hour, and back from the tap stretched the queue of bottle-holders—a representative from each group. You queued, filled the bottle, and immediately another member of your group tacked on to the end of the line, because by the time he arrived at the tap the group bottle would be empty. So the day passed in this bizarre activity while *Op-ten-Noort* steamed on.

Many of the men in the hold had not eaten anything for two days—since they have been given their rice ball aboard the Jap destroyer. On the first day aboard *Op-ten-Noort* a quantity of food had been left at the top of the gangway, but there had been such a rush by everyone that many had been missed out and had nothing at all to eat. When the Indonesian cooks had left a bucket of soup at the top of the gangway there was such a blind rush that most of it was spilt and hardly anyone tasted it.

It was obvious that some discipline had to be enforced. There were no officers in the hold—they were in messes under the main deck and had been given food and drink; I had even seen some of them smoking. While in the sick bay I had seen that many of the officers were able to clean the fuel oil from their bodies with wads of cotton-wool and medicated spirit. You can imagine how great my horror was to see what the ship's company were being subjected to in that dark, cramped hold. Those men, hungry and dirty and many in need of urgent medical attention, had in the previous three days taken part in two major sea battles and had seen their ship go down. For many it had meant a long spell in the water. Small wonder that they reacted in such a wild manner to the conditions they were experiencing.

Discipline appeared quickly in the form of a stocky figure of CPO Bert Diggle. Chief Gunner's Mate of *Exeter*, he had been used to giving orders and to having them carried out. With the minimum of fuss he called the Chiefs of the various departments together and told them that in future Chief Petty Officers would hand out the food, and at the daily issue every one of the ratings in the hold was served with something to eat before the Chiefs touched a thing. So lower-deck discipline was established and was to have important effects upon our later experiences.

It was during that second day that Captain Gordon came aboard, transferred from a Japanese destroyer which had picked up a group of survivors from a cork mat. The skipper had clung to an upturned boat for a while, but it became waterlogged and went under. He

swam to a Carley float a few hundred yards away, but it was hope-
lessly overloaded with wounded men, so he continued swimming for
another quarter of a mile to another float. There he was able to get
a handhold and there he remained for the next twenty hours.

During their night in the water the survivors had been brought
together in a group. The Navigating Officer, Lieutenant-Commander
Hudson, and Lieutenant Mark Kerr kept swimming round them all
night blowing a whistle to let anyone know if they were drifting away
from the main group, which was now clustered around a cork float.
This float was designed to support approximately forty to fifty men,
but there were now about 150 men in that area. Some had left their
rafts and planks to join those on the float.

It soon became obvious that the cork float was inadequate for the
number hoping to rest on it. As one after another joined the group
the float sank lower and lower, until everyone was merely touching
the float with the tip of his toes and was up to his neck in water.

They then agreed that the injured should rest permanently on the
float; the remainder would go into watches for 'standing', and the
watch would be changed on the blowing of the whistle. Through
that long night, as the whistle blew regularly, those on the float
swam off, and those who had been treading water came to hang on
for a welcome spell of rest.

As dawn came some of the faces were no longer there. Many men
were completely exhausted, but were being helped in every possible
way to keep afloat. There was no sound of complaint. Then at 1500
they were taken from the sea by a Japanese destroyer and later
transferred to *Op-ten-Noort*.

Our three days aboard the hospital ship were enough to show us
the hopelessness of our case and to give us a foretaste of our life in
Japanese hands. It also brought to the fore those men who were to
sustain their comrades under the most trying of circumstances. As
Bert Diggle commented later, 'I cannot pass over the period spent
in the *Op-ten-Noort* without acknowledging and appreciating to the
full the support of the heads of the various departments. Jock Dunbar
with his morale-boosting though noisy *Macnamara's Band*. God knows,
we had nothing to sing about, but it did fan the flicker of defiance.
The quiet, sincere Roy Ruse and never-say-die George Crocker.'

On the third day the ship slowed and we felt her nudge gently alongside. Soon after the hatch at the top of the gangway was opened, and standing there were the Indonesian cooks with a basket of rice topped to overflowing. Eagerly we eyed that rice, happy at the thought of 'big eats'. Then the cooks disappeared in a hurry as Nip guards crowded them out and a new set of guards poured down the gangway, shouting and screaming and swiping out right and left with their rifles. Under this noisy and violent persuasion we were pushed and driven to the upper-deck gangway and into the daylight.

As we passed the open rice basket we thrust out hands deep into the rice, but hardly anyone was able to get the rice near their mouths. So roughly were we pushed and hit by this new crowd of guards that we had to use our hands to fend off the blows. We were driven down the ship's gangway like recalcitrant sheep, the guards sitting on the rails so that they could hit us more effectively with the knotted rope-ends which they swung viciously at everyone.

Eventually, after more pushing and shouting by the guards, we found ourselves in columns of five. We were counted over and over again, and each time the guards shouted excitedly to one another and bowed incessantly. Time and time again the count must have been incorrect, as they shouted furiously, bowed and saluted one another, yet in the same movement managed to clout one of us as though it were our fault.

At last the count seemed to be correct and we were marched away, our officers in the first rows of five, walking along a jetty that smelt of decaying coconuts. In a welter of heat and noise and bruising we arrived at Macassar, in the Island of Celebes, and many who marched with us that day were destined never to leave, for we buried them in the red, ant-infested earth that we came to hate so much.

The heat was intense, the oozing tarmac of the road feeling red-hot to our bare and sore feet, and some men in desperation tore strips from their meagre clothing to give protection to their feet. Macassar is about 5° south of the equator, and we were marching under the full intensity of the midday sun.

Captain Gordon marched steadily at the head of our column as we left the docks, with their stores and 'godowns', and entered a little native town where all the streets seemed to have the name of a monkey, *orang*.[1] Up one street and down another we marched, obviously being displayed to the local inhabitants, some of whom held almond-eyed babies in their arms, some waving little Japanese flags. We passed rows of Oriental faces, expressionless, brown eyes wide open and looking right through us. Eight hundred of us marched through those streets, men of HMS *Exeter* and a handful of survivors from other vessels, paraded in all ignominy as a sample of Japanese supremacy. Finally we came to the gates of a Dutch army barracks well outside the town, where we were greeted by more Nip guards lying down in the road with machine-guns trained on us. We marched under an archway into a clearing from which branched off small huts, and into these we were herded, approximately ninety men in each. There was a central corridor in each hut with cubicles on each side, and to each cubicle were allocated six men.

It was as tight a squeeze as the one we had experienced in the hold of *Op-ten-Noort*. When we lay down that night to try to sleep we had all to keep stretched out; there was no room for the luxury of sleeping with our knees up. We also slept on empty stomachs — no rice at lunch, and, like a lot of songless Tommy Tuckers, we had no supper either. But we were dog-tired, and after we had been subjected to a grandiose inspection by the guard, who marched around in a group, armed to the teeth, we settled down to sleep. Our first night ashore, and mercifully most of us slept in blissful ignorance of how long we were to be in that godforsaken spot.

[1] Later I was to find that this was the word for 'man'.

Chief Ordnance Artificer W.E. Johns prior to leaving the Navy in 1948.

HMS *Exeter* dressed overall as she was in 1936.

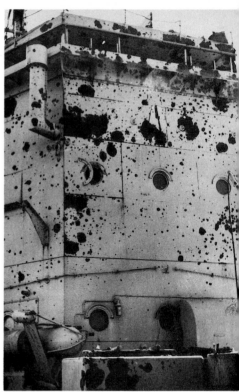

(After the battle of the River Plate) The one that got away. *Exeter's* deck can be seen at the foot of the picture.

Damage to the bridge and wheel-housing during the River Plate action.

The position of *Exeter's* forward turrets; both completely out of action after enemy gunfire.

The funnels, like the rest of the superstructure, were peppered with shrapnel.

Y turret's gun crew – the only gun crew to be left in action after the River Plate battle.

The *Graf Spee* being scuttled in Montevideo harbour.

Captain Langsdorff with his staff and the German Ambassador in Montevideo.

The new young Ordnance staff at Devonport before the *Exeter* sailed for her second wartime commission in 1941.

Admiral Sir Frank Twiss, KCB, KCVO, DSC, who was the gunnery officer of *Exeter* on her last commission, with P.O. Steward Pellegrini at Singapore.

HMS *Exeter* about to sink beneath the waves: the last picture, taken from a Japanese aircraft.

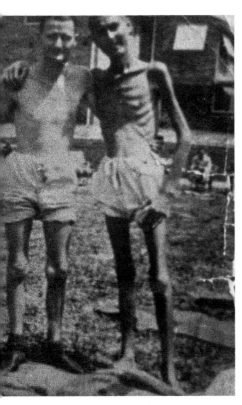

When we reached Australia after having been released from Japanese captivity, 49 of us who were very sick were taken into hospital. They wanted photos, but only two of us were able to stand.

The author shaking hands with the actor John Gregson at the premier of the film *The Battle of the River Plate*. (Photo: *Western Morning News*)

Celebrating the 'Battle Honour' awarded to HMS *Exeter* in commemoration of her final action at Sunda Strait during the morning of 1 March 1942. (Photo: *Herald Express*, Torquay)

During the commissioning ceremony of the new HMS *Exeter* I was given the honour of presenting a silver salver to start the new ship's showcase. I addressed the ship's company and both commissions of *Exeter's* wartime crews who had subscrib to the buying of the salver.
(Photo: Ministry of Defence, Portsmouth. Crown Copyright)

Chapter 9

MACASSAR

THOSE EARLY days in the camp were relatively inactive. We visited one another's huts and also began to get used to the idea of the Dutch prisoners who were already there and the new arrivals, American, Dutch and Indonesian, who were brought daily to the camp. We began to get some idea of the attitudes of the Nip guards, and we all sensed early that we were something of an encumbrance to the enemy. The island of Celebes had fallen to the Japanese Navy with ridiculous ease, two cruisers just steaming in and taking it. Even before the Nips had sorted out the Dutch and Indonesians on the island we were suddenly delivered into their hands.

Communication with the Nips was one of the most difficult problems at that stage. Guards would peep at us round corners, shouted strange sounds at us, and we would be able to make nothing of the noises we heard coming from their mouths. British prisoners would be shouted at, and, not understanding, they would walk unconcernedly away, only to be chased and hit and kicked. The guard soon found that we could be clubbed with rifles and that their superiors backed them up when they did it.

The Nips made signs with their hands which to Western eyes indicated 'go away', so our chaps obediently went away, only to find themselves beaten up because the sign actually meant 'come here'. Painfully we began to learn the rules of that *Through the Looking Glass* world, where a book started at the back and ended at the front, where officers lived in the bows of a ship and ratings lived aft.

We also learned the different attitudes towards food and prisoners of war. We had to be fed, or at least we mentioned that we expected to be fed, and at about eight o'clock in the morning we were given an ordinary bread roll—what Bert Diggle always referred to as 'our penny bun'—and it was not until the third day, late in the evening, that we were given a little rice also. One 'penny bun' every twenty-four hours! We tried to make it last by putting half of it away until noon, but as the days wore on into the second week of our captivity the supply of rolls stopped, the flour having run out. Now we had rice in the morning and rice at night, with no utensils, and this diet was ours until our release.

The rice issue was minimal, and, to supplement their diet, some of the men took to eating grass; but the effects of this new 'veg' soon drove them off it. Many of the men experienced severe stomach disorders, sickness, and black-outs, until eventually we all realized that it would have to stop and we should have to be content with our handful of rice. It was particularly at that stage that I remembered only too well Bill Eddey's little comment, 'If we don't look out it's a cod's head and a tin of rice for us.' We could have done with the cod's head!

We could also have done with our 'tot', but that seemed well in the past, and we had got out of the habit of bemoaning the fact that six bells did not bring us the pipe of 'Up spirits'. As for our 'victory bottle', that had gone down with *Exeter*, with one of our shipmates who had a particular affection for it.

The 'victory' bottle was a large quart sauce bottle which became part of the rum ritual. The duty Chief would, before he issued the ration to each man in the mess, measure two tots off carefully into the sauce bottle, which would provide a drink for the whole mess as soon as *Exeter* reached harbour for a rest. The bottle was then carefully stowed away in a cupboard in the mess. This happened daily, but *Exeter* stayed at sea, and during her final trials and tribulations there were many occasions when the bottle was in great danger.

One particular member of the crew was always first in the queue for his tot, and such was his liking for rum that he developed a personal attachment to the victory bottle. Even when the rum issue was delayed during the heavy bombing attacks he would try to nip in to the mess to see if spirits were yet 'up'. And when the bombing became fierce it was always this character who would be at the cupboard first to make sure no harm had come to the victory bottle.

When the end came, and the final torpedo ripped open *Exeter's* side, Chiefy had rushed to the victory bottle; but there was no one to share it with him. He could be seen through the open door clutching the half-empty victory bottle, as if he had known all along that it was there for him. Perhaps he sensed that those who jumped overboard were leaping into a desperate future which was not for him.

We were now concerned with a fair issue of rice, not rum, and the discipline which had been established in *Op-ten-Noort* was carried over into the camp, with Chief Petty Officers and Petty Officers establishing their mess in each hut and ensuring as fair a distribution of the food as possible.

Not only were we confronted with the rigours of an 'Eastern diet' — we really *belonged* to Nippon. One day we were all cleared from the huts and 'fallen in' before two Japanese naval officers dressed in white shirts and long shorts hanging over their knees and socks with the suspenders showing. One of them addressed us in pigeon English, telling us how we now belonged to Nippon and were formally and properly accepted. He warned us that we would have to do what we were told or be 'shotted to death'. Later our names, addresses, and ranks were taken, and we all wrote a short letter which never arrived home. But we were not to know that, and in those early days many of us retained a certain optimism. Life was not terribly hard in those first few weeks; groups of us would be taken outside the camp for a route march, and during the brief stop all sorts of queer objects were passed from the inhabitants into our ranks. For the first time the British members of the camp tasted the local titbits, and I remember one chap saying that he had been given toffee, when really it was the native brown sugar, *gula java*, rolled into a ball and wrapped in the usual green leaves.

On their return they brought all kinds of 'buzzes', and there were many wonderful stories that raised our hopes. I do not believe that anyone who was taken prisoner believed that it would be long before our chaps came along and got us out again. Our hopes were constantly rising and falling during the early months, particularly when other prisoners of different nationalities began to trickle and eventually pour into the camp at Macassar.

One day two tall, hard-bitten characters in green battle-rig were marched into the camp. They had sound boots on their feet and wore large green hats. It appears that they were survivors from an Australian regiment which had been landed on Timor with orders to defend it against the Nips if they tried to take it. The Nips decided that they definitely wanted Timor and disembarked thousands of their crack troops upon its northern shore. This first landing of troops outnumbered the waiting Australians three to one, yet so fiercely did the Aussies fight that after five days the Japanese decided to withdraw and wait.

More troopships arrived and more Japanese crack jungle troops poured ashore, so that when the Nippon attack was launched again the next day the Aussies were outnumbered almost ten to one.

For days the Australians held on, losing men in their hundreds, slowly being forced back across the island, until on the third day they saw the beach behind them and knew that they could fall back no farther. They were instructed to do the best they could for themselves, and these two soldiers, with a third, wounded comrade, found an old dugout boat concealed in the mangrove swamps. That night they slid it into the sea, paddling away as quickly as they could into the darkness.

When morning came they were out of sight of land. They had with them only one water-bottle, half full, and one tin of field rations; but they also had a tremendous hunger, for they had not eaten properly for the previous three days, so fierce had been the fighting on Timor. For a further three days they floated about trying to keep their general movement as westerly as possible, since they felt that any chance they had of being picked up by Allied shipping depended on catching those of our ships which were leaving the southern part of Java, from Chillichap, or from any port which was outside in the Indian Ocean, in an attempt to make it down to Australia.

On the third day they sighted an island directly ahead and decided to try to land. They pulled for the land and stopped that afternoon about 200 yards off shore to inspect it carefully before landing. They were indeed desperate for food at that stage, as their attempts at fishing had been unsuccessful; for a line they had dangled astern a jack-knife lanyard rope with a shiny Australian tunic button as bait.

The island looked quiet enough, and the wounded Aussie, his shoulder now covered with congealed blood, suggested they land. The other two began to paddle shoreward, when sudden shouts came from the beach as six Japanese soldiers came running down to the water's edge. Quickly they turned the boat and started paddling seaward, shots plopping in the water around the boat, one bullet tearing a hole in the hull just above the water-line.

Soon the firing stopped and no sign of pursuit was apparent. Next morning they were again out of sight of land when the sun came up. It was about midday when they saw smoke on the horizon, and soon afterwards about half a dozen ships came towards them from the east. They grew excited at the prospect of Allied ships, but soon recognized the red ball flying from the ships nearest to them.

The three men lay still in the bottom of the boat as the convoy passed, and were relieved when no attempt was made to stop and pick them up. Within an hour the convoy was moving out of sight.

Their relief was tempered by the thought that at least they would have been fed. There had been no shortage of water as the monsoons were starting and they had filled their hats during the heavy rain showers and had transferred it to the water-bottle; but the iron rations had long been expended, and it looked as if they were to spend another night afloat in their cramped boat. But this was the price of freedom.

As they watched the sun move swiftly down to the western horizon they were suddenly conscious of a strange gurgling noise behind them, and turned as one man to see what it was. They watched in horrified amazement as a large black submarine broke surface about fifty yards from them. The conning-tower was flung open as soon as it had cleared the surface, and before they had time to gasp their astonishment they were looking into the barrels of half a dozen automatic rifles gripped purposefully in the hands of the little yellow sailors leaning on the gunwales of the Japanese sub's bridge.

They were ordered to move closer, and as they bumped against the hull they were heaved aboard and pushed roughly towards the bridge. They were then directed below and told to sit down as the submarine began to dive. Two days later they were brought ashore, two of them to our camp, the other wounded Aussie 'somewhere else'.

On our forty-second day in camp there was a party of 'new boys'. The guards at the gate had become very excited; there was a great deal of shouting as all of them went quickly to get their rifles. As they mustered, the gates opened and very slowly and dejectedly entered forty weary, filthy, half-starved men.

A cry went up from those near the gates: 'It's our chaps!' And so it was—a group who had been picked up on the second day after *Exeter* had gone down, they had been landed at Macassar, but had been put in the local bug-ridden gaol, where they had gone without food for some days and then were on a daily ration of one rice meal. They were unwashed and, like us, in rags.[1]

Soon after our arrival at the camp we heard that the Dutch Army still held a key position up in the hills, that they had plenty of ammunition and a reasonable supply of stores and food. Three times a small Japanese naval force had asked them to surrender, but the Dutch had refused. Some weeks later, however, there was a great hoo-ha at the entrance to the camp, and in came a detachment of Dutch soldiers in their green jungle uniform with their large straw hats, carrying large kitbags and, of all things, still wearing their swords.

That night the new prisoners strode round the camp smoking cigars and stepping out like athletes well in training. Some of the English lads limped barefoot in their wake or kept them in view if they could not keep up with them, waiting for the moment that the cigar butt was thrown away. Then they pounced and puffed happily at the first tobacco since arriving.

This contrast between Dutch and British prisoners was at that stage very marked—they were completely kitted and smart in uniform and boots and we were dirty and in rags, hobbling around on sore, bare feet. The Dutch had made an impressive entry into the camp; what dignified entry could we have made in only dirty underpants, especially with no buttoned front.

When the Dutch Army surrendered there were many Indonesians in their ranks, most of whom were natives of Macassar and whose

[1] 714 officers and men from *Exeter* went into captivity.

families were in the area. They immediately spirited themselves away, burying or burning their green uniforms and changing at home into their sarongs, protesting in all directions that they had never been in the Dutch Army.

Gradually the Nips unearthed them and brought them into the camp, finding a neat way of keeping them under observation. It became one of the memorable early sights of the camp: a crowd of these Indonesians in their little tight-fitting black hats and multi-coloured sarongs, clustered up in the trees like large tropical birds. There they stayed until their cases were cleared up, most of them remaining with us in the camp.

Things did improve a little with the coming of the Dutch. Until now, when our rice had been served we had nothing but our hands to take it in; but tins began to appear, *blicks* as they were known to the Dutch, and with these empty, thrown-away tins there also came a rush mat to sleep on. Stretched on the hard stone floor, we began to come to terms with our new existence, learning to live with virtually no worldly goods.

Also, with the arrival of the Dutch Army came their tough Colonel, Johhny de Warr—tough but approachable. He used to walk round and talk to us every day, even though his English was none too good, and I remember his answer to one question we fired at him, 'How long before they rescue us from here?'

He pointed to the grass in the field and said, 'I think we shall see the grass die and grow again many times before we leave this camp.' It seemed a macabre echo of that fortune-teller in Miami, and he was only too right, although he never lived to see the day.

It was obvious from the beginning that the Colonel was in touch with people outside. He would, on the pretext of wiping his nose, wave his handkerchief to someone outside, and if you looked carefully you would see the person up in a tree. I never knew what he gained by these very obvious gestures, but he was a very popular man during the period he was in camp with us. About a year later he was given a house outside the camp, and he and his batman took up residence there.

All sorts of stories were told about Colonel de Warr. I remember one about his peace-time activities, when a new subaltern had just come out from Holland to join his staff and was being wined and dined by his brother-officers on the first night. Later in the evening the Colonel told the new officer that he was to be tested, and through the large doorway at the end of the mess was brought a rickshaw. The officers' mess was on the second floor of the building and had at one end very large french windows which were open. The young officer was told to pull the rickshaw round the mess and finally to rush at speed towards the open windows and jump with the rickshaw to the ground below. If he did this he was worthy to be accepted by the mess.

This was an oft-repeated situation, and more often than not the young officer would baulk at the idea, whereupon the Colonel without a further word would seize the rickshaw and rush out through the windows, with, I understand, disastrous results to himself, particularly his legs.

Such was the character of this Dutch Colonel, a man who married a local princess, and talked to us with all the ease in the world, breezily waving away our doubts and fears in his gruff but kindly manner. When he moved outside the camp we never saw him again. He was eventually accused of spying, and the Japs cut off his head and that of his batman.

Chapter 10

FLAG EIGHT

DURING THOSE first days in the Macassar camp we were roused just after sunrise to attend a camp muster, followed by a mad dash by just about everybody to sick parade. Then breakfast, such as it was, and during the period just after our capture we were then left very much on our own, everyone scurrying about the camp on the scrounge for anything that could reasonably be eaten.

Around the camp was a high wooden fence which was hidden from view where it ran behind the galley, easily the longest building in the camp. It was here that men in twos and threes could be seen most mornings strolling nonchalantly, or with an exaggeratedly fast walk, to disappear behind the wooden building with its billowing smoke. Later those same prisoners would appear once more with surprisingly contented expressions on their unshaven faces.

That area behind the galley would be cleared quickly at the warning cry 'Flag Eight' (the flag signal indicating 'Enemy in sight'), which indicated the approach of a Nip guard, and it was not uncommon to see a crowd of near-naked British sailors scampering away from the galley like a pack of stampeding animals before a forest fire. The 'fire' usually meant a couple of maddened Nip sentries who had caught the prisoners trading over the fence with local Indonesians.

In efforts to supplement our meagre diet, rackets and escapades of all kinds became our preoccupation. There were secret routes through the barbed wire and along the monsoon drains to the villages outside, and at night 'oddeggs' began to appear—peculiar types of food, invariably wrapped in green leaves, and shown surreptitiously by someone who had cultivated a friendship with one of the local Indonesian or Dutch soldiers.

At this time, very early after our capture, the Nips had enlisted the aid of the Javanese police to act as guards in the camp. One of these policemen came round the corner one day to see a young lad leaning over the fence talking to some Indonesians who were holding up a bunch of bananas. Obviously serious haggling was in progress. The policeman shouted and started running towards the young sailor.

Sam Langford, from the Rhondda, was just eighteen years old and very, very hungry. The bananas looked a treat, but, aware of the priority of self-preservation, Sam dropped from the fence and ran off towards the huts, the Javanese policeman in pursuit.

With a speed born of fear, Sam began to draw away from his pursuer, who by now had drawn his sword and was waving it threateningly in the air. The flashing sword and menacing shouts in no way reduced Sam's speed, and he had almost reached the shelter of the huts when the policeman stopped, poised the sword above his head, and threw it at the boy.

With a cry of pain that we could hear throughout the camp, Sam fell to the ground, the sword through his leg and blood spurting everywhere. By now other men had come from the huts and had pushed the policeman to the ground. Two Dutch doctors were attending to Sam, and he was quickly removed to the sick-bay and later in the day to *Op-ten-Noort*, which was still in the harbour.

A week later the Javanese policeman was found outside the camp with his throat cut and his own sword, bloodstained, by his side.

One of the cleverest and most daring of the food rackets enjoyed a surprisingly long and successful run and was operated by what were known as the '*benjo* men'. The word *benjo* means 'lavatory', and the food was in fact brought in by the lavatory men, who entered the camp twice a week with their sewage carts to empty the communal pool into which all the refuse went.

This pool was running wild with worms and bugs and with strange creatures such as Western eyes had never seen. Into this living mess went the long jointed pipes through which the *benjo* men's pumps sucked the sewage. When the cart containers were full the pumping stopped, the pipe lengths were disconnected, and the carts, dripping sewage and smelling to high heaven, would be trundled off by the *benjo* men, who by their coming had supplied food for those who had the money to buy.

The method was simple and effective. More pipe lengths were brought in than were actually needed, and these spare pipes were packed with 'contraband' which, by the use of their ample sarongs, the *benjo* men were able to pass out while the pumping was in progress. Their job finished, these men would leave much wealthier than when they arrived, for their charge for the *gula java* was high, and those Dutch prisoners who could afford it were only too glad to buy. One further important reason for the continuing success of the venture was that the stench of the cart was so fearful that no Japanese would go anywhere near it.

The *benjo* men had a good innings, but, like all the rackets, it had to face an eventual day of reckoning, and the subsequent punishment turned out to be one of the first mass beatings as it involved not only the dozen *benjo* men but about a dozen POW's who were in the vicinity.

Buying in those early days was very much a Dutch monopoly, the advantage of men who were 'playing on their own ground', for the prison-camp was the depot which had housed the Dutch soldiers before they went up into the hills. We also had Dutch sailors with us now, who had arrived dressed in their 'number ones', with all their kit, money and watches. We began to think for a moment that there were two different kinds of war. They had in fact walked off their ship with all their gear, and the ship was apparently still afloat. To think that *Exeter*, with all our personal possessions, lay a battered wreck thirty fathoms beneath the Java Sea!

The period of freedom after breakfast did not last. Working parties were organized, and many of us were out of camp for most of the day, leaving only the internal working party to carry out necessary construction and repair work in the camp, and those too sick for general work duties. These would later be taken into the compound, men with broken limbs and gaping ulcers—the fact that they could not walk was no excuse—and were placed in the charge of an Indonesian *mandoer* (leader or overseer), when they busied themselves making baskets and containers with rattan canes.

Officers were not let out of the camp and did not join the working parties. Certain of them would, during the day, prepare the lists of working parties for the following morning, first ascertaining the work requirements and then the numbers of men available. Most of the officers spent the entire period of their captivity within the confines of this camp or another.

All our activities both inside and outside the camp were carefully watched. Guards in German and Italian POW camps tended to observe the requirements of the Hague Convention. The Nips paid little or no heed to them. For instance, they did not remain outside the perimeter of the camp, but walked around everywhere, including the huts and lavatories. They were to be met at any time in any place, armed with rifle and bayonet. They were inside the camp day and night, and when two or three of us in a group would stare at something for a while we could be sure that we would be joined in our observation by an uninvited guest.

When this occurred the guard would usually see nothing of any importance and would begin to ask questions, only to meet with a number of queer answers. Communication in the early days was virtually impossible, but gradually the Indonesian tongue, Market Malay, became the bridging language. The Nips had to learn it to cope with the local population, and so naturally did we, but in picking it up from our Nip captors we adopted their faults, and when it came to talking to the Indonesians we found much bewilderment and misunderstanding.

When a Nip asked a question he usually ended his sentence with a *ka*. Our 'O.K.' was uttered by the Nip as 'O.K.ka', and this was also added in the Indonesian expressions.

Counting and numbering was in Japanese, and the orders for marching off working parties were also in Japanese, but if a question was asked at the gate it had to be asked in Indonesian. You can realize just how easy it was for things to go wrong even in the simplest of situations.

There was no privacy for us, even at night. The lamps had to be covered so that only a faint glow emanated from them, and often a Nip guard would walk into the obscurity of the hut with its ninety sleeping figures, and it was not an infrequent occurrence to be wakened and find him standing over you, his bayonet at your throat or resting on your bare stomach. To surface from an exhausted sleep to see this was, I can assure you, a very frightening experience and one you never grew accustomed to.

Sometimes the Nip guard would explain that he wanted you to talk to him, and sometimes this desire would be expressed by his offering you a cigarette or perhaps by giving you a spot of rough handling.

As the weeks moved slowly into months we began to get black-outs and dizzy spells through lack of food, and our reserves of strength were steadily dissipated. It was dreadful to wake with a feeling of hunger—if the hunger had not kept you awake all night—and to lie there wondering if anything would ever arrive to satisfy it. It was a desperately famished time between waking and breakfast, and even then the provision was never consistent—sometimes a small bread bun, sometimes a portion of rice. During the early weeks no one, except the officers, had anything to hold the rice in, and as it had only recently been cooked it was often too hot to hold in one's hands.

At that time we had occasional fruit and tomatoes and upon rare occasions a papaw fruit; but this soon stopped, and we were never to receive such delicacies again during our imprisonment.

One day we received what we thought was a terrible order: our hair had to be clipped off tight. As an example, our First Lieutenant, Lieutenant-Commander Cooper, had his shorn off, and we all followed, until the assembled prisoners stood with bristly heads looking like so many 'moon men'. That was how we were supposed to stay, and pair after pair of hair-clippers were worn out, until finally our hair was being clipped wih a large pair of horse clippers which could tear your hair out by the roots. If you could feel your hair it was time to get it cut, and we spent hours patiently waiting for the 'barber's chair'.

We also had to keep shaven, a problem without a razor. But I did eventually get hold of my very own, worn-out, rusty safety-razor blade. I made a frame for it from bamboo, and it lasted me for years, until we left the camp. There was one occasion later, however, when I experienced a somewhat macabre shaving situation. Working with us in the docks were Indonesian convicts, and one dinner break, behind a shed, I saw one of the convicts giving another a shave with a broken whisky bottle. It was fascinating to see the skill he had developed, and I arranged for him to 'do' me afterwards. He agreed, but only if I gave him some of my tobacco. Before I allowed him to start I fetched my pal along to watch the shaving. One false move and the bottle would have cut my head off, and I realized that he knew that I still had some tobacco left. Later I found that he was in gaol for murder, but he gave me a very close shave. In any case, I was always sick when I smoked that dreadful tobacco!

One evening, about three weeks after our arrival, rumours developed that some prisoners were to be moved, and that at least Captain Gordon and his staff were to be taken away. This aroused mixed feelings. We had some insight into what things could be like in Macassar, and we assumed that if anyone did leave it would be for Japan. Would things be any better there and, if so, in what way? There was little choice in the matter, however, because the party was selected by one of the Japanese. The Captain, Commander, Commander (E), Gunnery and Torpedo Officers — the bulk of the senior officers — were listed, and with them the wireless staff. Within a few days they were off on the long trip, to Japan.

Soon after this a larger party was listed, to consist mainly of engineering personnel. Our First Lieutenant, who was now in charge of the British contingent, tried his first ruse. The Nips wanted all men who could work machines, welders and fitters, etc., and into the party went seamen and stokers who were not the recognized ship's tradesmen. Despite doubts about their ability to do any engineering, the First Lieutenant was delighted to add them to his list of 'engineers'.

During the weeks of preparation there was time for the Nips to work out that there were very few artificers and trades ranks on the list, and when they tumbled to it the consequences were painful for Lieutenant-Commander Cooper. Angry and wild, they told him that he had lied, and further pursued the point by kicking him, informing him all the time that this was not to Nippon's liking. Then they amended the list, and I, with many of my artificers, found myself on Tokyo List 2.

Japan was not for me. Before the time of departure I had a queer growth develop in the back of my throat. It grew daily larger and more painful, until it was decided that my name would have to be removed from the list. I was personally more concerned at that time about the growth, and each day I was reassured by the Dutch doctor with the word *besake*—'tomorrow'. Then one night it broke open, leaving a large hole into which I was told every known disease in the East would penetrate and my chances of survival were nil. After a week it healed up.

Despite my recovery, I was not returned to the list, and the First Lieutenant continued to weed out the key artificer ratings. When the 'draft' finally set off it was of a very different composition from the one required by the Japanese.

The party was kitted with white clothing of an unsuitable type and of inadequate weight and thickness for the colder weather of the Japanese mainland. Some of our friends were later to die tragically, not from terrible, obscure diseases, but from simple but devastating bouts of pneumonia. During the weeks before departure they spent the days in the field next to the camp marching and learning Japanese drill. Orders were snapped out in Japanese, and there was great confusion caused by wrong interpretation of commands. It was common to see ten or twenty men at a time being beaten for what the Nips regarded as plain idiocy.

At this stage there were constant requests and demands for better hospital treatment. At the beginning of our confinement we had been able to send the badly injured and sick to the hospital ship *Op-ten-Noort*, but this procedure had been blocked. Among the camp medical staff we had our own Surgeon Commander and Surgeon Lieutenant and also a Surgeon Lieutenant form HMS *Encounter*. The Dutch had about twelve doctors and a staff of trained medical personnel considerable in size considering the numbers in camp. But medical supplies were scarce, and the situation was to become desperate.

The Dutch medical orderlies all wore a Red Cross armband and looked really smart in their uniforms and neat boots. As for us, our underpants and vests had become even more tattered and filthy, and we had no footwear. We looked like a lot of dirty old tramps.

The Nip footwear was usually a pair of rubber boots with the big toe separate in them, and on returning to their huts the Nips changed these boots for wooden sandals called 'klip-klops' because of the sound they made. The sandal was simply a piece of flat wood with a wired rubber strap under which the fore part of the foot was pushed. The Americans nicknamed them 'go-aheads' because, provided the walker kept going they remained with him; if he stepped backward. . . .

We copied the idea, making our klip-klops out of any old piece of wood we could find. We had no nice, tidy rubber strip for the toes, and were lucky if we could find an old piece of string in which we could fit our toes.

On one occasion as the Nips went indoors, each changing into his klip-klops, the little rows decreased until all that was left for the last Nip was one filthy, broken-down pair. The Nip looked at them. They were so dreadful that he would not even touch them, and he screamed and shouted in anger at the thought of the POW who had now obviously taken possession of his good pair. We all enjoyed that situation, but later that night all of us were searched before returning to camp. Needless to say, no nice, new klip-klops were found.

As some organization began to percolate down through the Japanese staff, working parties became more frequent, but it was almost six months before a relatively effective system of working parties operated, and by then we had used up much of our reserves of strength and nothing was being done to restore them. We were by then also beginning to experience the scourge of tropical diseases.

What a contrast from the time that I had walked into the sick quarters of Devonport Naval Barracks for my medical. It was a sweltering August day in 1936, and I sat, stripped to the waist, waiting for the Principal Medical Officer to arrive. It was my second time in that room, the first ten years before when I packed in with a crowd of Welsh lads leaving the workless pit areas for a life in the Navy, and now another draft.

I remember the Sick Berth P.O. calling me in, and I grasped my trousers tightly as I stood before the Surgeon Lieutenant-Commander. The PO cleared his throat and said, 'Ordnance Artificer William Edward Johns, going to HMS *Exeter* on foreign draft to the West Indies and South American Station, sir.' He nodded to me, and I let my trousers concertina down round my ankles.

'I see there is nothing on your medical sheets, Chief. You've not been through our hands at all. I wish they were all like you and my job would be an easy one.'

That afternoon I had climbed aboard the lorry that took us down to the dockyard, and when we arrived at the sea-wall alongside the huge beef screen where the Navy's meat was stored the driver shouted, 'All change for the *Exeter*. Change here for the land of the tango and bananas.' There was *Exeter*, straight funnelled and in all her shapely dignity. It was difficult now, sitting on the hard floor in the camp at Macassar, to realize that she had gone and that I was no longer the fit and eager young man I had been that day.

When would this end? Six months? Eighteen months? Perhaps. If anyone at that time suggested a longer period he was howled down as a gloomy Daniel. It could not possibly last that long, and we had to be optimistic about the end of our confinement. The question of escape was a very different matter.

Chapter 11

BID FOR FREEDOM

MOST OF US thought at times of the possibility of escaping from Macassar, and we discussed, in the early days, the possible methods; but a look at the map of the area will show how any urge to escape was tempered by the knowledge that the island of Celebes was in the centre of a group of islands all held by the Japanese forces. The jungle, full of poisonous snakes and wild animals, was often more of an enemy than an ally, and the shark-infested waters were another real hazard. The Dutch forces in the camp with us, who had long experience of the area, assured us that these were not the only difficulties. We would not have to move far from the camp to find ourselves in the territories of different headmen or chiefs. The general impression we gained was that it would be safer behind the wire of the camp than being an escapee running loose in the territory of those chiefs who had only recently been stopped by the Dutch from popping their enemies into the cooking-pot. It had taken severe penalties to restrain them from these habits.

Then one morning in September 1942, just before early muster, the news circulated through the camp that an escape had been made. Three Dutchmen had exercised their rights as POWs to attempt to break free and had got clean away into the hills.

Of all the prisoners these three were probably the best equipped to make the escape. One was a regular Petty Officer in the Dutch Navy, trained as a navigator and with a compass to guide the party at night. The second man was a Dutch Naval Reserve officer, an intrepid canoeist who, so my Dutch friend told me, had travelled, before the War, from Holland to Java by canoe. The third member of the escape group was a sergeant in the Dutch Army who had been stationed in this area for many years, knew it well, and was able to speak the various dialects used by local tribes. They had ample money to buy food and bribe their way along if necessary. They even had a boat arranged for them farther up the coast. Above all, each had the courage needed for such a venture.

Their policy was a sensible one, to lie up and sleep during the day and to move only under cover of darkness. It was particularly important that they should be under cover at least half an hour before daylight, but on the third day for some reason their caution deserted them and they decided to carry on for another half-hour. This was their undoing, for they were spotted in the early dawn light by tribesmen hunting for them. The Japanese had alerted all the headmen in the area, and it was a simple matter for the inhabitants to run them to earth and capture them as they slept.

On the morning of their escape we suffered the backlash of the event. When they were reported missing the whole camp was checked and double-checked. We began to worry about our breakfast, but later this was given to us, and soon working parties were leaving the camp, but only after very careful checking.

The three men were still missing when we returned from work that night, and there was no further news of them until the fourth day, Sunday. We were at that time allowed to remain in camp on Sunday afternoons, and I remember that an order came round to all chiefs of huts to muster outside the guardroom at once. Scenting trouble, we made our way there and were fallen in immediately in two ranks. The guards, armed to the teeth, were shouting and very excited. We began at once to wonder if this had anything to do with the three Dutchmen.

We had been standing there about a quarter of an hour when a green-covered van came in through the gates. Japanese guards, armed with rifles, seemed to be sitting all over the van, and as it came to a stop just outside the guardroom there were excited shouts as all the guards jumped off, and we heard scuffling from inside the van. Then, one by one, the Dutchmen were flung from the van; they were covered in blood, their faces unrecognizable and plastered with congealed blood. All had had their teeth knocked out. What was left of their black clothing had been torn to shreds.

Even as they lay there, unconscious and unmoving in the positions in which they had landed, two of the guards kicked them, screaming and shouting at those twisted shapes which showed no sign of movement however hard and often they were booted. The Dutch Camp Commander ran forward and tried to stop the guards, but his intervention only seemed to spur them on, and he himself was roughly pushed away by the screaming Japanese. God alone knows how those men must have been treated when they were first captured from the tribesmen.

They were taken from the camp cells to the town prison, and later the news filtered through that they had all been beheaded in the centre of the town as a warning to the local population that this would happen to them if they did not co-operate fully with the Japanese. Before the Dutchmen were beheaded they had to dig their own graves on some rough ground near the sea, at the rear of the spot that was later to be the site for Coconut Grove.

Those who had shared the same huts as the escapees were punished by being locked in one of the huts for weeks and on reduced rations. The camp was firmly informed that in the event of future escapes the room-mates left behind would also be beheaded.

This was the one attempt at escape. If it seems strange that escaping was not part of the POW routine in the Far East, there are other stories to indicate its futility. As that fortune-teller had declared in Miami, 'I see a fence or wall. It is insurmountable.' How right she proved to be; our only escape was death.

Chapter 12

WORKING PARTIES

As THE Japanese Navy began to recover from the surprise of so much territory and so many captives falling into its hands, so it began to organize. The heavy bureaucratic system ground into action and, in answer to the demand for space to accommodate the various officials, all the larger buildings in the island of Celebes were requisitioned and adapted. Gradually there grew a need for extensions as well as alterations to existing accommodation, and also a need to develop the various stores and buildings. The Japanese, having taken over the godowns at the docks, now made some attempt to deal with the contents, although I can remember in some of them the terrible stench of tons of rotting copra.

Such extensive operations naturally required a large labour force, which could not be provided by the normal supply of coolies, and soon the Japanese officials began to collect numbers of men from the camp, sometimes ten or forty. Later the numbers increased to as many as three or four hundred in a single party. It was not long before hundreds of POWs were leaving the Macassar camp each day to work at the docks, at the aerodrome, and in buildings and installations in the town.

There was also some attempt at organization within the camp, and an internal party of carpenters and fitters took over much of the repair work, including joinery for the Nip guard quarters and making most things from baskets to wheeled carts.

Other camp duties included cleaning the huts and keeping the grass in the compound reasonably short. For this purpose, the swords that the Dutch soldiers had insisted on keeping as part of the surrender terms were taken from them and used as scythes. Those not fortunate enough to have these swords were provided with pieces of bamboo, and to be faced with a meadow of an acre or two, equipped only with a piece of sharpened bamboo, was one of the soul destroying tasks we had to face.

As the demand for working parties increased, so we began to recognize the various Nip guards who came along daily to collect the parties, and became accustomed to their habits, usually sinister and sadistic. We promptly gave them nicknames: 'Gela' (stupid), 'Poko Merchant' (one who was always hitting people), 'Iron-Bar Orang' (the guard who used an iron railing to hit us with), 'The Bull' (a particularly nasty piece of work), etc.

We were still managing to get a day in camp once or twice a week, but this did not last for long. Nearly all the working parties were marched several miles to their place of work, still without clothes or footwear, making this daily trudge something of a test in itself. Gradually the dissipation of our reserves of strength, developed by our Western diet, left us weakened and in no state to withstand attacks of disease. We became particularly susceptible to mosquitoes, and I still remember the shock I received when I heard that the first of the *Exeter* lads to die in Macassar was one of my gunnery staff who had developed cerebral malaria after a bite and was dead within a few hours. That was in the September of 1942. We learned from this and subsequent cases that many types of malaria existed, and this, whatever clinical interest it may have had, piled further misery on our existence. Life began to assume a new grimness.

More Japanese were drafted to Celebes as warships began to call more regularly on their way south. New quarters were established at all the main buildings—the large central school, the main engineering works, the large garage, and even the Freemasons' Hall. The town administrative building in Macassar was taken over for the Admiral's residence.

To some of these new quarters would go as few as six POWs in the charge of Nip sailors, and many of the early trips were simply looting excursions. Led by the guard, we made off into that part of the town where stood the neat houses that had doubtless belonged to some of the Dutchmen now in the camp. We would follow our guard into various houses, ransacking the drawers and cupboards, the guard snatching everything of value—watches, rings, lighters, boxes of cigars, cutlery and above all, clothes. Where possible, our men tried to provide themselves with clothes, but to take coats and trousers would have been ridiculous—they made an almost naked man look suddenly overdressed. He would look odd enough with just the addition of a new pair of socks; but socks were much coveted, and were obtained only in this way during those early days.

The Nips had orders to send all things of importance or value to headquarters. Pictures were removed from walls, and it was ludicrous to see the choices made. I remember a familiar old hunting picture, a cheap and nasty print in many ways, taken outside and placed carefully with the other *objets d'art* destined to be sent back to Japan, while oil paintings of some merit, beautifully framed, were taken outside and burnt.

A little later those same houses were brought into use, many of them as Nip brothels, and there was the additional task of re-wiring the outside lamp and fitting it with a red shade or bulb. Beds were brought in from everywhere, and furniture was changed madly from one house to another. This involved some odd decisions on the part of the guard organizing the moving. I remember we had to struggle to move a huge wardrobe, and after much heaving and pushing we finally positioned it, only to find that it was firmly against a door.

True, the room had two doors, but we pointed out by signs to the guard that the wardrobe was blocking one of them. From the crescendo of growls that issued from the guard we gathered that he jolly well knew this and did not think much of our telling him. This was one of the first instances I had experienced of those difficult situations involving possible loss of face.

Later in the morning, when we had moved on to other jobs in the house, we were alarmed at a terrible noise coming from the first room. This turned out to be the cries of our guard, who, rushing impatiently from room to room, had used the door behind which we had positioned the large wardrobe. He had banged his face and split his lip, and in his confused rage he presented an amusing picture; but our grins were wiped from our faces as he rushed at us like a mad bull, kicking and hitting out at us for daring to laugh at him. This was lesson number two in the 'loss-of-face' situation. We were learning not to laugh if anything went wrong, however trivial the matter might be.

Geisha girls later arrived to live in these houses, and it was the job of POWs some two years later to work again in those houses, bricklaying and laying out communal concrete open-air baths. During the few weeks they were there the men found a certain sympathy and pity not only in the eyes of those girls, but in their actions and attitudes. They saw that the POWs had extra rice to eat, and they gave them cigarettes. Our boys at that stage were in very poor health and looked like walking scarecrows, a strange contrast to the short and fat little slant-eyed girls.

During one of the foraging trips one of the prisoners found a pair of large brown riding-boots which he managed to persuade the Nip guard to let him keep. Delighted, he returned to camp in his underpants with these riding-boots, only to be chased by an angry Dutchman who told him in no uncertain guttural terms that the boots were stolen from his house. The Englishman agreed, and an amicable agreement was reached, the Dutchman providing a pair of ordinary boots in exchange.

One of the largest working parties at that time went to the Japanese headquarters to be employed on the mammoth task of digging air-raid shelters. These were dug to a depth of twenty to thirty feet, and we were soon to learn that once you dug deeper than a metre the water appeared. But we had to dig, and as we got to the water-table we had to begin a continual process of bailing to enable us to continue digging and shovelling.

Despite this difficulty we reached the required depth, the inside face of the shelter was concreted, and the job finished. The long set of twenty or more concrete steps leading to the bottom of the shelter had set hard and the Nips were evidently very pleased with the result.

After this period of hard digging we reverted for a while to an orgy of grass-cutting with our sharpened bamboos, accompanied by some arduous pushing of the great ten-foot roller. Under a tropical sun this was a murderous task, with only the saving fact that we were not exactly encumbered with clothes.

A few days after the completion of the giant shelter there was a night air-raid warning, and in the pitch blackness of the tropical night the Nips poured down the concrete steps into their magnificent shelter, only to find at the third step down they were in water. Those at the back, urgent to get under cover, pressed on, until there were about forty frightened Nips swimming about in fifteen feet of water. We all thought it was a great pity that they did not drown.

It then became our job on arriving each morning to bail and pump out the water that had collected. It took most of the day, and by the following morning the shelter would be full again. Eventually the Nips had duck-boards fitted to the inside walls, a metre or so from the top, so that when they went down into their 'deep shelter' they stood on the boards, just under the roof, with beneath them fifteen feet or so of filthy water.

One of the Nips working there was the resident carpenter, an ordinary seaman, which normally indicated a young sprog; but he was somewhat older and had quite a family back in Japan. When air-raid warnings or alarms of any kind were raised he was expected to stand by as the sort of handyman of his platoon. Fleet of foot and extremely excitable, it did not take much to stir him into frenzied activity. During one air raid a fire was started in the village just along from Nip headquarters, and his section received orders to put it out. Our carpenter was naturally way ahead of the others. Outlined in the flames, he dashed ahead, only to disappear suddenly from view. As the others neared the spot they heard his voice calling plaintively, and found that he had disappeared into the deep, evil-smelling pit that the local villagers used for their latrine. He stank for a week afterwards, and even we POWs risked a hammering by holding our noses and 'wheewing' every time he passed.

It was while I was working with this party at headquarters that I noticed one day a long line of moving ants, thousands of them. I followed their trail until I saw them entering and leaving a dustbin. When I removed the lid I saw that the inside of the bin was swarming with them and at the bottom was the object of their attention, an old newspaper which had contained sugar at some time, because stuck to its pages were the remains—a sticky brown mess. I put my hand in and carefully removed the paper, not being able to shake the biting ants off my arm for fear of shaking any grains of sugar from the news pages. It was a delicate and painful process, but it meant that dinner that day was of sweetened rice, and there was enough to share with some of my pals.

The working parties soon became such a major part of our existence that we were spending every day except Sunday outside the camp. Our officers were not permitted to leave the camp, and I think that not one of them went outside unless it was to transfer to another camp or on the day of his release.

The parties were known either by simple alphabetical references or by certain uncomplimentary names that the POWs gave to them. From the very beginning some of these working parties were the reasonable equivalent of spending a day in hell—a long, tiring march, a day of slave labour, and then the march back again. Incentive to work was usually a blow from a stick or shovel, and as a consequence such parties became known as *poko* parties, *poko* being the term for stick.

Our working day started just after dawn, heralded by the notes from a bugle blown by one of the Indonesian boy buglers (ex-Royal Netherlands Navy). We simply clambered up from the hard stone floor where we had been sleeping and ran to the compound, where we fell in to be mustered. Once the hut numbers had been reported correct we washed, and the duty men from each hut went to fetch the rice. With the rice came a black mixture called coffee. I think I used this as often to shave with as to drink.

Breakfast over, and our tins cleaned (even though they might be old rusty salmon-tins), we joined the working party for which we had been detailed the previous night and waited, in lines five deep, under our *mandoer*, or leader. We were then called, one working party at a time, to the guardroom at the main gate, where we were counted by the Nip guards. This was a procedure impossible for the Japanese unless we were carefully lined up in fives. The guards would then either wet a finger and write on their palms with the spittle, or write signs in the air for their addition sums. Inevitably they ended up by hitting the *mandoer* and cursing him for giving them the wrong number.

We were then turned over to new Nip outside guards who had arrived to collect us, and were marched away to our places of work in Macassar. We always wondered as we passed through the gates what that particular day had in store for us, and our thoughts were seldom other than grim.

This procedure was the same for most working parties during those first months. When we returned from work just before sunset we cleaned up, had supper, and attended a final muster. The rest of the evening, two hours or so, we spent resting or talking and visiting friends in other huts. Each night the duty officer would visit the hut, just before Nip rounds, to read out the names for the various working parties for the following day.

Some of the working parties consisted of particular nationalities. B.O.1 was an entirely Dutch party, most of them engineers who were now working as prisoners in the workshops where they had previously been the bosses. The hospital party outside the camp was all-American, but A and B parties were British only. The rough hospital inside the camp was 99 per cent staffed by the Dutch. For a period most of the seriously wounded had stayed aboard the *Op-ten-Noort*, and cases of major illness and emergency operations such as appendicitis had been treated aboard. But the time came when all the patients, including *Exeter*'s wounded, were disembarked and placed in the camp hospital, while *Op-ten-Noort* was taken elsewhere for Japanese use.

From the beginning, medical supplies were scarce, and as the demands for treatment grew so the situation rapidly became desperate. My first experience of the problems in the hospital came when I was working on one of the parties building extensions to existing premises to provide clubs and canteens for the Japanese Navy. I stubbed my bare foot against a large stone, and the big toe got bigger and more painful, then turned septic, and eventually I could hardly put my foot to the ground. Considering that we were at that time working knee-deep in cement, there is little wonder that the toe 'went bad'.

I arranged to see the medical people, and the mere fact of not having to trudge out with the working party was some relief. The medicos eyed my toenail carefully, then squeezed the toe. A lot of pus flowed, accompanied by various inarticulate sounds from me, and it became obvious to all that the nail would have to be removed.

They stretched me out on a long stool, my leg held down by two of the staff and the rest of me being kept still by someone sitting on my chest. The nail was quickly split down the centre to the quick and, held in two separate pairs of pliers, was removed in one quick concerted movement. Within a split second I was upright, and the chap who had been sitting on my chest was flat on the floor.

A further examination revealed that the nail had torn off across the quick and another attempt would have to be made, this time by the Surgeon Lieutenant. At five o'clock that evening I attended sick-bay, having spent most of the day with my foot soaking in 'hot water'. A medical chit had made this possible, but it was only the water that had been drained from the cooking rice and was ready to be thrown away.

The final effort that evening was more successful, but no less painful. I am constantly reminded of this when, like today, I survey the thick, ugly nail that I now have on the toe of my right foot.

The following day I was back at work. The medical staff had warned me to keep the toe clean, and my feelings can be imagined when an hour later I found myself once more working knee-deep in cement.

Chapter 13

'GOLD TOOTH'

WHEN WE landed at Macassar that first day and arrived at this camp I had been the Chief put in charge of a hut of ninety-three men. We lived in cubicles, six men to each, off both sides of a central corridor, and it was my responsibility to make sure that the hut was kept clean, that the meals were served properly, and that some form of discipline was maintained. Most important of all was the responsibility of making sure that the men in my charge had as much to eat as was humanly possible, and particularly that everyone had an equal share.

One day, not long after our capture, I had joined an outside working party to see what I could do to bring back something extra to eat, but when I returned at the end of the day it was to find that trouble had come to the hut in my absence. Apparently one of the POWs in the hut had found an electric toaster the previous day in the town, had smuggled it back into camp, and had managed to tap the supply to make it work. While attempting a little amateur cooking he and his pals had been discovered by one of the guards, who was a recent arrival—a very junior Nip named Yoshida.

Yoshida had gone berserk. Throwing down his rifle, he tore the electric cable down and started to punch and kick the three POWs involved. Then he switched to throwing them judo fashion, though he departed from the rules of judo by kicking his victims in the face and privates while they were stretched exhausted on the floor. Anything seemed to go with him, and it was the first direct experience I had of this ferocious Nip who was to become the top guard and most hated man in the Macassar camp. Any civilized manner

that he had was a wafer-thin veneer which was easily stripped off
by the most trivial of happenings to reveal his thoughtless and cruel
nature. When the exhausted and bleeding men were finally left to
be taken away by their comrades one of them had his arm broken
in two places. This fiend incarnate who had come among us was to
stay until the end came; we were to feel his violence and suffer his
cunning, and hate and fear the very mention of his name.

Yoshida rose quickly from being an obscure ordinary seaman,
seemingly illiterate even by Japanese standards, to being virtual chief
of the camp, feared even by the other Japanese, even the officers.
He was utterly ruthless, and there were no limits to his savagery.
He saw what he wanted done, and once he had made a decision
nothing would stand in his way. He was the first and final law
concerning everything that had to do with the lives of 1500 forgotten
men, and the death of hundreds of prisoners in the camp could be
traced in some way to him. I would estimate that he contributed to
the deaths of 75 per cent of those who died in Macassar Camp.

Small and beady-eyed, he showed at no time any sign of culture
or breeding. He had gold teeth, and was named directly by those
who spoke Malay 'Gigi Mars' or 'Gold Tooth'. Yet he was not slow
on the uptake. In the early days he became personally identified
with the cry 'Flag Eight' ('Enemy in sight'), but he tumbled to this,
and we were forbidden to use the call. Other English terms were
also banned, and quite often he would swing at a POW who said
something in English. We often wondered if he did know some
English but would never let on.

Under the leadership of Yoshida in those days most of the guards
of the Japanese Naval Brigade grew in self-importance and cruelty.
Looking back, I realize that we POWs were providing them with a
means of promotion. Out of the fighting line, in charge of prisoners
of war, the guards slowly but definitely cottoned on to the idea that
we were the rungs of the ladder. Cruelty could be assessed for bonus
points they needed to work themselves up to the next rank. We were
handy to provide the means.

When a guard called a POW over to him to talk he would more
often than not find that the prisoner could not understand him.
In minor cases the unfortunate chap would receive the 'Emperor's
punishment', which involved the guard flicking his victim's forehead

with his fingers hundreds of times, until it produced a swelling on the forehead, a huge lump which remained sore for days. The most common punishment, however, was continued slapping of a man's face on both sides until his head rang. This was almost a daily routine, and was often administered for no apparent reason, least-ways to us.

I remember being on a lorry which was taking us from the camp on a working party into Macassar. We were a little surprised to see a Japanese officer suddenly run after the lorry, board it, and then set about us. Hitting out with his pistol, he made sure that he did not miss a single head or face, and later we were told that we had heartily deserved such a punishment and would be beaten again by the camp guard for it — and we were. It transpired that we had not saluted the Imperial officer, who was walking when we passed him in the lorry.

'B' Garage Party was notorious for the punishments meted out, and became known as the *poko*, or 'beating-up', party. Men came back from work bleeding and sick, not as a result of the hard work — Lord knows, that was bad enough — but of the general beatings they had suffered during the day. The party was in charge of a Nip Chief Petty Office, with a PO second-in-command, and an appropriately cruel and mean set of ratings who never missed the opportunity of savaging a prisoner.

At the end of the working day the prisoners, physically exhausted after non-stop cement-mixing, or carrying heavy loads, were told to fall in, while, grinning with delight, the Nip guards would rush off to fetch their implements. The POWs would wait apprehensively in rows of five for the proceedings to begin.

The Chief would then walk along the front row asking a question in Malay. If answered correctly he would repeat the question in Japanese. If no answer was then forthcoming the unfortunate indi-vidual would be pulled from the ranks and literally thrown to the waiting guards, who would start beating and kicking him, then throwing him judo style until either he lapsed into unconsciousness or his limbs gave under the assault.

On other occasions we would be drilled, with all the orders rapped out in Japanese. Soon chaos would ensue, as none of us knew any but the basic commands. A mass beating would then take place, no

one being excused. Tools for this beating would include baseball
bats, bamboo canes split so that they cut the flesh, the occasional
horsewhip, which usually managed to churn out pieces from what
flesh was left on our bodies. The most cruel and terrible weapon was
a solid, one-inch-diameter iron bar, whose owner was known as the
'Iron-Bar Merchant'. Such treatment was, to say the least, poor
recompense for a hard day's work.

The PO who was second-in-command of 'B' party was known as
'The Bull'. He always seemed intent on outdoing his chief in cruelty,
and would work prisoners beyond the point of endurance, standing
over them with a shovel with which he lashed out continually as he
rushed among them shouting and screaming. Men carrying large
bags of cement managed to develop rapid reflex actions to avoid the
swinging, cutting shovel; but if you were unlucky enough to stumble
or fall, the result was very painful indeed.

It was in such a manner that we built a large petrol-storage dump
at record speed. A huge field was quickly laid bare as we dug up its
turf to provide a covering for the dump. We stamped this down until
it looked like a grassy mound, an appropriate if sorry tribute to the
two prisoners who died making it.

Sometimes the punishment was not so severe and even had a slight
air of the ridiculous. One small working party was attached to a
guard nicknamed 'Annie Laurie', because somehow he knew the
tune and used to get prisoners to sing it for him. (Often he would
reward these vocal efforts with cigarettes and bananas, but at times
he would be critical of the singing and thump the singer heartily.)
The party was engaged in building an air-raid shelter for WT radio-
sets, and on the morning in question the shelter was all but finished.
It was now forty to fifty feet high, and had planking leading up to
the top of it while more planks led down on the other side. Up and
down those planks we went, carrying cane baskets of earth and
rubble, making the shelter higher and higher. Later in the morning
'Annie Laurie' suddenly said, 'All men work. I look,' and with that
he walked away and went into the Nip living-headquarters.

As soon as he was out of sight all the men stopped work, and
about fifteen minutes passed without anyone so much as touching a
bucket. Suddenly 'Annie Laurie' appeared from the quarters. He
came running, shouting excitedly, '*Serits!*' (Fall in!). Then, with all

fifty men standing wondering before him, be began to get angrier and angrier, shouting and screaming.

From that furious spate of incomprehensible language only one word seemed to be understood by the waiting POWs—'Marros'. Now, Marros was the name of the aerodrome outside Macassar which had been made by a permanent working party from the camp of about two hundred English prisoners. Realizing that something had to be done quickly, one of the POWs said, 'He must be asking how many of us have worked at Marros.'

Gradually we all put our hands in the air. Most of the men had spent some time at the aerodrome, and even those who had not, like myself, did not want to be left out of it. Eventually the whole party stood there, hands raised. The baffled Nip stopped shouting. He made funny little noises to himself. Then he pushed his hat over his eyes in sudden bewilderment, and tried to size up the situation.

Eventually he indicated that as so many had owned up he would give them only one hit each. This he did with a dirty split bamboo, which he picked up from the ground.

Everyone in the party realised that they had got off very lightly, but they also gathered that they had not hit upon the correct answer. On returning to camp they unearthed the Dutch interpreter, who was at first as puzzled as they were. They kept on repeating to him, 'Marros, Marros,' the word the Nip had kept using. 'Marros, the aerodrome,' everyone said.

Then he smiled. 'It wasn't *Marros*,' he said. 'He was saying *malos*, and that means lazy. You were all confessing to a man how idle you had been.'

The treatment we received was seldom as light and amusing as that experience. Usually, if we had had trouble out on the working party with the other guards, their officer or they would complain about it when they returned us to the camp at the end of the day, and so quite often Yosh or the sergeant of the guard would beat us up again. This in many cases would be the last straw for men who had literally slaved all day, been beaten up savagely, and wearily walked back to camp then to be savaged again by Yoshida and his sadistic guards. The example set by Yoshida to his ape-like guards made sure that a tyrannical standard of toughness and unveiled cruelty was maintained. And punishment was only a portion of the cross we had to bear—there was in addition hunger, disease, back-breaking toil, and the complete severance from our homes and loved ones. To them we were now of the legion of the dead.

Chapter 14

COOLIES AND GODOWNS

DURING THE early stages of our imprisonment I took charge of 'A' working party, which for the British POWs was the largest single party for the greatest period and was at times from two to three hundred strong. It was nominally the dockyard party, with its working headquarters about six miles from the camp amid the jumble of piers and landing-stages, in a building which had formerly belonged to the Dutch Oil Company. It was one of the largest buildings in Macassar, and had been taken over by the Japanese Navy to house the hundreds of Japanese coolies required for dockyard labour. They were a poor lot, dressed in a cheaper way, like a Nip sailor, and it was in company with these workers that the men in 'A' party spent their working day.

At the end of our barefoot six-mile trudge from camp we were halted in front of the building and formed into the requisite five ranks for counting and dividing into smaller work units. The Japanese No. 1 Chief Petty Officer would walk round, followed by his gang of coolie tradesmen, and as the turn of each came he would state how many required for the particular job. At first this was very tricky, as no one seemed to understand anyone else, and tempers at that time of the morning were very short; but soon our boys got around to counting better and faster than the majority of the Nips, including the 'bright boys'—our camp guards.

The coolies were in effect a kind of semi-sailor. They were really civilians but enrolled in the Japanese Navy and under the jurisdiction of the Japanese *Juto Hazo*, or Chief Petty Officer. They were all dressed in a light khaki uniform of shirt and long shorts down over their knees, and when you were following your particular coolie to a certain place or job you were immediately struck by the appearance of the odd rubber boot with special toe-piece which they wore. It always looked to me like a peculiar 'foot mitten'.

The coolies were in general short, fat and dull, generally the rejects from the draft board. They lived in the spacious office block which had now assumed the bleak appearance of a barracks.The coolies had built short ladders which were fitted to all the windows on the ground floor, and in and out of those windows and up and down the short ladders they went, like so many ants. The doors were large, but the windows seemed more popular for some reason.

Among the coolies were carpenters, steel workers, motor mechanics, drivers and bricklayers; but all of them could mix cement and seemed to have done most basic site-work—as rough a crowd of labourers as one could find anywhere. It must be admitted that they had a tremendous load of work to get through, and did it at tremendous speed, finish and finesse not being their strong points. Any pride of workmanship that we retained took a disturbing tumble when we were urged on by a bang on the head or back from a shovel wielded by a Nip who had rushed furiously to the next stage of the job, shouting and muttering his indication that this was the speed of work he wanted. It was always the same: the tempo of our chaps' work never increased without a major roughing-up.

There was some excitement and speculation about a job which, it was rumoured, would soon be given to 'A' party. It was referred to as the 'swimming party' and both Frank Clements, the Canteen Manager, and 'Ski' Turner, our Physical Training Instructor, had been very keen to join this party for a swim. Volunteers had been asked for on a number of days, and the men volunteering had varied from thirty to forty, but always at the last moment the 'swimmers' would be switched to another party.

About a week later, without warning or any request for volunteers, three hundred or so men were whisked off to the 'swimming job'. This included those keen swimmers who had daily been disappointed at missing their dip. The party was marched away, and steadily passed all those places where they thought they might be taken for their swim.

Finally, only one possibility remained: they were turned off the track to the left and on to an open, sandy beach, where they gasped with incredulity at the object in front of them. They had seen it being built, and it was now terrifyingly obvious why they had been taken, but not one of the lads believed for an instant that the job could be done.

They were marched across the beach to the object and halted in front of it. There it lay, seemingly immovable, a huge wooden platform about a hundred feet square with huge oil drums lashed in pairs beneath it, raising the platform about four feet above the sand. Standing by were hundreds of Nip guards who had come from everywhere to join in the launching of this cumbersome platform which the powers that be had decided should be floated out into the harbour and moored there as a seaplane jetty.

If the Nips thought the British prisoners were going to lift that platform, and place it in the harbour, they were mistaken. How daft could the Nips get? Even if there was any desire to lift it, it was blatantly obvious that we hadn't the strength. Every POW standing on that hot beach was sure that this was going to be a launching ceremony that would not take place.

Suddenly there was a shout, and within seconds all hell was let loose. Every guard on that beach had a stick, iron bar, or some weapon which he could crash down on the bare backs or shoulders of the POWs and they proceeded with yelling and lashing to drive every prisoner under the great platform. Many of the guards then climbed on to the platform and peered down between the planks at the struggling men beneath who were being flogged and screamed at to lift.

As the ring of guards around the platform drove the men into activity, so those on top found that they could push their sticks and bars down through the planks to give some added incentive to the heaving and straining designed to lift and move that platform some twenty yards down to the sea. Then, to the chorus of a crescendo of yells, it left the ground and moved slowly towards the sea; so, inch by inch, to renewed shouting and beatings, for four and a half hours the huge, incongruous pontoon was edged seaward until at last the leading men found their feet in the water. Before it was up to their knees they were driven from underneath and chased to the rear to add to the pushing and heaving until the pontoon floated gently offshore.

Once it was afloat, no one was allowed in the water. Some men who had volunteered daily for the 'swimming party' had to stand on the shore without the chance even of getting their feet wet. But I suppose that is the way they built the pyramids.

'A' party built houses, canteens, building extensions, and hundreds of air-raid shelters of different kinds. At first the Nips had scoffed at the cowardly concept of air-raid shelters, and even ordered those built by the Dutch to be destroyed. Later there must have been a directive from the top because it became a priority.

Coaling of ships was carried out by the dockside party, and there were also unloading jobs in the early days as many ships used the harbour at Macassar. As the war progressed we were pleased to note that the shipping dropped almost to nothing.

Unloading was usually packed with incident. I would arrive at the jetty with a working party of between two hundred and four hundred men, to be informed by the Nips that there were, say, eight holds in the ship to be unloaded. The men would be divided into parties of up to fifty to each hold and stood quietly by waiting for the Indonesians and the ship's crew to lift off the hatch covers and prepare the cranes and nets. On the sweltering hot dockside the barefooted working party waited with some interest for the first load to come out of the hold. Perhaps it would be a load of wood, iron or cement, and the particular group would work at this for a while; but gradually they would drift away to join the other groups to see what would come up out of the other holds. If, as sometimes happened, something to eat appeared in the sling, all hands were immediately at that hold, swarming like ants over sacks of sugar or tins of food, causing them to drop so that they burst open on the jetty. Personal tins would be filled with sugar and with water from the pump on the jetty. These sugar drinks were real luxuries, and faces became encrusted with sticky sugar grains, but who cared?

Such 'sugar orgies' never lasted for long. It soon became apparent from the irate cries of the ship's crew waiting to have the other holds unloaded that something was wrong. The guards would dash out of the office, shouting and kicking the sweating, sugar-coated prisoners until they divided once more into their proper groups. For a while some work would be done, but, with the taste of the sugar gone, fresh supplies would be sought, and all the POWs would gravitate back to the sugar hold.

There were also some nice little 'quiet numbers'. One of the coolies had three of our lads attached to him for work—trying to make a round hole in a tile. Each time they got near to completing it, somehow the tile broke. They tried to make that hole for at least three days.

Parties of prisoners on the move were always a source of trouble, and our dockside party was no exception. When we arrived at Nip headquarters in the morning we used to come through the entrance reasonably quietly without footwear, and we would be through into the compound before the coolies knew we had arrived. In front of us would be laden clothes-lines—shorts, vests and stockings—and it was not long before the Nips began to miss odd items. Immediately the losses were reported the parties would be inspected, but there was never any trace of the missing garments.

The coolies soon began to keep a watch for our approach, and as soon as we hove into sight up would go the Nip cry equivalent to 'Here come the so-and-so's.' In response the coolies would come streaming out through the windows to remove their washing from the line, a task which was often accompanied by the shouts and jeers of the POWs and cries of, 'What's the matter? Don't you trust us?' or, 'You don't think we'd pinch your clothes, do you?'

As we swung through the gates one day we found the lines packed with washing, but no one appeared from the windows to gather it in. The Nips just stood around looking at us, appearing very pleased with themselves, and as we approached the clothes-lines we could see why. Someone had hit on the idea of reeving the line through the sleeves or legs of the garments. It made us smile to think how hard they were making it for themselves each wash-day; but it also proved tougher for us whenever the chance came for them to hand out ill-treatment in return.

Hunger was our daily companion, and became one of our major concerns while out with the parties. We had long lost any finicky eating-habits, and kept our eyes peeled for anything in our surroundings which was in any way edible. When our large party made its way down to the docks we would pass along one of the main streets in Macassar where the Indonesian traders gathered with their carts of fruit on both sides of the road. The large band of POWs marched five abreast between the rows of carts, and time had taught the lads great sleight-of-hand. The amount of fruit that could be whipped off carts and out of barrels was astonishing; but finally even the long-suffering Indonesian cart-owners could stand it no longer. As the five-deep line of malevolent human locusts approached they would retreat quickly, and often in disorder, pushing their carts frantically and with such haste that the carts usually overturned, scattering the fruit all over the road. As 'A' party passed through with its scuffing, flat-footed gait it was as though a giant vacuum cleaner had passed. Not a trace of that fruit remained on the road.

Another source of extra nourishment was the Nip left-overs. For the price of washing up the dinner tins we could get the scraps in them after the Nips had finished. A queue for this would form outside the entrance to the mess building when we returned to the headquarters for our 'dinner break'. There was often fish for dinner, and the remnants made a welcome supplement to our meagre diet, but this had its snags as the Nips had a nasty habit of calling you over and emptying their fish-bones and cigarette-ends into your nice clean rice. Another habit was to spit their fruit-stones into your rice. This dirty and unfriendly habit turned us against the Nip coolie, who otherwise was a character rather to be pitied.

As 'A' party became established over the years, so different POWs blossomed out as tradesmen, particularly in wood and metal work, and some went regularly with the same Nip, who usually saw to it that he had the ones he wanted. There were some of the lads who were prepared also to turn their hand to any trade should certain conditions require it, and I remember one occasion when the Nip chief, followed by his coolies, walked round the assembled working party, taking ten for this job and ten for that, until the lads began to notice a strange Nip among the coolie party. They all listened carefully as he made his request to the chief for 'Ten *toekan batoes*' (ten stone-workers), and with great alacrity ten likely lads, all pals, stepped out to volunteer. They were quicker than the others to notice the new man's cigarettes showing in his pocket.

With his ten stone-workers, or bricklayers, the Nip set off along the straight road from the base. Suddenly the stupid Nip from the office ran out, saluted the Nip chief, shouted about something on the telephone, and ran to intercept the little party. The new Nip received the urgent message, while his ten workers stood by, wondering what was likely to spoil their day.

In bad Japanese, bad Indonesian, and dreadful English they were informed that there was now no call for ten bricklayers, but ten carpenters were needed, so he would have to take them back and change them.

'O.K. We're carpenters,' said his group, and when he was at last made to realise that his ten British bricklayers were in fact ten rattling-good carpenters he and the same ten men moved off up the road, ten pairs of eyes on the pocket with the cigarettes. They were determined to have a go at those cigarettes even if they had to turn into ten magicians.

Without doubt the largest cement job performed by any party was making the Admiral's air-raid shelter, sited in the courtyard of the municipal buildings in the very centre of Macassar. It was sheltered on three sides by large public buildings, and the fourth side opened out as the entrance to the main street. A strong, solid, reinforced foundation was first made, then cemented into this was a small but very thick iron box, which the man said was a safe. At a pinch it would hold about three men.

When the 'safe' was fixed, ton upon ton of cement was poured upon it, rapidly prepared and shovelled by hundreds of POWs. Day after day, week after week, this cementing went on, and the shelter rose higher and higher, until it grew to such gigantic proportions that we began to feel certain that the Allies must be dropping something pretty big and heavy if this was the only way to keep safe. We named the shelter Fujiyama.

Half-way through the making of Fujiyama a party of fifteen men was taken away each day in a lorry through villages deep into the country and about twenty miles up into the hills where there was a mountain river, fast-flowing and with a rocky bed. From the torrent it formed we had to remove large round boulders, anything up to a hundredweight apiece. We plunged in, searched for a suitable boulder, and staggered with it to the bank. Often we were tumbled over and over, but we always clung resolutely to our boulder, which had often taken us considerable trouble to find, perhaps with our feet. In most instances we had to submerge and tear the boulder loose from the river bed, where it had been lying securely for Lord knows how many years.

As more and more boulders were required we penetrated farther into the stream, and it became daily more difficult and dangerous for us to loosen the boulders and get them back to the bank. Success often depended on the Nip in charge, and we were often harried by flaying sticks, which were particularly painful on wet skin.

That mountain stream was too far for us to get back for our midday rice, and the party later went direct from the camp to spend the day there. We took our own rice, and were given a pot with a green vegetable in it which we called 'morning glory'. It looked like ivy, and it certainly tasted like ivy.

The occupants of the mountain village nearby were mainly rich Chinese who had shops in the town but had come up into the hills while the Nips were in occupation. We soon discovered how convenient this could be, and it became the routine for us to ask the Nip in charge if we could have our 'morning-glory soup' warmed up in one of the Chinese huts.

They would often agree to this, and two of the POWs would carry the pot of soup into the hut and turn it over to the care of an old Chinese woman. I saw her try the soup one day. She spat it out as though it was vitriol. I realized at that moment how far we had come down the 'gourmet' scale because we always ate it without fuss.

No words or gestures were exchanged when we left the pot; only looks passed between us before we rejoined the main party in the beaver activities. Out came the boulders to be piled high on the lorries for the trip to Macassar, to be used, as we found out later, for the final outer skin of Fujiyama. Then, when we stopped for dinner and collected the pot, there was always something added to the soup. Sometimes we would find chicken scraps or pigs' heads, or there would be the additional pleasure of bananas passed surreptitiously to us. I remember having a green jelly passed to me, presenting me with the problem of handing on to each man a piece of wobbly jelly in his rice tin, then cloaking it with rice—all under the watchful eye of our guard. There was the occasional and welcome cigarette. These little acts of kindness took me back to the day when we first marched from the docks to the camp at Macassar. The streets had been lined by those same Chinese, some waving little flags but no one shouting or cheering but just looking, their brown eyes expressing then what they were now able to do for us in a more concrete way.

Late in the afternoon we would climb back into a lorry on top of the day's last load of boulders, and ride back to Macassar through the paddy-fields, which we had now seen in their full annual cycle— the drought, the cascading monsoon, the transplanting, the fields of waving, ripening rice. On that drive back I always had the chance to think a little of the fields of Devon; then, those waking dreams would be rudely interrupted and we would be dodging heavy boulders flung recklessly from the lorry. With no footwear, and with soft damp feet we would swing into the mad tempo of work once more on the Admiral's shelter.

There were some amusing incidents connected with that shelter. We always had to smile when we considered the tiny steel safe inside that monstrous semi-spherical building, with its great coating of boulders. As we worked on the final stages we were in charge of an old Nip Petty Officer who could be a little 'rugged', and when one day he called one of us over and shouted to the poor chap to get him something there was good reason for him to ask our help in discovering just what was wanted. All he could gather was that he wanted something to help with what he was doing, and it was behind in the store.

I watched the Nip smoothing off the cement between the large boulders and told my pal that I thought he wanted a small trowel. Frank was not satisfied, and protested that it just wasn't a trowel that the Nip had asked for. But time was not on his side, and we eventually persuaded him to try to find a trowel in the store. Reluctantly he went, and reappeared clutching a small trowel which he nervously held out to the PO. When the guard turned to see what Frank was offering him he knocked him flat on his back, punched his face, kicked him, and behaved generally in Nip fashion, completely ignoring the fact that Frank hadn't the foggiest idea of the meaning of the words.

Frank crawled away and returned a little later, his lips puffed and bleeding; with a rueful look on his face he complained, 'I told you he didn't want a trowel.' Unkindly we all roared with laughter, for the Nip PO had angrily gone round to the store, returning with a leaf from one of the trees that grew there. Carefully he began to smooth the cement with this leaf. Even Frank grinned. At times life could be jolly difficult.

Whatever the difficulties, the work went on. We were beaten and whipped mercilessly on occasions, and in the heat of a tropical sun, underfed and ill, men would collapse and be at once set upon. Men with their bodies and teeth shaking from malaria would be forced to go on digging and shovelling until, completely exhausted and past caring, they would collapse senseless. The Nips, unable to beat them into activity, would heave them into a heap, muttering as if in disgust that they could not keep going.

Chapter 15

DESTINATION UNKNOWN

IT WAS A night similar to hundreds spent in the camp. Inside the huts of leaves, rotten canes and bamboo the prisoners rested after the day's toil, some crowded around the 18-inch circle of light from the shaded lamps trying to read the odd books or old magazines that had been smuggled into camp, others sitting on their rotten wooden, bug-ridden boards or flat out with exhaustion, too tired to join the others in their talking. Occasionally a figure would move into the half-light peering at the faces around, passing on when he could not find the person he sought, a man searching for a chance of *ganti-ganti*[1] for a soft working party the next day, prepared to wheedle, cajole, weep, or even threaten to get what he wanted, and craftily looking for those with the minds most scarred by imprisonment, those whom terror had clawed more deeply than the others.

Yet on this particular night there was something intangibly new, a whispering, almost telepathic, which suggested that there was something afoot which did not fit the normal routine, and this was brought to consciousness by the voice of the duty officer who had entered the hut. The murmurings were stilled as he reported that the British prisoners were to remain in camp the next day except for certain working parties, the Japanese special parties like the factory men and the basket-makers. There was to be a medical examination, and it looked as if some of the prisoners would be

---

[1] *Ganti-ganti* was the term given to a system of exchange. This is more fully described at page 171 *et seq.*

moved from the camp. Nothing further than that was definitely known.

Voices were raised in query and comment. 'Are we off to Japan?' 'It's an exchange of war prisoners.' And so on, the questions continuing on in men's minds for the rest of that night. It was only a few hours before we would know for certain.

The following morning the British prisoners were indeed told to remain in camp, and after the other working parties had left we were fallen in and marched off around the camp to the open ground near the main road where, to our surprise, we saw our officers also fallen in. Eventually we were told that we were to be medically examined, and a white-gowned figure came across and sat with his leg over the arm of a chair and waited there as first the officers and then the other ranks filed in front of him. If we were fit we said, 'Fit,' and he waved us past him. The chaps with broken arms and legs he more or less accepted as not being fit, but anyone who limped up to him and said, 'Not fit,' because his legs or feet were wrapped in rags doing duty for bandages, had to unwrap them and lay bare the deep running tropical sores which were immediately attacked by flies in the vicinity.

Eventually two hundred of us were chosen and marched to one of the sheds which served as a store. Five or six Nip guards were already assembled there, and we were kitted up with a pair of long white drill-trousers and a drill-coat; some of the coats belonged to the local band, others were civilian garb, both managed to fit grotesquely. Then we received a half-towel each and, the greatest joy, a new blanket; then a pair of wooden klip-klops and a green straw hat. Thus attired in a straw hat, a bandsman's outfit, and wooden slippers, I didn't exactly feel that this was the best line in gent's tropical rig.

We were then given two bars of soap and were told firmly to look after them and not to let them be stolen by the other men in the camp. If we had known then that it was to be eight months before we saw another piece of soap we would not have joked quite so much about that statement.

A few days later, when we came in after a day's work, we were warned to collect our gear together that night in preparation for an early start. Collecting wasn't much of a job, but we spent the greater part of the time visiting pals and leaving messages with each other just in case we got out first.

The next day we all assembled, twenty-six officers, three Merchant Service officers, and 169 ratings. We were counted and recounted and then marched to waiting lorries and driven off. We followed with eagerness each turn in the road, until we knew that we were bound for the docks. At least it was pleasing to know that we were going back to sea again—but to what destination? *Was* it to be Japan?

Chapter 16

PAMALLA

AT LAST WE should be free from Yosh. We all consoled ourselves with this bright thought as we sat in the dismal, rusty hold. We might find somebody almost as evil and ruthless, but never one worse than Yoshida was. We had no idea where we were going but were content merely to be sailing away from Macassar and that malignant presence.

The sea-trip was uneventful. One and a half days of coast-hugging, then a sharp run east until late in the day, and we were near land again. Occasionally during the trip the hatch covers would be lifted off to let in the sun and some fresh air, and a few of us at a time were allowed to use the deck latrines and return to the hold. Our trip had taken us across the Bay of Boni, to the port of Pamalla, and we learned that the ship in whose hold we had been confined was a nickel-ore vessel used normally to transport the ore from Pamalla to Japan, an important contribution to the Nip war effort.

We landed on the third day, carrying our 'belongings' ashore under the watchful eye of fresh naval guards, and were marched along very poor dust roads to a cluster of new rattan-and-leaf huts inside a stockade. We could see under the boundary fence as there was a clear gap of two feet from the ground. There were, in fact, two fences: an outer one of leaves to prevent looking out, and, about a yard away from this, an inner, barbed-wire fence, designed to keep people in. There had been no real attempt at putting the fences close enough together to be effective, but we knew already the hopelessness of any effort to escape.

The camp was at the edge of jungle, with the main road running past the entrance; on the other side of that road stretched a muddy beach, and across this, about fifty yards distant, was the sea. The beach was filled with trees which had fallen and been sucked down and almost swallowed by the mud. As far as the eye could see extended this rotten, dank, overrun, stinking forest, the grim legacy of some great tidal wave or earth disturbance.

When we entered the camp we were surprised to see two large Dutchmen, clad in white shorts and shirts and with bushy black beards. They were busy fitting electric lights in the huts, and the job was obviously not completed. Apparently we had not been expected and, with the usual Japanese 'planning', events were being left to look after themselves.

That evening we were mustered to meet our new guards and their officer, a Warrant Officer Murati. There were twenty naval guards to look after two hundred of us, but we were informed, through a civilian interpreter, Eta, that we had come to do a job of work for a civilian firm. If we worked well we should be treated well; food would be provided, and life would be made tolerable.

We spent the next few days tidying the camp, putting enough huts right for our needs. When this had been done and the galley tried out we were told that we would begin work the next day.

Our officers, chief and petty officers were mixed in two messes. The Commanding Officer was Captain McCahon, Royal Marines (the man we had cheered in his struggles to get out of the Java Sea), and he and the two doctors were the only men excused work. The rest of us took turns as cooks of the mess, which meant cleaning the hut and its contents—a long, rough table and two equally rough wooden seats either side—and brushing the red earth floor. We were also responsible for collecting the rice, and after meals we washed the pans and returned the empty rice cans as the culmination of our mess duties.

Next day, while the cooks of the mess swept and cleaned, the others marched back to the ship to collect picks and shovels. For the next ten days we dug and tidied our camp, completing the latrines and felling trees where necessary, but we had not been shipped to Pamalla for agricultural or forestry work and it was not long before we were directed to our real task. It was at that stage that we realized the significance of the small-gauge railway-line that we had noticed on our first march from the docks to the new camp. The line had come over the hill down towards the docks, ending in a built-up iron pier alongside the ship.

The civilians and the naval guards accompanied us to the other end of that line to organize our work in the nickel mines. This was to be the digging of ore at the mine face—at surface level, not in underground shafts. We dug at the face and shovelled the ore-bearing rock into iron bogies standing on the nearby track. Working in pairs, those detailed for 'pushing duties' trundled the loaded bogies, total weight about half a ton, along the level section of the track until they could gain some momentum on the slope down to the pier.

At the end of the track were two loading positions near the ship, to which the bogies were switched by midshipmen acting as points operators. Once there, the loads were tipped into the hold and the bogies joined the queue of empties already forming. When all were empty the pushing crews shouldered them back up the hill to the mine face, where the diggers would fill them again. So it continued, throughout the sweltering day. At noon the morning diggers became the afternoon pushers.

We quickly became accustomed to this work routine, speeds on the downward trip increasing remarkably, together with the development of the necessary techniques of control. The only method of braking was to use a hard piece of wood against the rim of the wheel and the frame of the bogie. With the half-ton of metal and ore accelerating down the track, two drivers clinging on grimly, the wooden brake would be forced harder and harder, until it began to smoke.

Sometimes the 'brake' would snap and the drivers would abandon ship, tumbling head over heels as they jumped from the bogie, which now hurtled down towards the pier and the waiting empties. Those drivers down below, prepared for such an event, would leap off the pier into the mud before the loaded bogie careered into the first empty and sent it off the pier into the mud, or into a mad telescoping movement of the long row of waiting bogies, ending in a mass of toppling metal, flying mud and nickel ore.

Even if the drivers retained their hold the midshipmen operating the points were sometimes nonplussed by the hurtling bogies, and diverting one suddenly at the points could cause nickel ore and a brace of drivers to be thrown together into the air. This could cause some really grievous bodily harm.

To the Japanese such activities were sabotage, a heinous crime for which the guilty persons were deprived of their 'driving licences' and compelled to dig for a week before being allowed to drive again.

Work in the mine was very arduous, particularly in the oppressive heat. It was doubly hard for men who were undernourished and suffering from the effects of appalling living conditions. Our guards were always fresh, a new batch of twenty coming in at the monthly change; but the civilians in charge of the mines and the loading arrangements were our real bosses, and they were certainly after more than their pound of flesh. They complained promptly if they thought we were not working hard enough, but to this our natural reply was that they were starving us—but this they denied. We said that we wanted meat and were not particular which kind as all we had eaten for weeks was rice. We were not even tasting the dubious delights of 'morning glory', the ivy-like weed we had at times back at Macassar.

It was not just a question of lack of food. The camp was infested with rats and mosquitoes, and although we had arrived at Pamalla two hundred relatively fit men, now we fell sick with malaria in increasing numbers. Less than two months after our arrival we were shocked to learn that one of our comrades had died. He was the first of many, the little cross inaugurating the cemetery at the edge of the jungle clearing. He was lain shallowly in the red earth with his name on the cross and the explicit statement that he was a 'Man of Exeter'.

Ironically, there were times when we actually fed on a rich man's diet, provided by the coconut-tree. Perhaps we could also have had coconuts from them, but we learned quickly that the nuts were difficult to remove and, even with the nut in one's hand, the husk was often so tightly grown around it that one was prevented from reaching the contents. Consequently there was at first not much enthusiasm shown when we were instructed to help cut down the coconut-trees.

As we set to work we were being watched by a large group of Javanese labourers. They were employed at the other end of the face at the nickel-mine, having recently been shipped into the islands as forced labour. We had been warned to keep away from them and not to talk to them if we did not want to be punished. Now they stood there, gazing at us with great interest and with a certain suppressed excitement. We could not understand this as there were no coconuts on the tree, but as soon as it toppled and fell twenty or thirty of them, with whoops and shouts, fell upon the tree, hacking at the top of its trunk with their picks and shovels. To our amazement, we saw them eating, and with our instinctive reaction to things edible we were quickly hacking and chewing alongside them.

It was delicious. Our objective was the part of the tree where the leaves were beginning to sprout and the fresh new leaves were pressed tightly together ready to burst. 'Millionaires' salad' it was called, mainly because during normal times it took the expense of felling a coconut-tree to obtain it. That day some of the most deprived men ate like Moguls.

This was an isolated delight. Our general supply of food was dangerously low. One day we came in from work at the mine to be told that no rice had arrived, and it did not take many repetitions of situations like this to lower our resistance. Lack of nutrition meant that we fell prey more easily to malaria and to the scourge of dysentery and scabies, both of these developing to major proportions.

Bandages and medicine for malaria were virtually non-existent, but the efforts of our medical officers never faltered. As we came in each night from work a large queue would form at the hut which was used as a sick-bay. At the end of a long table would stand our two doctors, both from HMS *Exeter*, Surgeon Commander Walsh and Surgeon Lieutenant Ryalls, RNVR. They would prod and cut and clean our wounds with improvised instruments made from a penknife blade and the rib from a corset. Green Dutch uniforms were cut up and used as bandages, but in time even this source of supply dried up.

I remember that, after endless requests by Captain McCahon and our doctors for medical supplies, the Nips one day handed over a single bottle of Vaseline. When this had been used up it was filled again and again with water which would be used on wounds demanding the greatest attention. It was all that was available, and we felt better even for having our wounds looked at or brushed with a feather from the water in the Vaseline bottle. Medicine we could not have, but faith we had to have.

It was not long before the camp was completely in the grip of sickness and disease, and death was to be faced as a daily affair. I became for the first time a victim of malaria, experiencing the bouts of severe shaking repeated daily at the same time. Before they went to work my pals would bring over their blankets and I would lie under about half a dozen of these and would also share with twelve others a large carpet. There I would shake, shiver and sweat on the bare boards under a roof of leaves, worried, miserable and at the mercy of my thoughts.

Quinine being unavailable, a special 'witches' brew' was prepared each day from the leaves of the papaya tree. It had a revolting taste, but it was the best that could be provided. The orderlies came round with the stuff in a bucket shouting, 'Come and get it!' even though no one was capable of moving. Each night they came round and helped us pour the evil stuff down our throats. None the less, many men died; others, like myself, managed to struggle back for a time, only to be struck again and again by the disease, a pattern which persisted until our return home.

Cases of dysentery increased, and were eventually removed to a separate hut where they were looked after by volunteers. Bandmaster Vidler—'Bandy', as he was called—was one of those devoted 'nurses'. 'Bandy' was a native of Cosham. He came to *Exeter* from HMS *Eagle*, and was Drum Major of the Mediterranean Fleet. He was also a damned good footballer. Now, as an aide to the doctors, he performed the demanding task of stripping off and washing down each patient before he was put into his place for the night. Because of the scarcity of clothes the patient was stuffed legs first into a rough, disused straw rice-bag, to lie there until morning, when he could again be cleaned for the day or prepared for burial.

Such was the incidence of sickness at this stage that the working party reached the low total of eight fit for work out of two hundred. We persisted in our demands for better food, not only to enable us to live, but even for the material reason that the civilian bosses would get no work done if we were not properly nourished.

We were always searching for something edible, and those who were fit were constantly on the look-out for something for their sick pals. 'Daisy' Adams tells how a particular supply of broth was obtained: 'One day we were at work clearing away the jungle near a house in which the Japanese doctor had taken up residence—a lovely spot overlooking the sea, with a small stream about four foot wide and two foot deep running along the lower edge of the grounds—and in this stream the doctor's pride and joy: four ducks. We looked at those ducks every day as we passed, until eventually Geordie Wilkinson decided that we must have one if not all of them. He and Taffy Robbins converged on the poor ducks, one from above, the other from below in the stream.

'Meanwhile I kept the guard, "Piccolo Pete", busy in conversation with a stock yarn using all the bits of Japanese I had picked up. I told him how the Nip ships had snatched us from the sharks in the Java Sea. Geordie and Taff grabbed one duck, then had to dive under a very low bridge that carried the road. They held the duck under water to keep it quiet, but neither of them knew how to kill it, so they bandaged its beak with strips of shirt and smuggled it back into camp for Hugo, the Maltese cook, to make broth for the sick.'

A yak—the local beast of burden, something like a water buffalo—was given to us on seven occasions only. One of the creatures fell and died just before it could be shot and just as the gun was being put against its head. Another was brought in dragging its left leg, which was rotten with sores and had a great gaping wound. It made its entry into the camp to a chant from the delighted POWs in the huts, timed to the movement of the rear leg, which was always late in catching up with the movement of the others.

On another occasion the sergeant of the guard, Petty Officer Kowataki, came into camp with a yak and, on being asked to kill it, stated blithely that he had never killed anything before and couldn't possibly kill the yak. 'I asked him for his gun,' says 'Daisy' Adams, 'which he gave me with one round in the chamber. I stood about three yards in front of the poor yak, but Kowataki was very concerned in case it charged me, and insisted that I stand behind a slender bamboo post, one of the supports for the cookhouse roof. I planted that bullet right between the yak's eyes, and the poor thing looked at me with a puzzled expression on its face. I looked in turn at Kowataki and said, "*Sato laggi*" (one more), and he handed me another bullet, which I promptly put about one inch below the previous hole. The poor yak sank on his forelegs and a drop of blood spurted, but he still looked straight at me. So once again the request, "*Sato laggi*", but this time I adopted a method suggested by the cook, Lofty Butterfield, and hit the yak just above the other two holes with the bullet travelling downward. This time he fell stone dead and Hugo got quickly to work; but the resulting feast was too much for most of us, and we were all sick as a result of it.'

Among the other odd things we were provided with in response to our 'No eat, no work' talk was a shark. It proved to be a wonderful meal, and I recalled the time, soon after our capture, when we were aboard the oiler looking down at the sinister sharks just off the stern. How I wished we had them now. Then one day there was a bag of monkey-nuts, and on two occasions duck eggs, the kind that are buried in the mud for years. They were black with age when we had them, and smelt terrible. Some of the men were so sick at the sight and stench that the eggs nearly finished them off; for the rest of us, we ate them, and I think they actually did us some good.

On another occasion a large green snake was seen in the camp and was furiously chased, but although hit often it escaped. It must really have had the wind up. Other creatures that managed to evade our eager clutches included iguana lizards and a wild boar.

The sickness continued to increase until the work done at the mine was negligible. Concern for food became master of our thoughts and action. By this time we had become friendly with the forced labourers from Java, and what little money we had we gave to them and asked them to buy food of any kind for us. This they would do, and some mornings, guided by stones that were thrown by them, we would slide away to a bush or clump of growth to find perhaps a bunch of bananas or some Java sugar. Life was hard enough for those Indonesians, yet they helped us, and many a POW who survived owes his life to the little extras they bought for us in the compound where they lived.

One day I bought twelve little green packets from a tiny local girl about six years old. I asked her if it was *banya makam* (could be eaten) and on her nodded assent I bought a dozen. When I had returned through the scrub to the working party I gave one to the Electrical Officer, Mr Smith (he had given me the first ten cents to start 'business') and opened one myself. Inside the green leaf, which was held together by a stick pushed through the ends, was a sticky substance which turned out to be tapioca.

Mr Smith 'borrowed' one for Captain McCahon RM and I shall always remember the Senior Officer getting down to this sticky mess with evident enjoyment. I smiled to think of him carrying out the same sticky operation in the wardroom in his tight-fitting red mess dress.

Our working party had indeed become a farce. We were now a definite liability after only six months, during which our original work force of some two hundred men had dropped dramatically to fifty.

During that time the Surgeon Commander had been able to grow a reasonable number of tomatoes from seed—not enough for the full number of sick, but sufficient for him to offer, on his daily rounds, a tomato to one person here and another there. Having been sick for weeks, I had seen him coming every day into the sick hut, where he would pad around in his bare feet, stained red from the earth of the camp, and stand straddle-legged over you where you lay too weak to move on the long raised platform. Every day he spoke to me, felt my pulse, but never gave me a tomato.

I felt left out of it. Ill-shaped though they were, those tomatoes were enticing and were being given to others and not to me. Then one day, as I sweated, ached and mumbled to myself, I received one, and with an awful suddenness I realized that it signified that I was very ill. Shaken though I was by this, my determination was increased, my willpower strengthened. It was so easy and even excusable just to give up and die; life presented so little hope.

It was one morning during that period that a huge aircraft was seen overhead. It came on several occasions, from different directions, circling overhead for some time. We did not know its nationality, but four days later we were no longer in doubt. Already the Nips were digging deep and solid air-raid shelters, and we were asked if we wished to do the same. When asked what thickness of wood we wanted for the coverings, the Senior Officer said he only wanted thin coverings to keep the sun off. Long, six-foot-deep shelters were dug and a roof of leaves put on.

Four days later they came. I was in the sick hut and heard one of our chaps in the door shouting excitedly, 'Look at them!' There

in the sky approaching the camp were the biggest aircraft we had
ever seen, seventeen of them in succession, making a tremendous
din.[1] Down into our shelter trenches we went, helping those who
could not walk, all except two whose moving was of little consequence now.

We crouched, waited and listened with some apprehension, for
just behind us were the mines and the new work-sheds containing
pumping engines and power-plant. From the few feet below the
surface we could feel the concussion of the great bomb bursts, then
the planes swept in turn, guns firing, across the camp. They stopped
firing as they came overhead, but now, close to the front entrance
to our camp—between us and the sea—the Nips had brought up
their HA guns. It was difficult for the aircraft to hit back at them
without destroying the camp and us, and we wondered if the pilots
knew we were there.

When finally they had gone we checked our casualties, and found
that the only hit inside the camp was a new tin plate which now
had a neat half-inch hole in it, bang in the centre. The owner,
'Pusser' Bund, viewed his damaged plate with great annoyance,
commenting that, with all the room available in the camp, the
Americans had to ruin his only plate.

After this raid we adopted a new meal routine, always placing our
plates outside in the sun to 'dry', neatly yet not obviously arranged
so that they spelt the word EXETER for any Allied plane to see and
report.

As malnutrition and disease caused more deaths, and as a result
of constant complaints from our senior officers and the doctors,
information was at last penetrating to the higher officials and
rumours began to spread in the camp that we were to leave. Eventually our Senior Officer was informed that this was now a distinct
possibility, but any delay was the fault of the Americans. The Nip
CO on many occasions explained to Captain McCahon that our
plight was the direct result of American action. The Americans sank
every ship they saw, either with subs or with aircraft. Very little
Japanese shipping was moving on the seas, and Japan therefore
could not send food or medical supplies.

[1] American B–29 'Flying Fortresses'.

Certainly no nickel ships had arrived for many weeks, until, one Sunday, one of them appeared in the harbour. That same afternoon we were all shaken out of our calm by the sound of gunfire. There was a general feeling of excitement—perhaps this was the time we had been waiting for. An Allied attack perhaps? Had they come for us at last?

The guards were all mustered quickly in the camp, carrying rifles and machine-guns; then, as suddenly as it had started, the firing stopped and all was quiet again. Tension eased, and after a while we were back in our customary feeling of hopelessness. Next day the guards informed us that it had been an Allied submarine, but, as usual, it had been sunk by Japanese forces. This was one indication of the stepping-up of Allied submarine attacks. We heard later that enough submarines had been involved to have taken us off Pamalla, but this was no doubt apocryphal.

The lone nickel ship remained in the harbour, and it seemed that our painful existence was to continue in its established pattern. It was now late in August 1943, and the effects of the malaria on us had been disastrous. Sixteen men had died. Lieutenant Mark Kerr, who had been such a source of inspiration during the night men were afloat after *Exeter* had gone down, had drawn himself back from death by a tremendous display of courage and determination. He had been thinned to the bone by malaria, dysentery and beriberi, and his condition was so extreme that few of us gave him any hope.

Then we heard one day that we were going to be moved. The Japanese officer told us that we were going to a place where the earth was not red, where we could wash, where there would be soup and the sick would have care and treatment. It could only be heaven; but how were we to get there? The nickel ship was still afraid to leave harbour because of the waiting aircraft and subs, and we certainly did not want to be put to the bottom of the ocean by our own forces.

It looked as if we would travel by road, a surmise that seemed to be confirmed by the Nip Commandant's question about how many of us, including the sick, could walk to the main gate. Could we manage to carry those incapable of walking? We said that we would get every man-jack to that gate.

That night they searched us and our huts, and we were told to be ready to leave early the next morning. Litters had been hastily constructed of bamboo, for there were only about thirty of us capable of walking any distance, and sixteen of the POWs were seriously ill.

Next day we mustered on the parade-ground, where our bundles were torn open and searched. Then we were all personally searched and the bundles tied up again. The Jap interpreter informed us that our work at Pamalla had ended and we were therefore going away. Actually we had become a complete liability to them, and the work was certainly nowhere near finished.

The litters were lifted and the move began towards the main gate, a hundred yards away. Progress was painful, and when we arrived at the gate there was nothing to be seen along the length and breadth of the road. The Nip guards kept the leaders on the move, with behind them the pathetic procession, still hopeful as we plodded on to the next bend, expecting at every yard to be overtaken by the transport. Bringing up the rear were the sick on their improvised litters and others on botched-up crutches. Many of those carrying or supporting their pals were themselves sick and weak in the extreme.

The road turned and twisted, but kept on in a direction we all knew—the quay and that nickel ship. Gradually it dawned on our tired minds that we were once again the victims of a typical Japanese trick and were to be taken away by sea.

I still do not know how we managed to reach the quayside, and getting our sick on board was a terrible task. After the long trek in the heat some of the lads were in desperate shape. Only the doctors and stretcher cases were permitted to remain above decks. The rest of us were battened down in the hold filled with nickel ore: rats in a hot-hole, and sicker rats than those who had come to Pamalla eight months before.

That same morning, filled with doubt and despair, we left harbour for the open sea. We had left sixteen of our men buried on the edge of the jungle, in the ant-infested earth we had come to hate—sixteen victims of that special brand of hell.

Chapter 17

COCONUT GROVE

As WE LEFT Pamalla our minds were part occupied with the bright picture painted for us by the Nip officer, but few of us gave it any real credence. The nickel island had been hell indeed, but this was obviously another face-saving manoeuvre—who on earth could believe that we were journeying to a land of plenty battened down in the loaded hold of a nickel-ore vessel? Nevertheless, there was always that tiny grain of hope that still lingered, that little sense of an unknown future that might perhaps hold some promise. Our hopes quickened a little when we were allowed on deck the following day and noticed that we were once more close to land.

Speculation increased as we steamed in a westerly direction, but during the afternoon our hopes were dashed as those on deck saw unmistakably unfolding before them the familiar coastline of Macassar. Heaven indeed! Here we were on a transfer from hell to that accursed camp where all our miseries had begun, and where we could imagine little hope of any improvement of our now desperate condition.

It is incredible how at the extremities of experience that faint flicker of hope can remain. After all, we had been away a long while and some changes could have been made. Perhaps the guards had been relieved; perhaps Yoshida had been transferred, or even died. Perhaps the war was all over.

Our ship drew alongside the jetty and the ropes were thrown and secured. There he was—the hated Yosh, shouting and gesticulating as usual, throwing orders in all directions and taking charge as he always did. Many of us were by now too ill to care and more concerned about the physical problem of getting ashore. Lorries were waiting on the quay, and into these went the worst cases—emaciated, dying men, in such a ghastly condition that I am sure that I detected a look of incredulity even on the impassive faces of our camp guards. It was difficult to believe that men could have changed so much in merely eight months. Many of us now weighed less than seven stone, and we were all stained a strange red colour from the nickel ore with which we had shared the hold on the journey from Pamalla.

On our arrival at Macassar Camp we were segregated from the other prisoners by barbed wire, and attempts to contact them were forbidden. Our clothes were stripped from us, and we were stretched on the ground to be hosed down before being graded into particular states of fitness. Then we were given a meal, and for a few moments life was upturned once more—that meal was hot, and it had meat in it.

It was not long before we were back on the customary working parties; then one day 150 men were held back from their usual tasks to form a special 'camp working party'. Nobody volunteered for this venture as it was to be supervised by the camp guards—any other new outside party would have brought a flood of volunteers to get away from Yosh and his henchmen, particularly if the new party provided possibilities of full 'loot bags' (see page 171). For the unfortunates who were held back for these unspecified duties, suspicions were rapidly confirmed. Yosh was in one of his driving moods, and when the other outside parties returned to camp that evening they were met by an even more exhausted group of POWs who reported that they had been taken to a nearby coconut plantation where they had cut down innumerable trees, dug out roots, and hacked generally at the jungle undergrowth to begin to clear a large space.

As the working party cleared this area, so they disturbed large nests of red ants—red tiger ants which bit like hell. This was bad enough for men working without footwear, but many had tropical ulcers—deep running wounds about the size of crown pieces. Into these unbandaged sores would crawl the angry ants, biting and sucking, a painful activity which would have to be endured without flinching as Yoshida was watching and was in no mood to stand for the slightest sign of slackening activity.

This was just the beginning; the clearing party became a terrible chore as the work continued into days and then into weeks. Men in that party described how crude rattan huts of the most primitive type were being erected in orderly rows. These were followed by a large galley, and as the area increased, so barbed-wire fencing was put up.

We realized quite early on that this meant a move to a new site, and to begin with we consoled ourselves with the fact that it was nearer the sea, though the thick jungle screened it effectively from us. It also had the advantage of being surrounded by coconut-trees, and this gave rise to the euphemistic but apposite title of Klappa Grove (Coconut Grove).

The completed project was far from resembling any of the exclusive clubs bearing such a name; the Dutch doctors, in fact, had grave doubts about the move. The Grove was damp and dank, a perfect breeding-ground for mosquitoes, and they gloomily predicted that the incidence of malaria would increase dramatically. It was already high enough in the stone barracks, and some of the Pamalla party had experienced as many as thirty attacks during their eight-month stay. Dysentery would, they said, be another problem. Lavatories in the present Dutch and Indonesian barracks had been properly constructed to suit tropical conditions, and dysentery had been kept under control. The new camp had been constructed without any thought of hygiene; deep wells had been dug with a latrine pit near by. Washing was from a bucket hoisted from the well, and the effluent from this and the near-by latrine joined to soak away into the earth, back to the well.

The move to Coconut Grove was made in one day, the maximum time the Nips allowed for the exercise. It was panic and mad rush from the word go, and at dawn the next day, when we were able to pause and take stock of our new surroundings, we found that we had really got down to the local way of living. The floors were of earth and the huts contained no furniture whatsoever. We had brought our bed-boards, mats and wooden pillows with us, and that was it. We were divided ninety to a hut and five to a 'mess'. Such were to be the conditions at the Grove that of the five in my mess only two were eventually to survive.

The camp had been laid out in a circular compound with four

roads leading from it in the form of a cross, a pattern which if seen from the air could be interpreted in different ways. When we expressed our fear that we might be bombed by our own planes in mistake for a Japanese Army camp we were told blithely that the roads had been so constructed that they would form a cross of red earth which meant that it was therefore a Red Cross camp. This was all we got out of Yoshida, but later Dutch injuries from Australian air raids indicated (if it had to be indicated) the stupidity of his reasoning or the intensity of his disregard.

With the move to Coconut Grove went the last of our civilized amenities; but what we grew to hate most, apart from Yoshida, was that damned red earth within the compound and inside the huts. It got into what clothing we had, into our bodies, and, for many of us, into our very souls.

The problems of hygiene were worse than anticipated. The cheap buckets wore out and were not replaced; the rope frayed and snapped, and no other was provided. Nightly, men returned from work to use the well, which was so inadequate that the last men to arrive at the dark, disease-ridden 'bathroom' threw wet mud over themselves. To the Nips the new camp was a work of art.

The move also meant that we had to walk farther to work each day, our working hours consequently increasing until the parties were barely back before evening muster. As this interfered somewhat with the process of counting—never a strong point with the Nip guards—there was a great deal of shouting and rushing about, a factor that did not make life any easier for the exhausted POWs, who were eager even for the discomfort of the hard bed-boards.

Constant protests were made to the Japanese about our treatment. As POWs we considered we had rights under international agreements; one of these was that of payment for work done, and after persistent complaints the Japanese, much to our surprise, suddenly agreed to pay us. After the initial shock it was wonderful to think that we would be able to handle money again: living in a world devoid of money, particularly paper money, needs to be experienced to be understood.

Every Sunday night we 'signed' for the work we had done, dipping a thumb in red ink and impressing it on a piece of paper. We carried out this elaborate routine for months, but no pay materialized, despite the fact that the Nips possessed thousands of these red thumbprints. Then the day came when they announced ceremoniously that we were to be given a little money, and the next morning we were each given ten cents.

Hundreds of men walked out to work that morning feeling like millionaires, but some guards refused to let the men in their working parties spend anything; other parties were able to buy bananas, coconuts, and the local sweetmeat, but, with a measly ten cents, our purchasing power was very limited.

The climax came a few days later. Apparently the Japanese had received a serious setback at sea, losing many ships, and on the evening of that day, when we returned to camp, a 'crash muster' was sounded on the bugle. We fell in before an angry and excited Yosh, trouble written all over his face, standing next to the Camp Commandant.

After a few minutes one of the coloured Dutch *mandoers* was pulled out of the ranks to face them. The Commandant began to ask questions, but was interrupted by Yoshida, who pushed him aside, grabbed the young Dutchman, and beat him mercilessly with a club until he sank to his knees and then into an exhausted heap on the ground. The young Dutchman took this treatment without a murmur, and it did not end until he was stretched insensible on the ground. Hundreds of men were to owe their lives to this gallant Dutchman who came later to work at the factory B.O.2 with me. He was the very brave son of a Norwegian father and an Indonesian mother.

We were then warned against buying anything to drink outside the camp. The Dutchman had apparently been punished because he had allowed his men to buy coffee. That same morning some of my men had brought coffee, but that seemed to be irrelevant. Yosh now had the excuse he needed to stop our money, and we were told it had to be returned at once. Never again did we receive anything but cuffs, kicks and cruelty for the work we did.

Those who had staggered back from Pamalla were particularly vulnerable to these conditions. As Bert Diggle records, 'I don't think I ever recovered from the effects of Pamalla. I just did not have the strength left for leadership, nor could I command by example. Yet, when I was *mandoer* of a working party and feeling really ill the Nip in charge set about me and beat me up. After several blows to the chin I was down and, like a boxer who doesn't know when he is out, I got up again. As my legs gave under me I kept thinking, "Stand up! Stand up!" and somehow I did. Then along came Moto San, the Nip educated in America who spoke and understood English perfectly. He set about me verbally: I was no good to anyone now, this once-proud Gunner's Mate. He knew me, my rating, and all about me. He had spies in the camp who kept him informed and told me things to prove his point. He knew all right.

'Then came his offer. I was to broadcast on the radio for fifteen to thirty minutes a day. Then I would have a bungalow, enough money to spend, and there were plenty of good-looking Indonesian girls I could have. Japan would win the war anyway. Where I got the strength from I don't know to this day. Perhaps a last desperate defiance — I thought I was just about finished anyway. I replied that I was still British and a Gunner's Mate. Again I was knocked to the ground and was told, "Don't forget I know all that goes on in the camp. Mention this to anyone and I'll have you shot." A Dutchman in the party gave me water, got me to my feet, and back to the camp. There I was found to have dengue and was put in the sick hut, where I was a long time recovering.'

As the length of the working day increased so did the demand for working parties, until they began to demand more men than the camp could reasonably supply. The source of manpower was drained by the sickness spreading through Coconut Grove. The Nips would still not supply us with quinine in anything like the amount required, so more men fell sick with malaria, and those who had it already just got worse. The guard insisted that these men go out to work, and gradually the damp-infested area we had moved into, coupled with the extra demands made upon us, began to have dreadful consequences.

It was not only the lack of basic medical supplies but the absence of the slightest human consideration. The medical teams were in trouble with Yoshida, who declared that the men were not sick but that it was a ruse to prevent the men joining working parties. When the doctors explained patiently how serious the conditions were Yosh would fly into a rage and the doctors would be beaten with rods and canes. Quite often when we returned from work we would be told of Yosh's visits to the huts now used as hospital accommodation, of how many of the patients had been beaten up, doctors knocked about and injured, and sick men forced from hospital beds back to their own huts to swell the numbers needed for working parties.

Finally Yoshida insisted that all men reporting sick were to be sent to him and he would inspect them himself. Sometimes men who were seriously ill, but still standing, would provoke Yosh into such a temper that he would attack them, often calling his henchmen out of the guardroom to lend a hand.

The tropical diseases we were prey to included Weil's disease, pellagra, tropical ulcers, beriberi, dysentery, apart from the now common malaria and basic malnutrition. Some of them were considered deadly even with the appropriate medicines available; but no cure could be attempted without supplies, and it says much for the skill of our doctors and their ability to improvise that they achieved results. Many cases of dysentery were treated by the patient eating burnt wood, a difficult task for men as ill as they were and requiring all their determination and willpower to get it down.

Our unbalanced diet gave rise to body sores; but the doctors had no calcium to make this deficiency good. They did suggest we forage, out on our working parties, through all the Nip dirt and refuse buckets to find eggshells. These we washed and added to our boiled rice, and if there is any meal less edible than tasteless rice with broken egg-shells I have yet to hear of it.

We had a Dutch dentist, and those with toothache were laid out on a long stool, the anaesthetist being a large Dutchman who held your head. The dentist pulled your tooth, patted you on the back, told you to rinse out and, if you could steal some salt while out working, to swill your mouth with salt water.

I knew one of the Dutchmen who had his appendix out without an anaesthetic, held down by eight other Dutchmen while it was being done. This, let me add, was before he came into the Macassar camp.

For major operations, such as amputations, an anaesthetic would be given. On one occasion the 'operating theatre' had been prepared and the patient was shaved and ready. The anaesthetic was just about to be administered when in burst Yoshida. Someone had upset him, he was angry, and into this atmosphere he came yelling and screaming and clouting one of the doctors. In a flash he wrenched off the anaesthetic bottle and vanished. As the doctors left they said apologetically to the patient, 'Oh well, perhaps another time soon.'

The senior surgeon was a Dutch doctor called Schmitt, older than the others and a very clever man. It was he more than any other man who could get anything from Yoshida. On rare occasions he obtained anaesthetics and he also received Yoshida's interested attention, for even in the quiet and earnest atmosphere of the operating theatre Yoshida was to be found. Dressed in a smock, he would join the ring of doctors around the patient, and as the poor chap passed into unconsciousness it was with the memory of that dreaded face and slant eyes.

Our physical condition was further exacerbated by a reduction in the rice ration, and, as a *mandoer* responsible for doling out rice, I was only too aware of the way things were heading. As *mandoers* we had to carry a measuring utensil—a flat tin fitted to a wooden platform part of which was shaped into the handle. As the men came up for their rice we filled the measure and levelled it off under the watchful eye of the individual who was holding out his container. Every grain of rice was scraped out of the measuring tin and transferred before the man would move on and let the next one move up for his issue. If a little was left over at the end the queue re-formed and some rice given to as many as possible. Most men went to a different working party each day, but in the fixed working party a strict list was kept and priorities were religiously observed. Every man knew where he stood, and the rice issue was a ritual which was never abused.

As the issue dwindled, so we had to fit false wooden bottoms to the measuring utensils to make sure it went round and each man had his fair share. With the thickening of the wood came signs of severe malnutrition and a general slowing down of work. This in turn enraged the guards, who began to cut loose and beat up men so badly that this in itself caused a significant increase in the number of sick men. Repeated appeals by the leaders of each community, Dutch, American and British, for medical supplies were ignored, and men began to die who if they had been given the simplest of medicines would have been alive by the end of the war.

It was not always the older men who suffered more. *Exeter*'s ship's company had included 'boys', aged just sixteen and for these young-sters, not fully developed, camp life was indeed ghastly. It was little wonder that their suffering was often greater, and when one of them fell ill his health collapsed, and with it his reason. He became insane and had to be put into solitary confinement, the only available place being the cells behind the Japanese guardroom. From there he would shout, in such Malay terms as he had picked up, all sorts of threats at Yoshida and the other guards. They could hear him clearly enough, but in a way they were afraid of his madness.

Each morning two of the sick men who were left in the camp would take him out of the cells and hose him down. He had gaping tropical ulcers on his legs, was suffering badly from dysentery, and would foul himself in his cell, where he would lie in his excrement. Yet, under those terrible conditions, the ulcers on his leg actually began to heal. He always insisted on being told the latest camp news and 'buzzes', but as we discovered later that he was shouting out all this information to the guards, the men who looked after him began to make up the news. He would play merry hell if he was told nothing.

In the door of his cell was a peep-hole with a slide-flap which could be pushed aside for the guard to look in. One day, Yoshida strutted to the peep-hole, unaware that the young lad was waiting for him and standing ready for the flap to be pushed aside. As soon as Yosh put his eye to the hole the boy poked his fingers through into the Nip's eyes. Yoshida never went near the boy again.

It was during this period that the dock party were confronted by some unexpected visitors. At the end of their six-mile tramp to the docks they noticed that two ships were alongside the wharf, one of them flying a swastika flag. The party did not work on the German merchantman but on the other (Japanese) ship, which they unloaded under the eyes of the German crew, who looked down on a scene which obviously shook them. The POWs were forced to double with loads far too heavy for them, and were beaten and kicked with great ferocity, this turning out to be a particularly nasty day.

One of the German crew called out something in German or Dutch, thinking that they were Dutchmen who were being man-handled by the Nips. When they found that they were British sailors they seemed dumbfounded. Someone aboard who could speak English asked them why they were not wearing boots to unload the ship. When told that the prisoners hadn't any there was a brief conference on board the merchantman, and a little while later many pairs of boots were thrown on to the quayside. They were acknowledged by cheerful thank-you's, and later the German crew passed over their dinner-time potatoes and bread. There was little doubt that they were horrified by what they saw.

The following day the new working party swung excitedly around the last corner of the docks. Having heard of the kindness shown by those German sailors and of the extra food, they hoped that there might be a few more pairs of boots. Then, as they turned the corner, their hearts sank into their unshod feet: the German merchantman had gone.

The mosquitoes and disease-bearing flies were still with us, and to add to our many duties the Japanese passed the somewhat odd order that every day in future the chief of each hut, when reporting his numbers correct at evening muster, was required to produce 300 flies and 250 mosquitoes. This meant that the members of each hut had to find between them this number of insects each day, so that in effect the 'hunting' task fell to the lot of those left in camp, usually the sick and infirm. Men out with the working parties had no time to indulge in fly-catching. The order also insisted that the mosquitoes had to be stuck to a piece of paper in the inevitable rows of five deep and given to the Nip Petty Officer of the day. The flies were tipped out of a tin into a bucket alongside the Nip PO.

British naval ingenuity soon found a way to overcome this problem. The inside of the fly-collecting tin was smeared with grease so that when the tin was tipped over the bucket, flies would stick to the grease, thus obviating the need to catch so many flies every day, and leading eventually to each hut building up a stock of spare flies. In an emergency one could always rely on borrowing flies or mosquitoes from another hut – an important reserve source, for failure to produce the required number would mean that the entire hut of ninety men would be beaten up.

One night that remains vivid in my memory was when I was bringing back a working party of about four hundred men. At the factory office where we were working the Nip on telephone duty had to swat flies all day long and kept his victims in a large glass bottle,

which stood on his desk, an untapped store of fly wealth. Whenever
the opportunity arose and he was out of the office I would dash over
and tip out a few hundred to bring back concealed about me. Proper
concealment was vital, as on entering camp each night the working
parties were searched, and when things were discovered, particularly
foodstuffs, it ended with a beating for the individual and for the
working-party *mandoer* and sometimes for the entire party.

That particular evening a Royal Marine in one of the earlier
parties had been caught smuggling, and the searching of all the later
parties was intensified, extra guards being called in to help. Anyone
who aroused the slightest suspicion was hit or kicked, and the time
taken to search so increased that about three hundred men eventually
stood waiting in the queue that stretched back to the main gate.

This was the state of affairs when I marched my three hundred
men in, and there was I loaded with dead flies; but not for long. I
started to unload, the flies falling in their hundreds about my sweating legs, many remaining stuck fast, while others fell between my
toes and lodged there. As I tried frantically to shake them loose I
was pleased to receive the order to turn my party about and return
to the main gate. In the respite gained I was able to unload and
brush away the remainder of the flies.

The Marine, Micky Dodds, had been on a working party with
'Geordie', Stoker John Wilkinson. They had managed to salvage
some food and clothing while helping to clear the debris caused by
a recent American air raid, and were determined to bring it back
into camp. They had decided that, in spite of advice not to try to
smuggle stuff in, they had to continue to bring in what they could,
taking it in turns to do the actual smuggling. 'On this occasion',
says Geordie, 'we pooled our smuggled stuff and Micky loaded his
legs and waist and I came in empty. There were fifty of us on the
working party, and Kay Koy, the sergeant of the guard, counted us
in, then started his normal search, as we thought; but, having Yoshida there, we felt that there was something special going to happen.
Kay Koy proceeded to search every individual from head to foot.

'Micky Dodds and I were nicely placed in the third and fourth
ranks from the front, about centre. After the first two ranks had been
searched with no success, I thought that by the time he reached me,
Kay Koy would be rather sick. There were only two of us with

trousers, and I think by now that Yoshida and Kay Koy knew that anyone with long trousers would be a recognized smuggler.'

Geordie was searched from head to foot, and then had to drop his long pants; but, to Kay Koy's surprise, there were no smuggled goods. He continued into the fourth line and approached Micky Dodds, telling him to put up his hands and down with his trousers. Micky refused at first, so Kay Koy smacked the marine across the face and repeated the order. Down went the trousers, but instead of dropping to his ankles they stayed on his knees, so full were his loot bags.

'Yoshida', comments Geordie, 'was delighted now he had found someone smuggling in a big way. The whole of the camp were ordered to muster, bugles were blowing, and Yoshida was furious. About two thousand prisoners had to muster—British, Dutch, Americans, Indonesians, the lot. We fifty had to do a front support and stay like that for an hour and three-quarters as punishment, and during this time two of the Nip guards walked up and down each file, booting in the stomach anyone whose body touched the ground, or hitting with a baseball bat the behinds of those whose bodies were too highly arched.'

The rest of the camp looked on, and at the end of the period Yoshida announced his punishment for the fifty men. Each would receive twenty-five strokes with the stick on his behind.

'I knew he meant it. I had not long been out of hospital after having 207 strokes on the behind with the baseball bat, and I knew I couldn't stand another 25. That bout had put me in hospital for nearly six months face down, unable to sleep, eat or do anything. But our *mandoer* shrewdly selected the strongest of the working party to be first to receive their twenty-five strokes. Yoshida was full of fight and energy, knocking them down left, right and centre, but they were still getting up for more, and as they were finishing their twenty-five they were asked to stand in a separate place. When it came to my turn I wasn't going to be as foolish as I was previously. After about five strokes on a bit of raw meat on my behind that wasn't quite healed I took a dive. Yoshida lapped this up, seeing a big man like me take a dive. He sent for stale water from the fire buckets in the guardroom, and poured it over my face and head. He also held my nose while half of it went down my throat. I shook my head and was ordered to get up again. I took another couple on the backside and down again.

'By then someone else had stepped up for his turn. Yoshida thought he had me, or had killed me, and turned away. Looking out of the corner of my eye, I could see that he was busy on someone else, so I got up and crept to the section that had already been beaten up and hid in the rear of it. I didn't get the full twenty-five, but I had had enough.'

Then it was Micky Dodds's turn. The assembled camp stood waiting for Yoshida's verdict, and it began to look as if the Marine would be beheaded. They marched Micky to the small rostrum about thirty yards from the guardroom, and he was told to put his head on it while Yoshida stood sideways with his sword out ready. Yoshida had already called for our padre to say some prayers, and after these had been solemnly said by everybody the Dutch captain began to plead with Yoshida, until the Jap asked the captain what punishment he suggested.

After some discussion it was decided that Micky Dodds would do thirty days in solitary confinement—that is, in the tiny cell in the guardroom. 'I had experienced three days of this', recalled Geordie, 'and would not want any more. Very little to eat. No toilet—just do what you had to in that room. Millions of mosquitoes; filth, smell, no air, and the tropical heat. I remember that I wanted to get in touch with Micky the first night he was in, and the only way to get near was via the British officer's block, which was almost adjoining the back of the guardroom. I made my way there in the dark, and was about ten yards or so from the ventilation window of the cell. I called out to him and got the reply, "Is that you, Geordie?" I asked him if he wanted anything. "Yes, it's cold in here. Can you get me a blanket?"

'I obtained a blanket for him and handed it through the small opening between the rails. I didn't know what would happen the next morning when the Nips came round and saw the blanket, but I didn't care. I went round again the next day. "Anything else you want, Micky?" "Yes, I'm hungry." I had to be careful with the food, but I did get a bit through to him, until someone found out, and I was ordered not to go near him or both of us might have our heads chopped off.'

Micky Dodds did not do his thirty days—no one could last that long—but he did manage more than seven, which was some achievement. His health never fully returned, and it was amazing that he was still with us on the day of release.

During the previous year we had received some evil-smelling dried fish in our diet, but this had been missing for some while now. Constant requests and even demands for extra food did eventually result in the arrival of thousands of flying fish, which were put out in the centre circle at the junction of the four roads, open to the sun and the millions of flies and the dirt which settled upon them and remained until the fish was issued for eating.

It was at this time that we were beginning to feel a little optimistic and 'buzzes' were rife in the camp, being based mainly on a story that the camp guards now all had horses and were regularly going outside the camp to learn to ride them. This suggested preparation for a quick get-away via the mountain roads.

The new situation meant more work and the formation of a special 'P' working party composed of the sick men. It turned out to be a wonderful job for them, but to begin with they had the arduous task of making stables for the horses, first hauling in the now familiar green bamboos, trimming and cutting them to length. Then they stripped the long rattan canes and placed them in bunches ready for tying. Within a surprisingly short time the bamboo structures were rigged and the horses stabled.

'P' party had no intention of giving up this job before it paid off, and they wheedled their way into feeding the horses. Every day sacks of coarse corn were brought in, but as soon as they were left alone to their task the lads tucked into the fodder, and a great deal less of it went to the horses. The men, their bellies stuffed, would go out in turn for a drink of water. Within minutes their stomachs would be round and swollen with the expanding grain. The horses became thin and ill, quite often swaying from side to side in the stall, hardly able to stand up. In this condition they could not have carried the fleeing Nips very far had the island been invaded, a comforting thought to the fat-bellied 'horse-minders' rolling back to their huts.

At one evening roll-call we were all mustered in the compound watching the red ball of a sun diving quickly towards the mountains, when through the gate rode a dozen guards. They spurred their horses through our ranks towards the cross-roads and the centre circle covered with our stock of fish. Instead of keeping to the road they drove their horses on over the circle, squashing the fish and kicking pieces into the red earth roadway. The final act of degradation was when two horses stopped and with legs astride covered our fish with muck, to the evident delight of the Nips, who screamed excitedly, '*Benjo! Benjo!*' revelling in a situation which so obviously disgusted us.

Yoshida was by this time taking it out of everyone. The doctors and their staff were frequently beaten up, and it was quite a common sight to see them all doing 'press-ups' in front of the guardroom. The guard, often a fat, ignorant bumpkin, would sit in a chair in front of them, feet on a desk, watching the sweating men who had to keep going or have that gorilla around them, using the butt of his rifle in persuasive beatings upon the back of some unfortunate doctor or orderly who had finally collapsed under the strain of this and the hot sun.

Our numbers were reduced also by some transferring of prisoners, mainly to Java. Our First Lieutenant, Lieutenant-Commander G. Cooper, was included in one of the parties, together with most of the other officers. But still over 1000 prisoners of all nationalities remained in Macassar. Many of them were destined never to see freedom again, while others were doomed to return home after the war in a state of chronic illness.

Chapter 18

DETERMINATION TO SURVIVE

FOR MANY POWs survival was linked to their initial physical condition and to the amount of hardship and punishment they were able to withstand. Those who were tough and strong when they first marched through the gates of Macassar camp had a head start on their less fortunate brethren, and though nearly all of us eventually fell sick, those chaps who had the initial reserves of strength managed to weather those critical early years of imprisonment.

'Geordie', our champion boxer, was one of the toughest men aboard *Exeter*, this toughness supplemented by a recklessness which was to stand him in good stead as well as involving him in some difficult situations. Geordie always had an eye to the main chance and a pair of 'loot bags' about his legs in which to store the valuable 'finds'. Ever on the search for food and the means of survival, he became the source of supply for a number of items, sometimes a little unexpected.

Working one day with the party under the supervision of the notorious 'Bull', he was one of a group of eight POWs working near one of the outhouses in the Nip barracks. 'Seeing an opportunity to slip away, I entered one of the outhouses and found two full tea-chests, fully sealed and containing dried tea. What a surprise! Coffee growing on the island, but imagine tea to an Englishman! The greatest demand for this was in the sick-bay, where, once the fusty smell had been dispelled by drying the tea in the sun, it was brewed, and upon occasions smuggled-in limes were squeezed into the unsweetened beverage, proving a tremendous relief to the dysentery sufferers. Many were the journeys to and fro with my loot bags, until every grain was purloined and found refuge with our boys, leaving the empty chests to enrage some Nipponese owner.'

On Christmas Day 1944 Geordie was with the dock working party helping to unload some cases of unknown content. They turned out to be Christmas-boxes from Japan for the men serving in Macassar, and many contained chocolates and sweets, but some contained a really festive cargo.

'I was in charge of a section unloading these boxes on to the jetty as we were not allowed to board ship. As the order to lower had to be given by me to the Indonesian in charge of the crane, I waited until the Nip guards were relaxing their vigilance and caused one of cases to drop at excessive speed. It burst open to reveal quart bottles of Japanese whisky.

'As much as we desired to drink, it was impossible under the eyes of the guards, but I was able to fit one bottle on to each leg in my loot bags. Making a trial walk up the jetty in order that my pals could tell me if it was noticeable, I received the tip that a Nip was following me, and eventually he called, "*Piggi manna?*" [Where are you going?] "*Benjo!*" [Toilet!] I replied and flew down the jetty steps, bursting the two bottles against the wall and facing the furious Nip, who could see that I was not going to the toilet.

'I took a lacing from him with his fists in my face and his boots in my stomach. The chagrin on his face had to be seen to be believed.'

Geordie was determined to get some of that whisky back into camp, and when the last load of the day was ready for transporting to the warehouse about a mile away, and the two Nips climbed into the driving-cab, Geordie managed to get into the back of the lorry as it pulled away, purloined two more bottles, then faced the nigh impossible task of getting off that speeding lorry with the bottles intact. 'I made several attempts to pace the speed of my withdrawal with that of the lorry, but with a bottle of whisky in each trouser leg it was difficult and must have been comical to watch. Eventually I made it, dusty, dishevelled, and delighted. I regained the working party, answered the roll, and made the camp. Imagine if you can the impact of half a gallon of whisky suddenly appearing in the hut. From the medical point of view and also that of conviviality, it made our night one to remember.'

More important than whisky to the sick men was the provision of vitamins, and by a lucky chance a source of supply was discovered. Bill Guy, who was in the sick men's working party, discovered a broken case of small bottles containing a powder he could not identify. He passed it to Geordie, who contacted Dr Schmitt. The Dutch doctor confirmed that the bottles contained concentrated vitamin B.

'The following morning,' says Geordie, 'I ganti-gantied [exchanged] with Bill Guy at a cost of one month's rice ration and took his place in the party. On my first day I forced open more of the cases and found multi-coloured bottles which I loaded into my loot bags—fifty bottles in each. They proved to contain a range of vitamins.'

This valuable source was plundered for about a month, Geordie giving up his rice ration to remain with 'C' party and to keep the doctors supplied with the much-needed vitamins. He also kept a case of them available for his mates, and countless Nip searches failed to bring to light any of the supplies. There is no doubt that the smuggling in of the vitamins meant new opportunities of life and survival for many of the sick prisoners.

Geordie was not always lucky: his strength and recklessness made Yoshida his enemy. On one occasion Geordie had been caught smuggling in food. This maddened Yoshida, who was both angry and delighted at catching Geordie in the act. He shouted for his baseball bat, and with all his strength he flung blow after blow at the Englishman, expecting him to fall under the ferocious attack, but Geordie remained standing. Yoshida lashed him across the buttocks, back and legs, but Geordie refused to go down. Screaming now with uncontrolled fury, he lashed and yelled, kicking and letting the blows fall across his victim's legs. After 207 blows Yoshida was exhausted, and in his fury he pushed Geordie over. That hammering earned Geordie the respect of everyone, even the Nips. A weaker man would not have survived.

On another occasion the punishment was not a beating but a spell with the 'Bull's' party, digging and shifting earth. The POWs would shovel the earth into a Dodge truck, and when it was full twenty or so of them would jump on and travel ten or fifteen miles up to the aerodrome. By the time they arrived the earth in the truck was nicely compacted and difficult to shift. They shovelled it off the lorry, while the 'Bull' sat atop the cab watching and yelling, '*Kura!*' (You!) if anyone slacked.

'After about a week I found that the first five men off the lorry entering the barracks got a good job. I made sure in future that I was one of the first five and was working in the garage with some of the Indonesians. They used to go home for lunch and bring us some tin-tin and handy-andies [Indonesian titbits or sweetened biscuits]. During one of the lunch hours I walked around the barracks, which occupied what was previously a girls' school with an attached chapel, and came across a church. This had been barricaded, and entry was forbidden, but my curiosity had been whetted when I learnt that some goods of value were stored there.

'At the same time a few days later I went to investigate. I was really sticking my neck out when I forced the door, slipped inside, and locked myself in for about an hour. I found a large quantity of savings stamps, originally owned by the Dutch Army and taken over by the Nips at capitulation. I put samples in my loot bags and got them back into camp, where I showed them to one of my Dutch friends. I asked him which were the most important ones and those which I should bring back. "All, Johnny," he replied. "You bring all in. All very important."

'The next day I was back inside the church, filling both loot bags and bringing the rest of the stamps back. On the third day I went along with one of my mates, "Baron" Aindow, and we cleared all the important items, even the curtains, which we brought back into camp wrapped round our bodies. That curtain material came in jolly useful.

'I got hold of two biscuit tins, stuffed the stamps into them, sealed the tops, dug a hole near the boards where we slept, put the earth back over the tins, and carefully hardened down the surface. The stamps were still there on VJ Day, and are possibly still there now. I was very ill with dysentery on the day of release and couldn't get to them, but I am sure I could find the spot again if it has not been dug up or built on. When we were liberated and transferred to HMS *Maidstone* I was only too glad to be on a British warship and going home.'

Chapter 19

JOURNEY TO JAPAN

WE OFTEN wondered what had happened to our shipmates who had marched out through the gates of Macassar camp for unknown destinations. Those of us who had spent eight months in Pamalla were to return with our story, but other parties had gone without anything further being heard of them. Captain Gordon and most of the officers were in a party of about thirty British and Americans which sailed from Macassar in the *Hakusan Maru*. They were four weeks at sea, calling at Formosa and Kyushu before arriving at Yokohama. From there Captain Gordon and others were taken to the specially built naval interrogation camp at Ofuna, a carefully hidden place whose existence was not known to the representatives of the Protective Powers and where the captured men were not regarded as prisoners of war.

Captain Gordon endured four and a half months of the Ofuna treatment—largely solitary confinement, near-starvation diet, kicking and clubbing, and hard physical exertion in enforced silence. All attempts were made to demoralize the prisoners in preparation for the periods of interrogation, sometimes conducted by a circle of ten inquisitors.

From there many of the prisoners went to Zentsuji camp in Shikoku Island, a dreary but relatively reasonable camp.

In September 1942 a thousand prisoners left Macassar camp, 150 British (all Royal Navy), fifty American naval personnel, and some Dutch Army and Navy men. Among them were some of *Exeter's* crew, including Alf Carne, the Dynamo ERA. He recalls that they were all clad in jumpers and trousers of the Dutch KLM line, and were bundled aboard a Japanese Army troopship, the *Asama Maru*, where they were stowed in the hold of the ship on double bottoms. The British sailors were put in the worst spot because—so the Nips said—they were the best sailors; the others were in tiers up the ship's side, the only access to the upper deck being two vertical iron ladders to hatches above. Fortunately the trip was in good weather and the food was reasonable; in fact, the rations for the Japanese soldier. Half an hour a day for exercise was permitted on deck under heavy guard.

Eventually they arrived at the busy port of Nagasaki, where they were transferred to inter-island ferries and kept between decks with shuttered windows and ports. They were still very heavily guarded, and there was much pushing and shoving by the Nip guards until they reached an island in the mouth of Nagasaki harbour, disembarking across an unmade landing of about a foot of mud.

It was bleak, cold and wet as the large party of prisoners marched the two or three miles to camp, but they were pleasantly surprised at what they found: new huts, new straw mats on tiered bunks, and tables laid with bowls by young girls. This was definitely it. But how wrong can one be. 'Army guards were soon around, shouting and letting us know who was boss. The girls disappeared. We were given our ration of rice and vegetable stew and were later divided off fifty to a room with a senior rating as *hancho*, or room chief.'

Reveille was at 0530, with a muster in the room, all reports being given in Japanese by the room chiefs (see Appendix 5, p. 219). This was followed by breakfast at 0600 and work parade at 0630. Sick men who were unable to work had their rations stopped; this meant that fifty-two rations became forty-eight if four men in the room were sick. Those who were fit enough marched half-way to the dockyard with the camp guards, and were then turned over to the naval guards, who escorted them to the dockyard, where they were split into working parties with a Nip *hancho* and one prisoner *hancho*.

'The first two days', says Alf Carne, 'were spent forming working parties—welders, machine-shop fitters and turners, platers, etc.; but, needless to say, there were not the skilled men to do those jobs. I was among the twenty detailed for a drawing-office party, mainly Dutch and British prisoners. This lasted for about six months, with all design work deliberately sabotaged, and it was amazing what we got away with under the inexperienced eye of the eighteen-year-old high-school student in charge of us.

'Then one day we were confronted by a Japanese graduate of Indiana University, who had spent forty years in the United States as a professor of marine engineering. We feared the worst. A fortnight later he told us that an examination of all our drawings showed what we had done. For this we could be executed; and we all sweated a bit. Then he told us that his son and daughter were both in the US forces, and he would be there too, but had been kept in Nippon after coming for a holiday. We breathed again. He said that he would say that we were not as good as we claimed to be, and that he would get the party out of the drawing-office.'

They were then formed into Group 16 (Punishment Group), labouring, carrying cement, unloading oxygen bottles from barges, all at the trot, with clubs behind them every few yards.

Food at the camp was steadily reduced. The Nip Medical Officer was apparently keeping a graph of lessening calories as part of his research into how much a man needed to enable him to carry on working. Illness also struck fairly rapidly, and during the first year in Japan many prisoners died of pneumonia. There were no warm clothes, no protection against the rain, and after a hard day's work prisoners returned to huts unheated even in the depths of winter. This was a very different situation from tropical Macassar: the climate in that part of Japan is similar to that of England—damp cold with plenty of rain. It is no wonder that between October and April over fifty men died of pneumonia or other respiratory diseases. The only treatment was to leave them in the hut, stop food rations, supply about two aspirins, and hope for the best.

'Our doctors did what they could, but were unable to get any help from the Nip medico, who was too concerned with his diet charts. We managed to steal some M and B powders and sticks of blue caustic from the laboratory in the school where the drawing-office party was working. The doctors used the caustic to burn round the tropical ulcers before treating with the powders. This was about the only medicine, apart from aspirins, available for about twelve months.'

The dead were crated in orange-box coffins and carried about two miles by their comrades to a jetty from whence they were taken by boat to Nagasaki, another mile or so to the crematorium, and later the ashes were placed in urns in the crypt of St George's Church for eventual return to Britain. Fate in Nagasaki decreed otherwise.

During 1943 the camp expanded. A US National Guard regiment of artillery came in from Java, followed by a RAF contingent, both groups cursing 'Wilhelmina's Warriors', who were less than helpful at that stage and were decidedly unpopular. Then a crowd of American civilians arrived, contractors from Wake Island who should have been treated as civilian internees but were lumped in with the POWs. They were taking things badly. Many of them were over fifty, and one in particular, a man of about sixty, was put in the confinement cell, a bamboo cage about 4 feet 6 inches high, 4 feet deep and 2 feet 3 inches wide. Unable to stand, sit or lie properly, he was dead within three days.

After about twelve months all the prisoners were issued with Japanese Army padded uniform and British Army boots; but they were only allowed to wear this gear in camp, because the Nips did not want the civilian population to see that the Allies had decent boots while the Nips had only rubber sneakers. So it was rags and rubber footwear at the docks, but at least they could change into something warm and reasonable when they returned wet through at the end of a working day.

No books were allowed, no concerts permitted, and no prisoner was allowed out of his room after 8 p.m. No prisoner was allowed to visit another room, and was severely punished if he was caught doing so. The official policy seemed to be to degrade the prisoners both mentally and physically. Punishment usually took the form of standing in front of the guardroom with hands raised above the head, or a beating on the buttocks with a baseball bat. If the prisoner was knocked down—usually with a blow on the hamstrings—all the guards watching joined in with boots, rifle-butts, etc.

After about eighteen months the death-rate at the camp lessened. Probably the prisoners were getting tougher or more dehumanized. There was a great rise in the incidence of pellagra; all cuts and sores turned septic, and nearly everyone suffered from some disease or other. Men were doing strange things at times, actions quite out of keeping with their normal character.

Some letters arrived from home, and prisoners were given these after several weeks' censoring. 'Twice in the time we were in Japan we received letters. One of mine had a snap of my wife, and this was certainly a great day. Obviously millions of letters sent via the Red Cross had been detained by the Nips. I found out on repatriation that my own wife had written and sent money for parcels every month. No doubt thousands of other men's relatives had done the same, but only on two occasions were Red Cross parcels distrib-uted—Canadian and American, if I remember correctly. Two parcels per room of fifty!'

There were many small acts of sabotage in the docks where the POW working parties went. 'Although, despite protest, we were working for the Son of Heaven, most of us did our worst. I must say I was astonished how we got away with it, but in general the stan-dard of Nip workmanship was bad anyway. The civilian labour at the yard was in the main semi-skilled and consisted largely of boy and girl teenagers conscripted from their homes, living in a set of barracks we christened "Boys' Town". Apart from a little better food and an occasional day off, they were not in much better shape than we were.

'It was, however, impressive to note the outlook that the more skilled men had on the future of Japanese shipbuilding. They were convinced that one day they would lead the world; indeed, much of their preparation was towards that aim. The war was only an inci-dent, and if it took ten or a hundred years they would win it eventu-ally. Some of our laughter then has turned to less than wry smiles today.'

More troops, mainly Australian, were brought into the camp from the Singapore area, until by 1943–4 the camp was about four thou-sand strong. In the new year deaths began to increase again as the long drag began to tell. In April 1944, when Allied bombing was stepped up, the POWs all sensed that it was a time of change.

'A few of us used to get together and try to see what we could organize if invasion came. We decided that if there seemed a possi-bility of massacre, then at least we would rush the guns and take a few Nips with us. We had to be very careful in our talk as there were informers even among the prisoners. An extra bowl of rice went a long way with some people. All our plans were nebulous, and before we really got off the ground there was another shake-up.'

All executive officers were transferred to another camp, and fifty of the recalcitrant prisoners, including Alf Carne, were taken by boat across the bay to Nagasaki.

On 2 October 1943, all the officers at Macassar Camp, except a few specially picked to stay, were part of a draft of two hundred prisoners—including twenty-eight British—who were marched to the jetty and manhandled into the after hold of a cargo ship called the *Rio de Janeiro Maru*. They arrived at Tanjong Priok on 5 October, and were taken to a camp at Batavia (now Jakarta), in lorries. Later some of the prisoners, including *Exeter's* First Lieutenant, Lieutenant-Commander G. Cooper, were again moved north to a camp at Bandung.[1]

After this draft only the Padre and Lieutenant David Chubb, together with the Warrant Officers, remained at Macassar. The men of *Exeter* were now scattered over a number of camps in Japan and Java, separated not only from home and any contact with their loved ones, but now divided from many of their friends, with no knowledge of where they had gone and what had happened to them. In most cases we tended to fear the worst.

[1] Some experiences in these camps are related in *Ordeal in the Sun*, by G. Cooper and D. Holman (Hale, 1963).

Chapter 20

'TIDA BOLIE'

WHEN 'PUTTY' Churchward came ashore from *Op-ten-Noort* his shattered ankle was still in plaster, and he lay on his back in camp for
about two years while it slowly mended. I vividly remember him in
the roughly constructed bed, its four legs standing in tins of water—
an odd set-up, but one with a definite purpose.

'I awoke one morning,' recalls 'Putty', 'with a tickling sensation
around my neck and right ear. As soon as it was light I could see
the reason. An army of ants was coming and going in an orderly
fashion from my right shoulder across me diagonally to my left leg.
After I got over the initial shock I realized it was my wounded leg
they were after! As I felt no pain or stings I kept quiet until the rest
of the chaps were awake, then told the Dutch orderly, who called
Doctor Fraeder.

'When he saw what was happening he said in his Dutch-English,
"Dot is goot!" and explained that the ants were not infectious and
were probably cleaning up the wound. However, for future comfort
my bed was stood in four tins of water to prevent further invasions.'

I can remember how horrified I was to see the procession of ants
climbing over one another in their anxious pilgrimage up the bed
leg, across 'Putty', and down to his ankle; and they came in at the
window!

By the time the camp was moved to Coconut Grove, 'Putty' was
hobbling about with the aid of a crutch and joined the other invalids
in the compound making baskets. This band of sick men was the
permanent inside working party, keeping the camp clean, 'mucking
out' the toilets, and somehow—in what spare time they had—con-

triving to collect 250 mosquitoes and 300 flies to be handed in at evening muster.

'Putty', apart from being ship's painter, was also of a strict sect and regarded very seriously the problem of worship in the camp. Church services were banned, despite the fact that we had our ship's Padre in captivity with us, though segregated with the officers. Except on such rare occasions as the Nips permitted, church was *tida bolie*—not allowed. The Padre was at times kept busy enough with the funeral services.

Despite the ban, 'Putty' would lead a service on Sunday evenings in a quiet part of one of the huts. Frank Clements would chalk up the hymns on a bed-board, and we would sing them in a strange *sotto voce* manner, for singing at any time in the camp was also *tida bolie*. We enjoyed 'Putty's' services, but there was no doubt about the fate that he and indeed the rest of us would have met had we been discovered.

One of the other invalids in that party was a Dutchman who possessed great skill in woodwork and who after a year's work suddenly produced a complete violin and presented it to one of the musicians from *Exeter's* Marines band called Kayser who had been a first violin with the Hallé Orchestra. The violin was a superb piece of craftsmanship, complete with strings and bow. How he got hold of them I do not know, but it indicated that there were still some contacts with the outside for those Dutchmen whose homes had been in Macassar.

The instrument played beautifully. On Sundays, with our own guards and pickets keeping watch for snooping Nips, we listened enraptured to the music. Unfortunately it was seldom without some interruption.

There was 'craft' of another kind in the camp, stemming from the earlier *ganti-ganti* days. *Ganti-ganti* was the term referring to 'exchange', particularly replacing one person with another. One of my earliest memories of this activity was when I had a small working party of thirty men, fifteen British and fifteen Dutch. We were working on a new wireless building, shifting earth and sand in pairs. As I watched the work I began, as I usually did, to count my party, only to realize that I had a man too many. I counted again and still made it one over. The Dutch section contained both white and coloured men, and on a further count I realized that I had one dark Dutchman too many.

As I walked alongside the pair I suspected, I was immediately urged to keep quiet and help them. They were brothers, one of whom was a prisoner, the other still free and living in Macassar. While they worked the brother from the town passed on all the news about the prisoner's family. This *ganti-ganti* would involve the non-prisoner remaining with his brother's working party and returning to camp in his stead, while the brother spent the night with his own family. Next day, when it was convenient, they would change places again. Simple, but it required considerable courage to carry it through.

The easiest and most humane of the working parties was one known as the Store Party. It was supervised by the Nip civilian storemen and was exclusively Dutch. The same Dutch *mandoer* and most of the same men went on this party each day. No beatings had been reported, and upon occasion the prisoners received a coconut or two to eat before returning to camp. Their work was in the large stores or 'godowns', concerned with a full range of goods from needles to large furniture. The party was therefore carefully controlled, and no kicker against discipline or 'kleptomaniac' was allowed to join that party. The Dutch made sure that it was so carefully tied up that nothing could disturb its relative calm.

One day a dozen British POWs were required to go along with this working party, with myself detailed as the British *mandoer*. This was to be my first visit to the stores, although there had been rare occasions when British POWs had gone along, returning to sing its praises so loudly that I was looking forward to a quiet, restful day away from the camp and its attendant worries. My party would be no problem as the officers arranging the working party would usually send those chaps who were in poor shape and who could do with a rest and something extra to eat.

Imagine my surprise when, next morning at muster, I was confronted with a bunch of very healthy 'racketeers', twelve of them, smiling broadly at me. When I questioned their being with this special party I was told that they had *ganti-gantied* with the sick men, who were now on the working parties to which these worthies had originally been assigned.

There were many motives for such changes. The duty officers came round to the huts each night to read out the names of the working parties for the next morning. The racketeers would listen carefully for the names of those in the particular party they wished to join, then they would offer bribes to those individuals. The bribes varied from an extra rice supper for a whole week to an actual sum of money. Extra supper was a great temptation to a man, particularly if he was ill. If this method of bribery failed, some of the racketeers were not averse from a bit of 'persuasion'. *Ganti-ganti* became a shrewd business in which some people flourished and through which some tragically died.

The racketeers would take tremendous risks to get their hands on anything they fancied, loading it into special 'loot bags' which hung down the calf of each leg inside the long green trousers. It was amazing how they managed to avoid discovery, particularly as once they had smuggled the loot into camp they had the return trip to make to get it out to their Indonesian contacts for bartering.

As contacts could often only be made via certain working parties, these men had to operate the *ganti-ganti* system to enable them to hand over the goods and receive the money or other payment. On certain working parties it was possible to buy food if you knew the routine, and foregoing supper (such as it was) for the chance of going out to spend money on better food was a fair bargain for the racketeer. But often when they took the rice to the man with whom they were making the exchange they would find the poor wretch too beaten up or too sick and exhausted even to eat his own rice ration. I was now faced with twelve of them—my entire work group—and my hopes of a restful time vanished. The Dutch *mandoer*, who knew the men for what they were, was greatly alarmed and muttered nervously, 'Trouble will come. We shall all get beaten up.' I was inclined to feel as pessimistic as he was.

We moved off with the other working parties to the main gate, were counted, and put in charge of our armed civilian guards, who put us aboard a lorry for the journey to the stores. That morning the monsoon broke, and we drove through teeming rain. On our arrival we were told to jump out and run for the store, where we sat for an hour. We were each given a cigarette—so different from the other working parties I had known.

Morning wore on until dinner-time, my twelve 'boyos' getting noticeably and appreciably more impatient. They got up in twos and threes to have a look round the store, discovering that it contained mainly tables and chairs. I am convinced that the only reason some of the furniture did not disappear was simply that they could not stuff it inside their trouser legs.

At midday we were ferried back to camp in the lorry, passing uneventfully through the gate and back to our huts, with an obvious sigh of relief from the Dutch *mandoer*. The respite was brief. When we left the camp after dinner we were stopped suddenly by Yoshida just as we were marching out. He demanded to know where my twelve lads had got the white straw hats they were wearing. They told him that a Nip had bought the hats for them, but Yosh said he would find out and wait for them on their return that evening. If they were lying he would deal with them himself.

Those hats certainly stood out. By this time most POWs had been issued with a green straw hat of Dutch Army pattern; but the white hats these lads wore made them look like a bunch of holiday campers.

We drove away, filled with apprehension, the rain still bucketing down; but this time we were taken to a different store, and as it was raining the Dutch *mandoer* told us we could *yasume* (rest) all afternoon, provided no one wandered about. All men would be searched thoroughly before leaving, and anyone found with anything would be punished and reported to the camp guards. With Yoshida waiting to deal personally with anyone who stepped out of line, we felt sure that no one would attempt to take anything in that night; but half an hour later I heard boxes being broken open, the rustle of paper wrappings, the low murmur of contented voices. I walked around to see if I could talk sense into them, but it was no good. They continued packing box after box of playing-cards down into their loot bags.

Later that afternoon I heard the rustling sound again from behind the large packing-cases; I went to look, and, to my relief, they were busy unloading the packs of cards from their trousers. At last they must have seen the red light—but no; they had found and opened another box, which contained needles and reels of cotton, a much more marketable commodity and one which would mean a lot to the Indonesians. They loaded themselves to the waistline.

At the end of the afternoon, when it was time to return, the Nip civilian asked if any man had taken anything. There was no reply. He looked carefully at us, then said, 'O.K. Campo.' When my men tried to climb back into the lorry they could not bend their legs. We had to push and pull to get them in; but they made it and we were driven back to camp, where we knew a guard waited to ask questions about those white straw hats.

The rain was still falling when we made a kind of orderly approach to the guardroom in fives. Soaking wet, we stood in front of the Nip guard secure within his oilskin cape while he laboriously counted us. This task had been made a little easier for him because the Dutch *mandoer* had informed me on the way back that he was going to separate his men for counting. He did not wish his Dutchmen to be mixed up with the thieving British. But their luck held once more. Yoshida was not there, and the rain was too heavy for the guard to bother to do more than count us. We were dismissed without a search, and the twelve 'loaded' characters were able to go to their hut. The Dutch party had doubled away smartly from the guard-room; I kept my chaps at a walk—anything faster and they would have been flat on their faces.

During the next few days Indonesian housewives in the Macassar district began to sew with bright new needles and fresh supplies of cotton, and another commodity appeared in the camp of which I had not been aware, as part of the smuggling episode. Thousands of cigarette papers were on the market, and that evening I was presented with fifty packets as my share, even though I had been in many ways an unwilling helper.

It is only fair to say that these 'racketeers' were in the minority. They followed the basic rule of the survival of the fittest; but they also gave considerable help to the sick. A man whose pal was really ill could go to them, and by an offer of his 'good' working party would be able to take his pal a little something that was otherwise unobtainable. The racketeers themselves did not go sick until the last year of captivity, when even their resistance was broken; the sudden deaths of two of their leaders subdued them and gradually brought their better nature to the surface. They still used their craft in acquiring extras, but these were for the large number of men who were now desperately ill. Unfortunately, there were by then many sick men who were beyond any assistance.

Maybe the racketeers were at times unscrupulous and callous, but they showed initiative and surprising courage in dealing with our captors. It needed guts to risk a tremendous beating and consequent maiming, just to get enough to eat or some extra clothes to wear. Some of them persisted in their defiance until the end.

Chapter 21

THE FACTORY KNOWN AS BO2

IT WAS early in the third year of our captivity that the First Lieutenant sent for me and told me that I was to take charge of a new
working party, a large one consisting of British, Dutch, Indonesian,
and American tradesmen, acting as 'town engineers'. I remember
that this 'appointment' came at a time when we were beginning to
be aware of the turn of fortunes in the war: the Japanese were
becoming increasingly short of food, and in consequence our rations
were further reduced. Mass beatings became more frequent as frus-
tration and vexation increased.

It was during that period that we had to eat blackened rice from
a godown which had been bombed and burnt by our planes. The
diet was intended as a punishment for the action of our forces, and
it was surprising how long that tasteless food lasted; but, like all
good British tars, we told each other it was good for our dysentery
and stuffed it down somehow. At other times our daily rice was
replaced by Indian corn, the stuff they normally fed to the chickens.
It was really expecting too much to get a day's work out of men who
had been fed on that diet. There was always a great crowing set up
by the prisoners before they ate it.

The engineering project was to be a permanent job for those
mainly involved. The Dutch already had an exclusively national
working party of a similar kind, known as BO1, in the town. That
group had now prepared a new workshop for BO2, a more cosmo-
politan group of those British tradesmen who remained after the
various groups had been sent off to Japan and the remaining Dutch
and American tradesmen. These specialists, about two hundred of

them, formed half the party; the other half was composed of non-tradesmen who were not permanent but replaced every day to ensure a fair distribution of men to rough and smooth working parties. These non-tradesmen were referred to as coolies.

BO2 was housed in a compound that had been fenced off from the outside world. There was a large workshop block, built in the local fashion, just tall roofs on bamboo posts. The floor was of sandy earth, and growing through the roof of the large workshop were coconut-trees, left there, I gather, to act as some kind of camouflage. In the machine-shop were eight lathes, mounted on cement beds, two drilling-machines, and a shaper. At the rear of the workshop was an engine-house with an electric motor and a large flywheel which drove the counter-shafting for the other machines. This ran almost the length of the shop. Benches were set at different positions throughout the shop, but only one steel vice was fitted. Adjacent to the workshop were acetylene welding and electric welding plants, together with two large blacksmiths' forges with hand bellows.

Farther down the compound was a large carpenter's shop, the other end of which was fitted as a drawing-office. Many of the Dutchmen in the party had before their capture been the bosses and civilian draughtsmen for Macassar, doing precisely the work we were set.

Over on the far side of the compound was the motor or auto shop, manned by Dutchmen who naturally made the best use of their knowledge of the language and outside contacts. Food was smuggled to them daily by the Indonesians who worked there, and occasionally this was discovered by our captors, the resultant beating up involving not only all POWs but any Indonesians unlucky enough to be standing near by.

This was to be my final working party, and one which was to keep me fully occupied. I had such a large complement of permanent workers that I was able to write their names on a large blackboard, keeping for them a correct roster for their turn, if any, of the extra rice.

When we first started the engineering work we made just about everything. Miracles were enacted daily on lathes, and our tinsmiths made all sorts of queer objects out of sheet tin. The acetylene welding plant settled quickly into an efficient routine, but there was trouble with the electric welding unit from the very beginning, a fact which brought a great deal of trouble on my shoulders, literally as well as figuratively. The dynamo was on the point of overloading for most of the time; then that one thing more and everything in the compound would stop with a crash. The boys thought this was great fun, though they did try to conceal their enjoyment. After a dozen such failures the Nips were fed up and showed it in their own distinctive manner.

One of our first jobs was to make vices to add to our single steel one. We made two dozen screwed spindles and then two dozen pairs of steel jaws. The Nips later produced two dozen large wooden posts which were dropped into holes in the earth and cemented. Another piece of wood had a steel jaw screwed into it and—hey presto—two dozen vices à la Japanese. Those vices were still there eighteen months later when the war was over.

Many of the men in BO2 were returning to skills which they had not used since the day the *Exeter* went down. For the coolies the working party meant a quieter 'number' after the navvying involved in the panic of cement-mixing, air-raid-shelter building, etc.

My knowledge of Malay had improved a great deal by the time I took up this job, but because the situation was now different there were real language difficulties. I had become accustomed to general work and tools such as shovels, picks, and buckets; now I had to cope with Malay terms for 'drill a hole', 'cut a thread', 'turn a taper on a spindle', 'steel', 'brass', etc. At first these difficulties seemed insurmountable, but the Dutch Senior Naval Rating who had been responsible for building the workshops was sent as an interpreter. Although his English was not good by any means, we struck a bargain. I asked the questions in Malay and he answered in English, or vice versa. In this way we managed to get along, but not without some trouble and the occasional beating.

As the workshop site was the nearest one to the camp, it proved a popular party for sick prisoners. Their number had increased dramatically, but the Nips refused to allow them to remain in camp. Better that they should be in my coolie party than out on a distant and tougher assignment.

Every day a large percentage of sick men arrived at the factory compound, where they would line up ready for work allocation. I

would muster them very quickly and tell them to fall out while I
started up the engine. In the few minutes needed for that job those
poor, sick wretches would crawl away and hide, often merely under
the benches because they hadn't the strength to find anywhere safer
or less obvious.

When Nito Hazo, the senior Nip, first encountered this he got
tough with them, cursing them for being lazy. I explained to him
that they were *stinga mati* (half dead), but he would not have it.
'They would not be out of camp if they were that bad.' Yet gradually
even the Nips began to realize just how seriously ill many of those
prisoners were. For our part, we who were able to work worked
twice as hard to make up for them.

Our first 'production lines' provided community requirements.
We even produced watch cases, and the amount of private 'favours'
increased tremendously. Such work brought us certain items in exchange. We made steel saws and swinging saws for the carpenters'
shop. This was the first time I had encountered a swinging saw, and
when I first looked at the working drawings I could not see how it
could possibly work. I explained this to the Nips and was hit and
pushed around for my pains. The sketch plan was returned a few
days later, altered as I had mentioned, but according to them nothing
had been done to it. I learned to be more tactful in future so that
they would not lose face. The result would be less painful for me.

Most of the designs given to me were drawn in the sand of the
workshop floor. Sitting on my haunches, I would watch the Nips
draw the lines in the sand with a stick, accompanying the drawing
with instructions in a language which I could seldom understand.
Often I would add to or alter the sketch to help me to understand
it, but if I drew a line which was not considered necessary I would
be pushed over. After this session in the sand I would make a real
drawing on paper and give it to the man who was to make the item.

Cans, buckets and funnels were made by the hundred in the
tinsmiths' shop, but one day a Nip came in with dozens of motor-
car leaf-springs which we had to break apart, sending the large
leaves to the blacksmiths' forges. There, under Nip supervision, the
springs were hammered and shaped into what looked to us like
swords: *kutana* was the name we came to know them by. Later they
were ground, filed and finally stoned and tempered. From there they

went to the carpenters' shop to be fitted with a wooden scabbard. The top of the sword had a hole drilled in it and a fancy handguard and handle were fitted. Then a pin was driven in to lock it all together.

Sometimes the scabbards were covered in leather, but I discovered later that this depended on the person who was to receive the sword and how much the purchaser could afford to pay. (Every Nip seemed intent on making money in every way he could in order to own a sword.) We turned out many fine-looking swords, and although they were lethal weapons we felt delighted to think that the Nips thought them so necessary. If they sensed that they might need them for fighting at close quarters or for surrendering or even for *hara-kiri*, then the Allies could not be far away.

One job was a little disturbing. Hundreds of pipes arrived in the compound, drain-pipes that had been dug out of the Macassar streets. I was shown a real blueprint, all in parts, but I could recognize the completed job. Crude and completely welded, it was one of the most incongruous and dangerous mortars I have ever seen. The material was already rusting, such corrosion making the metal not only unsafe but unpredictable. I protested at once to the Nip chief, and on getting back to camp that evening I reported to the officer-in-charge that we were being given work involving the manufacture of mortars. I asked him if I should refuse to let our men work on it; but after I had explained the situation fully my British Senior Officer and the Dutch CO agreed that for the sake of all concerned I should not object. It was generally agreed that the mortars would kill more Nips than anyone else.

At that time we were also making a Heath-Robinson-type hand-grenade from a weak-seamed steel tube. Each grenade was basically an eight-inch length of the tubing, the sides having three grooves turned off. It was also cut by the shaping machine four times along its length. The base plate was welded to the tube, and the head cap was a piece of wood. These grenades were sabotaged by cutting one of the flutes much deeper than the other—just the odd grenade here and there—and it paid dividends. We could keep some kind of score through the American working party at the hospital. When a Nip died the Americans had to prepare him for burial, and most of their work came as a result of our sabotaged grenades or the lethal bursting mortars. Our only concern was at the too obviously effusive congratulations that came from the American party. A misplaced remark and zimbo—off with his head.

In charge of the carpenters' shop was a Nip PO who was 'beating happy'. He was known as 'Tidda Appa' ('It's nothing'), and was usually to be seen with a heavy piece of wood in his hand. On this particular day I had gone over to the motor shop where the Dutchmen worked and found them standing with a large, round piece of steel in their hands, obviously not clear what they had to do with it. They told me in their mixed English that 'Tidda Appa' had given them the job and that it was impossible to do. I had a quick look, then took the steel away from them and threw it into the monsoon drain. As I did this I was aware of a strange look on their faces and the sudden onset of fear. I turned to see 'Tidda Appa' in an attitude of pleased anticipation, his stick ready. I walked straight up to him, saying as I went, '*Mow lakass*?' ('Want quickly?')

I explained in some haste that the way the Dutchmen were going to do the job would take too long; the way I suggested was much quicker. I got away with it; but I had to think pretty rapidly of the quick way!

On one occasion, reasonably early in the morning, I had to go to the Nip office, and as I entered I heard the angry voice of the Jap Commandant. He was smacking the Chief's face many times, during which treatment the Chief was bowing again and again. I imagined that he was thanking the Commander for punishing him and telling him that he deserved it. I did not wait to find out anything else; this was no place for a POW.

Half an hour later I heard the Chief shout for the PO, 'Tidda Appa', and inside the office the same scene was re-enacted, only this time one step down. 'Tidda Appa' was now on the receiving end. The downward passage of this strange scene was continued during that morning, as the elaborate routine of 'face-saving' was acted out.

One of the Americans who worked with me at BO2 could open any lock that was brought to him, so lock-making became one of our specialized illicit jobs. We made locks for the twenty or so young Nip tradesmen who were working as permanent staff and needed locks to keep their personal belongings safe in their communal mess-room. For this work we demanded cigarettes: no cigarettes, no lock and key. Without the lock and key the young Nip could lose his kit, and that meant real trouble. They could not order us to make keys as their Chief would tan them if he found out. Soon they were all fitted out with their locks and keys, and business quietened down until it was renewed briskly when we were commissioned to make them keys for each other's locks. For this task we would take nothing less than a whole packet of cigarettes.

Those cigarettes were a real treat. Our normal smoking mixture was a kind of coarse bush which was dragged into the hut every so often and split among the prisoners. It made a non-smoker out of me, except when I had the chance of a Nip fag. Many of the POWs made themselves wooden pipes, but the pipe got hot like a boiler and burnt the tongue. Rolling one's own cigarettes was normally out because of the lack of paper. It is difficult to realize what it can be like living for nearly four years without paper of any kind. Paper just did not exist, other than occasional cement bags, which were at an absolute premium. One of those bags, carefully washed and dried, could be peeled into four layers of thinner paper; a real token of friendship was to be offered a 'roll' and given a piece of cement bag for the task.

BO2 turned out to be the most useful of all the working parties, but its success also turned upon the courage and determination of the young Dutch *mandoer* who had been so badly beaten up. He played upon the cupidity of the Nips to obtain medicine badly needed by the sick men in the camp, first by arranging for a macabre supply of gold. This he obtained from the dead men before they were buried: a gold ring, gold fillings, or perhaps a watch was passed to him, and these he showed as a form of barter to the Nip Chief, telling him the particular *obat* (medicine) that the doctors needed.

The Nips would barter for the medicine at the hospital, not using the gold, but the swords that we made at BO2. The medicine would come into the Dutchman's hands for him to organize the tricky routine for getting that medicine back into camp to the doctors.

For several months it had been one of our party chores to take wood each night into the camp on a hand-cart. This was wood from the carpenters' shop to be used for the galley fires. A special carpenter had the job of finding a suitably shaped piece of wood to hold the medicine being smuggled; then he carefully removed the outside bark, hollowed out the inside sufficiently to take the medicine, replaced the outer piece, and sealed the bark. This completed piece would be thrown with the other firewood on to the cart and brought back to camp. It was added to the huge pile behind the galley, and later, when the coast was clear, the wood was retrieved and the medicine turned over to the doctors.

This arrangement worked until our release, and as a consequence many men living today do not know that they owe their lives first to the men who died, for the gold they unknowingly 'bequeathed' them, and to the Dutch *mandoer* who exploited the Nips for the vital medicines.

The problem of the sick men who came with the BO2 party involved not only the wizened, weak and emaciated, but also the particularly unpleasant manifestation of beriberi. Men with this disease could not sweat or urinate, became terribly swollen, and unable to walk or lift their limbs properly. When they did arrive at the workshop they would sit around the forges as soon as they were going. Then, in that tropical heat, and with the fire at full blast, we would move them nearer and nearer. In some cases we even helped them to lift the seven-pound hammer and work on the anvil—all in a desperate effort to make them sweat.

Sometimes, like a miracle, it worked. Hilarious with joy, they would sink exhausted to the ground, sweating, urinating, and coming alive as the fluid left them. Others, sitting waiting their turn, would remain as full of water as ever, and at the end of the day they would stagger awkwardly back to camp. They were always part of a special party which went ahead of the main body because of their snail-like progress. It was essential to have the whole party and the correct number at the main gate at the same time.

Many of those unfortunates did not come to BO2 again. Many were never to join another working party, but, realizing how bad they were, they found it much easier to die, just like that, overnight.

One of our Royal Marines who was in such a plight sent a message for his particular pal to go over and see him. This meant running the gauntlet of the guards because sick quarters were out of bounds. Sneaking past the guards and under the barbed-wire fence, the Marine came to the sick hut, peered through the window, and called softly. His sick chum turned his head painfully, looked for a moment at his pal, a sad smile on his face and his hands clasped on his monstrous stomach. Slowly he unclasped his hands and turned first the thumb of one hand up, then slowly the other, and died.

Chapter 22

TROUBLE FROM YOSHIDA

ALTHOUGH work at Factory BO2 became almost a steady routine, there was always the element of tragedy present. My first duty each day on arriving at the compound was to walk to the large board where I had chalked the names of my standing party of about 250 tradesmen. I would stand there with the Dutch interpreter, crossing off the names of those who had died. One morning there were six of these names to delete, but I would not do it until I had brought the Nip Chief to the board. Then I crossed them off one by one, saying as I did so, '*Mati! Mati!* ('Dead! Dead!')

Every day the Nip Chief wanted the same amount of work done. I could not get through to him the fact that the men who were dying were tradesmen and consequently irreplaceable.

'They are dying,' I would say repeatedly. 'They need medicine. Give my men medicine and they will work; otherwise they will die.'

'But you still have four hundred today.'

'But they are not tradesmen. They are coolies and sick men.'

The Nip Chief would look at the sick men lying around him— even their numbers depleted—shout at me, and then walk away to his hut. The jobs would keep coming in, the Chief saying that all were wanted *lakass* (in a hurry), but even the best of my men had three or four sets of work to do on the bench in front of them.

As the third year of our captivity drew on, the deaths mounted. It seemed a long while since we had been shocked by the news of five men dying in one day. Now the death cart was kept waiting at the end of each day, waiting just in case of a 'late departure'. Then it would be rushed off to the burial ground, where the prisoners were interred with indecent haste and virtually unmourned. It made my blood boil to realize that in the hospital less than a mile away were medical supplies that could have put the cart out of business.

Such was the apathy at this stage that as the grim burial party passed through the camp entrance only one question was asked: How many today? The eerie parting note of the bugler sounding the 'Still' was the only record of their departure; but they had gone beyond the walls of the camp and the guards would molest them no more. It was at moments like this that the words of the fortune-teller in Miami rose in my mind. 'There is blood, and I see a fence or wall. It is insurmountable; also I see pain and cruelty for a long while.' How much longer could it go on?

Virtually everyone in the camp was now sick. All men who could stand, and many who could not, were forced out of the camp to work. Men plagued with dysentery were made to stand in the tropical sun writhing in pain and constantly fouling themselves — just to prove to the guards who watched them that they did really have dysentery. The guards showed a sadistic delight in the pain and torture endured by those poor wretches.

I was very sick again with maleria, about my twentieth bout. Both my feet, swollen painfully with beriberi to twice their normal size, were very, very sore. I became as a consequence very clumsy, walking against projections and stones. Tropical ulcers had developed on my festering feet, forming holes the size of a five-shilling piece which became filled with flies sucking at the sores and causing intense pain. There were no bandages, and the flies were unchecked.

As if this was not enough, the left side of my face and mouth, together with my tongue, had gone completely dead: pins stuck in me and a lighted torch placed near my face had no effect. These were the manifestations of pellagra, a few days later supplemented by the onset of dysentery.

This was shattering news to me as most of the deaths in the camp had dysentery as a contributory factor. I experienced the dreadful stomach pains that particular day as I marched my 350 men towards the guardroom to be counted and turned over to the factory guards The pain doubled me up, and I arrived there like a wizened, bent-up old man. I was able to get the men halted, counted, and off through the gates, but the customary routine of saluting first the

guardroom to the left and then the private Nip soldier on outside
guard duty to the right seemed to take years.

My condition grew worse during the morning, and I began to
stagger about. Eventually I was unable to stand up, and was also
near the period for another bout of the malarial shakes. I was so
bad, in fact, that the Nip Chief decided to send me back to the
doctor in the camp. I was joined by another Petty Officer who had
been sick for many weeks, and together, under the eye of a Nip
guard, we tumbled and fell on our way back to the camp gate, where
we were reported as very sick men and sent to our huts.

We did not reach them. The young Dutch bugler boy came running after us to tell us to return to the guardroom, where Yoshida
wanted to see us. No sooner had we returned than Yoshida pushed
me back against a coconut-tree and set about me, beating my back,
seat and legs. Blow after blow fell on my pain-racked body, until
finally I sank exhausted to the ground. Buckets of water were thrown
over me; I was dragged to my feet, thrown back against the tree,
and it started all over again. Finally I lost consciousness and came to
in my hut, bleeding and wanting very much to die. My punishment, I
was told later, was because I shirked working and dared to come
back into the camp before the day's work was over. The Petty Officer
who had staggered back to camp with me and received similar
'treatment' died two days later.

Even in my state I was not excused work the following day, but
was flung back into the usual routine of mustering my working party
at the gate, being counted and checked before we left. How it went
off without incident I do not know; I was too ill even to hold up my
head.

The climax came three days later. I was at the factory, and the
usual group of four men had gone back to the camp with the handcart
and one Nip guard to fetch the dinner rice. Some minutes after their
return the 'buzz' went round that there was trouble in camp, and
that there was to be an interrogation when all the working parties
returned that night. Personally, I felt so ill that I could not care less.
I knew that I had done nothing incriminating in camp to cause me
trouble—or so I thought.

Before we returned to camp that evening all men were warned
that trouble was expected, and they were urged not to try to smuggle

anything in, but to try to keep the sick men moving. Even our Nip guards looked apprehensive.

As we turned in at the camp entrance and halted outside the guardroom we saw a pile of illicit objects—coconuts, hats, tins and other objects. The Dutch Senior Officer who was Camp Commandant was standing there looking very worried. We were searched and dismissed to our huts, where we were eager to know what it was all about, and who was in trouble. There could be something in it for me, because apart from being *mandoer* of the BO2 engineering party, I was also senior member of a hut of ninety men, and although I was away from it all day, and did not know what went on, I was nevertheless still responsible for it.

All hands were to 'clean', and there would be a muster as soon as the last working party had returned, all working parties having been told to get back into camp as early as possible. When the bugle eventually sounded for muster and we doubled over to our positions we saw extra guards marching in at the gate. All the off-duty guards were, in fact, inside the compound.

Above the usual noise associated with the muster of about two thousand men could be heard the excited voice of Yoshida ordering a quicker muster, careering around with a great solid stick which he was obviously impatient to use. One of the working parties had that day brought in a load of wood for the galley fire, conveying it on a long, flat-topped, four-wheeled wagon which was now clear of wood and had been drawn down from the galley to a position in front of the guardroom.

The muster over, we were told that the men whose names were called out were to fall in in front of the guardroom. As soon as they were in line the Commandant started to question them carefully: 'Is this object yours?' 'Is this . . . ?' Before any answers could be given Yoshida rushed in with a roar, grabbed the first man, and flattened him against the flat-topped cart, where he was beaten by a guard on either side of him. Finally he collapsed on the ground, only to be revived by the usual buckets of water and again beaten, anywhere on the body.

The guards then seized other men in the line, until there were three or four beatings going on at the same time. When the victims were beaten into insensibility they were thrown to one side, and

others from the line were driven against the wagon. Any vestige of
civilized behaviour had departed from those guards. They jumped
about, hit and screamed, showing a terrifying ferocity that continued
unabated as the pile of moaning bodies grew.

As we in the ranks watched, nauseated and weak, our first feelings
had been of relief that our names had not been called, but that relief
was quickly replaced by a deep revulsion. Appeals from the Dutch
Commandant that the beatings were too severe were met simply by
snarls from Yoshida, who was now immersed in his activity, his shirt
hanging out over his trousers, his face running with sweat and
transfigured with cruelty and fury.

When, and only when, those sixty men had been beaten insensible,
there was a momentary pause in that barbaric scene. The sun had
almost set, but cries and shouts brought out the hurricane lamps to
enable the orgy to proceed. There was more shouting and more
protests from the Commandant, until the order was given that all
chiefs of huts, being responsible for the items found in their huts,
were to be punished for permitting smuggling.

With the other chiefs I limped into the arena, close to the human
mound, the blackness of the night now lit by the flickeroil lamps. I
was still sore from the tremendous beating I had taken from Yoshida
only three days before, but I had no time to feel sorry for myself.
We were grabbed and pushed against the cart for our share of the
punishment. I was knocked flat by the weight of the blows that drove
me against the cart, and, as if this was not enough, a Nip Petty
Officer, Kay Koy, walked up and down the flat top of the cart,
carrying a split bamboo. As we were forced back over the cart, so
he would dig the end of his bamboo stick into our faces, eyes, and
nostrils. The resulting cuts were to remain with us for weeks.

Bleeding, sick and unable to stand, we were then informed by
Yoshida that this punishment would be repeated, only more severely
next time, if objects were found in our huts. Then we were dismissed.
The human mound was slowly removed, body by body, by those pals
who did what they could to ease the pain and make us comfortable on
wooden boards and wooden pillows.

The next morning was hell. At the early-morning parade I could
hardly stand, and my whole body had turned a shade of yellowy
green. I was shown to the Dutch doctor with the idea of being sick-

paraded as too ill for work, but the doctor said that anyone who had been beaten up the night before, if sick-paraded, would drive Yoshida berserk. It was in my own interest to get to work if I could.

I managed it, but, instead of being Chief of the party, I had to be held up in the ranks by my friends. When we were counted out that morning I met Yoshida's eye and could tell that he knew how ill I must be to need support in the ranks. Limping painfully, I arrived at the factory compound to see almost the entire Japanese staff looking at me from the Nip factory office.

I was at work in spirit only, if that. It was impossible for me to interest myself in anything. All I could do was to clutch at my drawing-table, head hanging, reluctant to ease myself down into the rough chair where I used to sit and work at the drawings. The youngest Nip from the office slipped into the workshop and quickly put on my chair a rubber sorbo cushion, muttering, '*Juto hazo kasi*' ('The chief gives').

When I realized what had been given to me I picked it up and hurled it away in disgust. It was picked up by one of my lads, Bill Dagleish, who was in such a bad state that he had to limp across to pick it up from the floor. He disappeared with the sorbo cushion into the store, and when I was able to look in there later he was sitting on it with some sign of contentment. I do not think it was really of much help. Bill had taken over the store from Tubby Hand, the previous storekeeper, who had recently died. I had never had the heart to turn Bill out of there and back to his proper place at the bench. He was young and ill, and was one of my own young ordnance artificers in *Exeter*.

Chapter 23

THE MINES AT YOSHIKUMA

WHEN ALF CARNE and his fellow-prisoners were taken to Nagasaki they were housed in a transit camp overnight, and next morning they were marched a couple of miles through the city to the main station. By this time they were about three hundred strong, being joined by prisoners from other camps: about thirty Royal Navy personnel, about twenty Royal Marines, and the rest RAF men, Australian and other soldiers. Some left the party *en route*, until eventually only the naval and Marines element of the draft arrived at the destination.

'We entrained in about four coaches to the accompaniment of the usual shouting and pushing. Blinds were drawn and we were off. The Army guards on the train relaxed after a while and we managed to scrounge a few fags. We also managed to peep under the blinds occasionally, and I know once I glimpsed an airfield with several wrecked fighters on the ground. This cheered me, and I passed the "buzz" around. The journey took about six hours, although we were in sidings for about two or three of these.

'We arrived at Yoshikuma and marched about half a mile to the camp, which appeared to be brand-new, although a few POWs were already in: Australians, a few RAF men, and from seventy to a hundred men of the Loyal Regiment. The Senior Officer was Squadron Leader McCarthy, a RAF medico.

'The Nip Commandant was a retired schoolmaster of about sixty-five who was on the Reserve of Officers. Apart from the Sergeant-Major, who appeared young and vicious, the guards seemed to be middle-aged and unfit for active service, and indeed much better than any we had previously encountered.

'We formed a Camp Committee which dealt directly with the Nip Commandant—all very civilized. The Committee comprised the two medicos, an Australian RQSM, myself, a sergeant of the Loyals, and a Royal Marine corporal. The work of the camp was in two groups, plus a few camp employees—cooks, sweepers, etc.

'The prisoners at Yoshikuma were to work in the Japanese coal-mines there, one group by day, the other on the night shift. These were weekly shifts.

'The mine entrance was about half a mile from the camp. We were marched there, then split into groups for different jobs under Korean *hanchos*. I was in charge of one main group for marching to and from the mine, and started as the Day Mining Party. I was detailed, with two others, as a shot-firer under an old Nip (a gentle-man, this one). He was somewhat akin to a "deputy" in our coal-mines—he selected the places to drill, we drilled, placed the charges, and retired. Then he fused and blew them.

'As we were in such a small group we were lucky with our boss. He used to smuggle in little sweetmeats that his wife made for us—rice cakes with raisins and suchlike. Perhaps nowadays we wouldn't look at them, but they were luxury to us then. I cannot think of his name now, but his very existence proved to me that the Nips were not necessarily all sadistic devils.

'The main shaft was 700 metres deep, and no cage descended. We had to walk down. Half-way, headlamps were drawn and signed for. The worst part of the whole shift was walking up; the shaft ran about 1 in 4 or 1 in 3 in places and some of us were literally dragged out by our mates at the end of a shift.

'The mine was a soft-coal mine, long disused until just before we arrived. Minor falls were frequent, and many accidents were caused by large lumps disintegrating while being loaded into trucks. Injured miners were formed into a gardening party reclaiming land (similar in a sense to the duties performed by Dartmoor inmates) for produc-ing vegetables. Armed with "chunkles"—a kind of chopping hoe—they advanced in line abreast, rooting at the bushes and grass.

'The worst enemy we had was the Head Man of the mines. He hated us and we hated him. On one occasion a minor fall had trapped three or four prisoners, but he would not allow us to try and get them. Professionally he may have been right; I did not think he was. But what really annoyed us was the fact that he said they were only POWs and not worth bothering about. When the war ended this man paid the penalty for his action in his own mine. This is the only instance I know of cutting loose and stepping out of line.

'About early August, after one of our blasts, a faulty seam caused a slight fall. No one was injured, but on trying to clear the debris I crushed the tip of two fingers, and as a result I was transferred to the gardening party.'

Japanese women worked alongside the men in the Yoshikuma mines, and were usually hard at work by the time the camp working parties arrived. The POWs, who had very little clothing, worked in a thin piece of cloth (a *fandooshie*, or loin-cloth) which just managed to hide their genitals. The Japanese women worked completely in the nude, and it was hard, tough work, demanding continuous action and energy to move out the coal as it was dug at the face.

The women always finished work before the POWs so that they could be first in the communal baths. Others from different coal-mines in the vicinity also used these large communal concrete baths, and when the POWs finished work for the day and marched down to the baths they were met with shouts and screams from the Japanese women, who saw rushing towards them sweating, coal-covered men, naked and scrambling to rid themselves of the filth and coal clinging to their skeleton-like figures.

Meanwhile Allied bombing had increased and small, obviously carrier-based aircraft were seen flying over the area. 'Our morale was very high now, though the death rate even in this small camp was beginning to rise. I think most of us were nearing the end of our tether; our reserves of strength had dwindled; food, which was daily scarcer, had never been plentiful. Men were beginning just to lie down and die. The diseases of malnutrition were rife, and though hope was now keeping us going we were dreading another winter.

'We had constructed a form of air-raid shelter made of bamboo reinforced with earth, and on several nights we were herded into this death trap with machine-guns covering each exit. I think the idea was to keep us under control rather than to protect us. Early in

August we were told that the Allies had started to bomb with a great fire-bomb which burnt everything for miles, and now we were told that during an air raid we had to cover ourselves completely in our blankets.

'A few days later, busy "chunkling" with the gardening party, I saw lots of large bombers overhead and heading eastward. We all cheered like hell, while the guards got very excited and threatened us with all sorts of punishments if we didn't take cover. We still stayed cheering and took no notice. Suddenly, away to the west, a parachute appeared, and then a second one. The air was very clear. Someone said, "Some poor bastard has had it." Shortly after, a tremendous flash lit the sky, and then a great column of smoke went up. The explosion was several seconds after the flash, and shook us even where we were. The Nips went crazy and set about us with rifle butts and flats of bayonets as we cheered like mad, thinking it must be some great ammunition dump. We couldn't care less; we sensed in that huge mushroom cloud over Nagasaki that something big was happening. Then we were all driven back into the camp.'

The next day they were all back in the mine, lame or arms in slings or not. Rumours were rife, and within a few days the working parties stopped. The Camp Committee called on the Nip Commandant, to be told that the Son of Heaven had called off the war to spare us all. Next day the Committee took over the camp and put the Nips to work.

Orders from MacArthur's headquarters were received over the wireless; the prisoners painted POW on the camp roofs and made sure that everyone stayed put. Discipline was good, although the POWs were naturally concerned at the lapse of time between the end of the war and any real sign of repatriation. After five weeks an Australian recovery team arrived, and within twenty hours the ex-POWs marched out with home-made colours flying and heads high. Even then tragedy was not far away as two members of the Loyal Regiment died that same day.

'We took the train to Nagasaki, now a frightening place. Less than four months before we had seen it a booming war town; now it was acres of nothing, the huge girders of the Mitsubishi factories lying like so many burnt matches in an ashtray. Devastation everywhere, and with one bomb. It frightened all of us.

'There were huge marquees on the devastated jetty. Hot water was available, and we could step out of our lice-ridden prison clothes and, after a hot shower, into clean underwear, G.I. shirt, and trousers. There were the delights of pyjamas, toilet gear, candy, tobacco, malted drinks. Was this not very heaven?'

Chapter 24

NO FLOWERS
FROM NIPPON

As TIME went on, every so often men would be taken from the camp and sent, as I found later, to a large camp in Java where thousands of prisoners were being massed. Whenever this happened, sixty-five of my key men and myself were always taken apart from the rest of the men in the camp, and slowly we realized that we were doomed to remain at Macassar. We began to wonder why this was, until it became obvious, when it was known that the Nips were massing POWs in Java, that we were regarded as the little nucleus to remain in those islands like the Celebes where the Nips did not want to have a lot of POWs to contend with and perhaps turn on them, particularly as the garrisons were not very large.

We also found later that the Nips had tunnelled into a big hill where they had made a massive workshop. We had been uprooting one or two of our machines, which had been taken away at night; now we knew where they had gone and also why we had really been retained. We were to be boarded in this mountain workshop until the end of the war.

'Buzzes' were coming thick and fast into the camp now. The Americans had a large fleet in the Pacific. Thousands of tons of bombs had been dropped on Germany. There were stories of great battles and of sweeping American victories. Our planes were, in fact, beginning to raid Celebes more frequently, and there was a strange eagerness on the part of the Nips to run us all back to camp when the air-raid warning sounded. We wondered whether Celebes was on the list of sweeping victories and invasions. But if it was, what would the Nips do with us? Shut us in the trench-cum-shelter that we were pushed into?

News eventually filtered through that the Allies had landed in Borneo, at a place called Balikpapan. This was a great disappointment, as we realised that our island was one that the Allies were leap-frogging in the rapid advance.

Then about fifty new arrivals turned up at our camp, a group of tired, travel-stained soldiers under the command of an RGA Major. They had come overland on their way to Java, placing their large number of sick and dying in specially dug pits on the way, leaving a little rice, while the fitter men continued through the jungle and swamp to Macassar, being pushed on by their Jap guards.

Work went on as usual, but the 'buzzes' became more numerous, until one evening when we returned to camp we heard the story told by two of our chaps who worked on repairs to bicycles at Nip headquarters. The guard in charge of them, one who had been with Yoshida, usually met them each morning with a dozen or so bicycles to repair. Imagine their surprise when they found no bicycles but hot coffee and local cakes. The Nip sweetened their coffee, asked them to sit down while he waited on them. He asked them if they thought he was a kind man, and asked that if the situation be reversed they would remember that and treat him kindly too. He would not dream of their doing any work that day.

Next day we went on our usual working parties, carrying out the same routine, without any significant change, until later in the morning I was asked to go to the office, where the Nip officer told me to stop all men working. I was to get brushes and whisks to clean the workshops 'Besar clean'—Admiral's clean-up.

When I shouted to everyone to stop work I was bombarded with questions, but I quietened the chaps down by telling them simply that work was to stop, even on the officer's motor-cycle. The workshop was to be made clean and tidy, but apart from that I knew nothing more than that 'something was in the air'. Later we were told to return to camp and take our rice back with us.

When the workshop had been tidied I mustered the men and reported to the Nip Chief. As the men fell in in the usual fives to be counted and reported, we all looked for some sign from the Nip. As I saluted he replied smartly, gave me a peculiar look, half grin, half apologetic, and as I marched my men past him on what was to be our last time out through the compound gate he saluted time and time again, bowing as my party passed him. The lads, their spirits rising, shouted all kinds of comments from 'Goodbye' to unprintable epithets.

Nothing was yet certain. As we marched down the hot, steaming lane back to camp we passed the Dutch Camp Commandant on his way to the Nip CO's house. As we eyes-righted him innumerable questions were called from the ranks, but he walked on in silence, his head down as usual. A little while after, we met the British Senior Officer, the Gunner, Mr White, dressed in his 'number ones'. All he could say was that something was up, but he didn't know what. So on tenderhooks we arrived at the camp gates, where I had the nigh-impossible task of keeping the party reasonably subdued. I did not want any trouble at that tricky moment.

Inside the camp there was much speculation. One story was that the war was over, another that we were all to be shifted in a rush. Fresh guards had apparently arrived that morning, doubling the numbers and giving rise to the cheerful rumour that we were all to be shot up.

We ate our dinner rice, but still no news. Then came the order that all prisoners were to get into the new white shorts and shirts that had been supplied to everyone a few months before. This brought the 'buzz' that a top Nip Admiral was to visit us, or that at last we were to see someone from the Red Cross. No letters or parcels had ever reached us, and the Red Cross as far as we were concerned had never even heard of us. It looked as if we were to be dolled up to show them how well the Nips had looked after us.

'Fall in at the double' was sounded off, followed by the quickest muster ever. Full of hope mixed with fear, we fell in and waited, until through the main gates of the camp came all the guards in full battle order, together with another fifty Nips armed to the teeth. This formidable party, steel-helmeted and with fixed bayonets, halted and turned to face us. Trumpets blared, guards saluted, and we stood grimly to attention as the Nip Commandant approached, followed by Yoshida and our Dutch Camp Commandant. Behind them came the Senior British American and Dutch officers in the camp.

We waited apprehensively as the Dutch Commandant climbed on

to the platform and began to speak in Dutch. We listened without comprehending, but as he spoke we began to sense his meaning, confirmed for us by Dutchmen in the ranks who muttered, 'The war is over. The war is over.' Then the English major, who had only recently joined us, told us tersely that there was a three-day armistice, that the war was not yet over, but that we would not go to work. We were to avoid any fuss or trouble; the guards were still in charge and would shoot if anyone did anything silly.

I clutched the hand of my friend Frank Clements, who stood by me. As I looked at him out of the corner of my wet eye I could see his eyes too were wet. After a moment of silence we were dismissed, and pandemonium broke loose; tears, shouts, screams, kissing and handshaking. I walked away by myself behind the huts, staggered by the news. I do not think I really believed it. As I passed the Dutch huts I went in to find the Dutchman who had been with me on that factory working party, a man whom I had grown to love and respect. We spoke animatedly in Dutch, Malay, and broken English. We were so very happy.

Then I went over to the hut where my sick pal Don Geake was lying. A short while before there had been three of us lying there weak and helpless, and even now Don had been too ill to attend the muster. Tubby had died two weeks before, but there was a good chance that Don would survive with medicine and good food. So it proved, and today he is fit and well, still serving as an officer in the Royal Navy.

The three-day armistice passed; on 14 August 1945, Japan accepted the ultimatum, hastened by the dropping of the atomic bombs on Hiroshima and Nagasaki. Our next move was to get away from Coconut Grove, with its mosquitoes and memories of death, so groups of us went 'house-hunting', but the places the Japs offered us were not suitable, and finally we settled on the large Dutch hospital. The Nips protested that we could not go there because the hospital housed their sick and wounded; but this was no time for such considerations. We told them to get out as we were going in the next day.

We moved in, as planned, with our 'property': bundles of rubbish and rags slung on bamboo poles or in the handcart pushed by a small party of men. I remember one of the Nip guards, who had always been a tough guy with the poko stick, trying to make one of our chaps get away from a wheelbarrow he was taking. Weak and emaciated as the POW was, he pushed the Nip away and told him to go to hell. For the first time we saw a Nip give way.

It was a long trek to the hospital; we had to rest frequently on the way. But if it had been necessary we would have walked all the way home to England.

In the hospital we found beds and mattresses and pillows. We laid our mattresses on the floor, and several of us fixed up our beds on the verandah; it was bliss to lounge around in comfort without being disturbed or molested. There were still dangers: the Nips were still the only people who were armed, and they had the ticklish job of protecting us from another source of trouble, the rising Indonesian nationalist feeling which was aimed at the ejection of the Dutch from the islands of the East Indies. As we were now very brown skinned and were dressed in green Dutch uniforms, we were likely to be mistaken for the 'enemy' by these elements of the nationalist movement.

Soon Allied aircraft came in with supplies, but not to land on the local airfield which we had made. There were hundreds of craters on the runway as a result of two recent Allied raids, and we had to clear an open space at the rear of the hospital so that supplies could be dropped by parachute. The planes managed to do this from a surprisingly great height, from where it was difficult for us to distinguish their markings. I remember two American lads boasting, 'There go our boys! You Limeys take a good look at the American planes.' We just stood around waiting thankfully for the parcels to fall, but were more than amused to read the initials on the first pack to fall: RAAF!

The Aussies dropped us a large number of rubber jungle boots, soft and with real laces, together with green jungle trousers and comfortable, thin green shirts. We eagerly shed our old clothes and put on some self-respect with these new uniforms. Then the food and stores began to flow freely, supplies that were vital for the large number of us now filling the hospital. The very ill had been placed in blocks which remained the hospital proper; the rest of the wards were used for the other POWs still under orders not to leave, but being fed now with cooked rice and greens with the usual bamboo shoots.

There was other food. Around the hospital ran a small wall, and to this each day came Indonesians from everywhere with fruit, bananas, and papaya, eggs by the thousand, and live chickens and geese. Over the wall in return went mattresses or beds. One chap even had a horse in the hospital grounds—swapped for a mattress! Now he could enjoy riding the horse; a few weeks earlier and he would have enjoyed eating it.

We had our personal 'fireplaces' where cooking or 'brewing up' went on day and night. We were eating a dozen eggs at one frying, chicken was permanently on the menu, and for days this perpetual eating went on. There we lay, a rough-looking lot, stretched out on our mattresses on the floor, with piles of fruit and eggs, and with clucking chickens attached to nearby beds. The Japanese guards came round each day, smiling, friendly, ingratiating, offering us cigarettes and sweets in exchange for our filthy, ragged clothes. We took the sweets and cigarettes, but we held on to the rags.

Suddenly we were no longer quite so hungry. Life was making no serious demands upon us, so instead of eating the chickens we set them to fight and laid odds on them as they battled. A dozen eggs against a bunch of bananas; a packet of cigarettes against a bottle of frying oil.

Then we managed to obtain an old short-wave radio-set which we quickly repaired and used for daily transmissions, telling whoever would listen about our plight, our nationality, and our longing to be taken away from the accursed island. It all seemed such an anti-climax, and our hopes began to die as the weeks passed without anyone coming to relieve us.

One day our message was picked up by a RAF station at Balikpapan, the oil refinery in Borneo, and soon a plane was overhead asking us what chance there was of landing.

It had taken us a long time to build the air-strip at Marros. A rough, unofficered working party, composed entirely of British, had made the Marros road and then built the runway—3430 metres of macadam on rocks which had to be broken up by men working in their bare feet—with its accompanying control tower and buildings.

To supplement this work a grass runway was made alongside the macadam-strip, but this was never used by the Nips.

Allied bombing had left well over two hundred craters on the surface of that landing-ground, but the RAF pilot asked what chance there was of filling in the craters on the grass runway. This could obviously be done, but the only workers up at Marros were about a thousand Indonesian coolies, the working party of forced labour brought over from Java by the Nips. Now the war was over, and they refused to do anything for the Nips.

It was obvious that the Nips would not be able to get that large labour force into action; but four British *mandoers*, ERA 'Chilley' David Chandler, Bernard Preece, a sergeant of the Royal Marines, SPO Archie Mort, and another man went up to Marros with promises of returning the unhappy Indonesians to their homes in Java as soon as the craters were filled in.

Within a matter of days the craters were filled in and a Mitchell bomber landed, from which stepped a tough-looking Australian major. He looked a little suspiciously at the four dark, thin figures approaching him, and showed his surprise when they addressed him in English. When the four lads told him there were more like them at Macassar he asked to be taken down to the camp.

Taffy and the Australian major went across to the Japanese CO's house at Marros and called him out, saying they wanted a car. The Nip officer took them to the garage and pointed to the old crate just inside, but the two men had their eyes on the other vehicle—a De Sota limousine, that was concealed in the shadows farther back. 'We'll take that.'

On arrival at Macassar the major saw the Nip admiral and informed him in no uncertain terms that he held him responsible for the safety of all the prisoners in the camp until they were relieved. He would also hold the Admiral responsible for the good behaviour of the Indonesian population in the town. Arms were to be stockpiled and only those Nips who were on guard duty were to be armed.

His duty done, the major returned to his plane, and the four *mandoers* returned to Macassar, each smoking two cigarettes at once. There were planes with food to follow.

It was as well that the Nip guards were armed. Relations with the Indonesians were not easy. Although the armistice had been signed in Japan, the situation was not so simple in Celebes. For years the Indonesian Nationalist Party had been agitating for home rule. Now the war was over, but, with the Dutch owners still in captivity, the nationalists began to stir. There had not been so much as a squeak from them during the Japanese occupation, but now there were angry meetings and demonstrations, and one night they arrived at the hospital, lighting their way through the night with burning torches. It seemed that we would end up by being murdered by the Indonesians.

The Nips had quickly accepted their responsibilities. Their armed guards massed along the roads being taken by the nationalists, and they stood their ground. The Indonesians shouted abuse, but at bayonet point, and facing loaded rifles, they gradually retreated, and soon their shouts and cries died away.

Things now began to move. Event followed event, sometimes in bewildering confusion. Lieutenant-Commander Cooper, First Lieutenant of *Exeter*, had been released from the camp in Java, and arrived back in Macassar to see how the crew were and to make sure they were taken as quickly as possible back to England.

There was also the formal surrender. A small Allied party was sent by General Sir Thomas Blamey, who was the senior officer responsible for accepting the Japanese surrender in that part of the Dutch East Indies (see Appendix 6, p. 221). It was an Australian party, arriving in three small ships, one a captured Italian sloop, and we watched with a strange anxiety as these vessels drew closer to the shore. In preparation for the surrender ceremony the Japanese had rigged a large marquee on the dockside, plentifully stocked with refreshments.

As the Allied ships came alongside, the waiting Japanese were lined up, at their head the Japanese admiral (who, incidentally, had not needed that massive shelter we had built for him). He stood, impassive but a little ridiculous, in his white shorts and vest of thick cloth, behind him his staff officers dressed to the nines. To their right, twenty weak, emaciated POWs waited — a tattered guard of honour.

We could hear the orders being sounded aboard the sloop, and at the bugle-call there was an echoing command of *'Kioski!'* from the

Japanese officer, at which the assembled Japanese and the band of prisoners jumped briskly to attention.

The Australian officer walked slowly down the gangway, preceded by determined Australian guards with rifles at the ready, coolly surveying the Japanese onlookers. The Japanese admiral moved forward, saluted, bowed, and took from his aide a bunch of flowers which he offered to the Australian.

The officer ignored the Admiral and the reception party, heading instead for the wizened POWs, shaking hands with each member of that special guard. With that clasp of the hand we returned to our own world and our self-respect. To this day I can see the look of disdain on the Australian officer's face as he tossed the proffered bunch of flowers into the Java Sea.

POSTSCRIPT

THE MEN OF *Exeter* came home; but, as with all those men returning from Far Eastern camps, their repatriation was not easy. Sick in mind and body, these emaciated figures had to be transported almost around the earth to their homes in Britain. Many of them came home only in body and uniform; their minds are to this day locked in the horrors of Macassar.

Pellagra, dysentery, malnutrition, malaria, Weil's disease, tropical ulcers, foot rot and heat: couple these with loneliness and desperation, and what are the cures? Brutality experienced on all sides; seeing shipmates die; unclothed, unwanted and unclassified; for disposal only. No news, letters or parcels. What was to be done with men who had suffered in such manner?

A struggle for rehabilitation began at Queen Mary's Hospital, Roehampton, and continues to this day. Thousands of ex-POWs were to pass along the 'Long Corridor' at the hospital and enter once more the tight community that the camp had engendered. They knew now the extent to which dedication could be taken, and the devotion of Sister O'Hara and Colonel Caplan, the doctor who has given his life to this service, is a story which deserves its own separate telling. For many of *Exeter*'s ship's company the miracle of recovery was achieved; for some the battle was already lost.

HMS *Exeter* did not return. She lies at the bottom of the Java Sea, victim finally of the superior odds which she and that earlier vessel of her name had been called upon to face. The battle honours of the Plate and the Java Sea were but the culmination of a tradition established on 17 February 1782, off the coast of India, when *Exeter*, one of nine large ships-of-war in Sir Edward Hughes's fleet, was in action against French men-of-war under the French Commodore Suffren.

Exeter was at the heel of the line and came under heavy fire from the French ships, until she was virtually a wreck. At this hopeless stage the Master came to Commodore King to ask him what to do with the ship as two of the enemy were bearing down on her. This dilemma, which was to be mirrored in later actions, was no problem to the Commodore, and the reply was quick and laconic:

'There is nothing to be done but to fight her till she sinks.'

APPENDIX 1

The Four Days in Montevideo

After the Battle of the Plate *Graf Spee* entered the harbour at Montevideo at 10.50 P.M. on Wednesday, 13 December. On Monday, 18 December, she was blown up in the estuary of the Plate. The story of the four intervening days is told in the following abstract of a description by SIR EUGEN MILLINGTON-DRAKE, KCMG, then British Minister at Montevideo.

First day (14th December)
My instructions were to demand that the *Graf Spee* should not be allowed to stay more than the twenty-four hours allowed by International Law (though we would not have objected to forty-eight hours, the compassionate concession previously given to certain British warships visiting Montevideo since the outbreak of war). According to International Law, the *Graf Spee* could only claim an extension of that time if it were necessary for repairs to make her *seaworthy* as distinct from any other repairs or refitting. That she was seaworthy was shown by the fact that she had travelled at full speed for over twelve hours since the major battle in the morning.

Captain Langsdorff had asked for fifteen days for repairs, and though he no doubt believed that he could achieve this in a *shorter* time, he probably wished to have a margin within which to break out at a time of his own choosing, without it necessarily being known to the blockading ships; nevertheless it is extraordinary that he did not seem to realize that even within one week at the most, overwhelming allied forces would be waiting for him outside.

Two Uruguayan officers went on board at seven o'clock in the evening and remained an hour to be shown all the damage. They were not allowed below the armoured deck, as Captain Langsdorff told them that everything below it was secret, and in any case no shell had pierced it. The chief damage affecting seaworthiness directly or indirectly was a big shell-hole in the bows on the port side sufficiently near the waterline to make her unseaworthy, in Langsdorff's opinion, in the North Atlantic in the month of January, when he hoped to get through and back to Germany, taking advantage of the moonless nights. Indirectly, but of much importance, the auxiliary boiler operating both the apparatus for making fresh water and the one for the oil purifying plant was much damaged. Apart from this there was considerable damage to fighting equipment large and small, but of course such damage could not be taken into consideration.

The look-out from the top of that great control tower of the *Graf Spee* reported that he had observed a battleship on the horizon. At the very most it could only have been one of the light cruisers, as the much bigger *Cumberland* did not arrive until that evening. But the officer in question was the gunnery officer of the ship, Commander Ascher, a very able staff officer who was eventually to be a gunnery officer in the *Bismarck* and to go down with her. Therefore Captain Langsdorff entirely believed his report, the more so in that he had told his departing prisoner, Captain Dove, that very morning that the light cruisers would never have made that desperate attack on him 'like destroyers' had they not been relying on big units somewhere at hand. So that what I have called 'The Charge of the Light Brigade' (that is, of the light cruisers) had been not only magnificent but had served an important warlike purpose. Nevertheless, that evening Captain Langsdorff retained the optimism for which he was well known in a meeting with his officers; but we know that they did not share it.

Second day (15th December)
I received new and quite different instructions from the Foreign Office, supported by an urgent code signal from the Commodore out in the Plate, conveyed to the Montevideo wireless station by the Falklands. They were that I was to do anything I could to retain the *Graf Spee* in Montevideo till the following Tuesday when the two big units of the British Fleet would arrive off the Plate. The only

open way to do this was by means of a rule of International Law that in wartime if a merchantman of one belligerent and a warship of another are together in a neutral harbour, and the merchantman sails, then the warship must not follow till twenty-four hours later— a sort of cat and mouse rule to ensure that there should be no scrap just in front of the neutral port. We therefore arranged that a British merchantman, the *Ashworth*, should sail at 6 P.M., and I presented a note to Dr Guani, the Uruguayan Minister of Foreign Affairs, to this effect, pointing out that *Graf Spee* could not go out until twenty-four hours later.

Dr Guani read the note with a puzzled expression, and then said with a somewhat sarcastic smile: 'Surely this is a great change from your note of yesterday?' To which I replied: 'Only a change of tactics, Señor Ministro.' Frankly neither I nor my Naval Attaché thought that it would stop the *Graf Spee* if she really wanted to go out, but fortunately Captain Langsdorff was far from wanting to go out.

That morning he attended the burial in the Protestant cemetery of his thirty-seven dead, and when he returned to his ship he received two bad bits of news—that Commander Ascher had observed on the horizon another big British unit, no less than an aircraft carrier. (It is only fair to say here that when I said in a lecture at Plymouth that this further error by such an expert was difficult for a layman like myself to understand, the C.-in-C., Sir Richard Onslow, told me that I had been 'a bit hard on that Gunnery Officer', as he himself in comparable circumstances had made the same mistake of thinking he had actually seen a warship that he was half expecting to see.) The other news was that the Uruguayan Government had decreed, in accordance with the report of the two Uruguayan naval officers, that seventy-two hours would be sufficient to make the ship sea-worthy and that this time would count from the return to shore of the said officers at eight o'clock the previous evening. In other words the deadline for *Graf Spee* to leave would be eight o'clock on the Sunday evening.

If only one of those supposed major units had actually been there, then *Graf Spee* was doomed; therefore, that evening Langsdorff reported to Berlin that there could be no question of a break-out to the Atlantic, but that he would endeavour to break out *up* the estuary towards Buenos Aires, if with the ammunition remaining he could do any appreciable damage to the enemy. These were the operative words, for he had only 186 shells for his six big guns which would be enough for an action of some forty minutes. Failing this he requested instructions as to whether he should allow the ship to be interned, or should scuttle her in the shallow water of the Plate, after destroying all equipment.

Meanwhile repairs were going on feverishly on board and we have evidence that the crew, which had entire confidence in their beloved captain, were doing this work with remarkable efficiency and indeed enthusiasm.

Third day (16th December)
The courageous decision of the Uruguayan Government had astonished the world. Now, in the spirit of their enthusiasm for soccer, the population, knowing that *Graf Spee* was in the harbour but would have to go out before evening to meet the three British cruisers waiting outside, began to regard the expected encounter somewhat in the nature of a Cup Final, and all day trains from the provinces brought in crowds to the capital.

Meanwhile we had decided to sail another merchantman, the *Dunster Grange*, at 6 P.M. so that the *Graf Spee* could only leave after 6 P.M. the next day, Sunday, and before 8 P.M. when the seventy-two-hour stay expired. When I handed Dr Guani this note, at first he smiled and then suddenly got serious and said to me, rather like talking to a naughty schoolboy, 'Now, don't you sail another and give the *Graf Spee* an excuse for staying on because we want to get rid of this unwelcome visitor as soon as possible.'

At about one o'clock Captain Langsdorff received the reply from Berlin approving his endeavour to break out up the estuary towards Buenos Aires if he could do so with any prospect of success. Alternatively he was under no circumstances to allow the ship to be interned but she was to be scuttled after a very thorough destruction of all equipment. Meanwhile every effort was to be made to obtain a prolongation of the stay in Montevideo. However, in the late afternoon Captain Langsdorff had practically decided to give up the break-out, mainly for the reason that his ship drew 22 feet while the British cruisers drew only 16–17, and that as the water intake for cooling his engines was at the very bottom of his ship, it was only too likely that mud would be drawn up and the engines would stop, when he would become a sitting-duck target for the cruisers.

We knew that most of the essential repairs had been completed by that evening, and were expecting the *Graf Spee* to break out *that* night. So did the Uruguayan authorities, who closed that port that evening for merchant shipping. So did Harwood, who had prepared a battle plan. Though he had ordered the third degree of readiness for that night, the men in the three cruisers volunteered to remain at action stations all night. There could be no finer example of the spirit of the British Navy.

When, about eight o'clock that evening, the German Minister had failed to obtain any prolongation of the time limit, Langsdorff quickly decided that he must scuttle his ship. He only awaited final confirmation from Berlin, and then he started to write a long letter of protest which was to be handed to the Uruguayan Government when his ship went out the next evening. He did not get back to his ship till the early hours, and to his senior officers waiting in the wardroom for his return he made the laconic and dramatic announcement '*Das Schiff wird gesprengt* [The ship will be blown up].' All repair work was immediately stopped, and elaborate instructions were given for the destruction of everything on board, which was then done in the early hours as unobtrusively as possible.

Fourth day (17th December)

In London the tension had risen, and Mr Churchill was writing to Mr Chamberlain in France, anxiously wondering what the *Graf Spee* would do. We now know that her crew were systematically destroying all her internal equipment and seeing to the placing of torpedoes and the remaining ammunition where their explosion would cause the most destruction. Captain Langsdorff had at first intended to set off the explosion himself on board and so go down with his ship, but he was dissuaded by the Gunnery Officer, who felt that the captain should personally conduct the crew to Buenos Aires.

It was not till one o'clock that a telegram came from Rio de Janeiro, from the German embassy there, saying that the battleship *Renown* and the aircraft carrier *Ark Royal* had just entered the harbour—just the two ships that Langsdorff believed had already been for two days off the Plate. But it was too late—the die had been cast.

In the night the German merchantman *Tacoma* had changed her position in the port to block as far as possible the view of *Graf Spee*, so that it was difficult to observe that in the course of the afternoon some 800 to 900 of the *Graf Spee* crew were transferred to the *Tacoma*, disappearing below with their personal belongings.

At 6.15, conforming with International Law, the *Graf Spee* weighed anchor and moved out slowly and majestically, followed at a distance by the *Tacoma* without clearance papers. Not, as we then thought, for a death or glory break-out with a suicide crew, but with a skeleton crew of forty-three to operate the ship to her last anchorage.

Crowds were watching from every conceivable vantage point, down by the many wharfs of the port, on the top of every building and on the slopes of the hill right up to the lighthouse, where the President of the Republic, General Baldomir, had gone with Dr Guani to observe what would happen. There was some disappointment in the crowd when the *Graf Spee*, arriving at the well-known point where streamers turn westwards to make for the channel to Buenos Aires, in fact took that course instead of turning eastward towards the mouth of the estuary, where the British cruisers were waiting. These were visible to me as small dots on the horizon, placed as I was on the top of the highest skyscraper in Montevideo.

Presently the *Graf Spee* hove to well beyond the three-mile limit and soon afterwards four launches could be seen leaving her. We had not noticed that her flag was lowered, but this was the signal to her officers and men on board the *Tacoma* that the fuses had been started to cause the explosion in twenty minutes.

The sun had almost set on the calm waters, when at 7.45 there rose a great flash skyward, followed by a vast mushroom-shaped cloud of smoke like the pictures of atomic explosions with which we have become familiar. For a few seconds there was no sound, the crowds hushed into absolute silence, while the sound of the explosion travelled to us like the thunder that comes after a particularly bright flash of lightning. Then followed several lesser explosions, and the ship was in a short while in flames from stem to stern.

Meanwhile the tugs from Buenos Aires had gone alongside the *Tacoma*, and the crew were climbing down several rope ladders into them, rather like the assault on a medieval fortress in reverse. Though the Uruguayan guard boats and port authorities at first tried to delay them the Government ordered that they should be allowed to go because they were obeying its decree by getting out.

The *Graf Spee* crew reached Buenos Aires next morning, and on 19 December the Argentine Government decreed that they be interned. In the evening Langsdorff made a last address to his men, saying that they must be content that they were in a friendly country where internment would not be a great hardship. Certain other things that he said were not understood till next morning. He dined with his officers and was apparently quite cheerful. He was last seen by his Flag Lieutenant writing in his spacious room in the officers' headquarters in the Naval Arsenal, where he was to find him dead next morning. He had shot himself alongside the battle flag of his ship.

His decision to blow up the ship, for which he took full responsibility in his last letter, was much criticized at the time but we can now appreciate that in deciding to do so he had courage in two respects: the moral courage to refrain from a spectacular breakout of the death-or-glory kind that might be expected of him in the circumstances, and physical courage because he decided that to do this with honour, and so saving the lives of his crew of over a thousand men, he must take his own life, not only in accordance with the tradition of the sea, but to prove to the world that his decision had not been from any lack of personal courage.

He had said, 'I prefer a thousand young men alive to a thousand dead heroes', and in fact 'he did better than he knew', because some forty-five out of fifty of his highly skilled officers would escape and get back to Germany, two of them to become successful submarine commanders and one of them to sink more Allied tonnage than had the *Graf Spee* during all her raider cruise.

APPENDIX 2

Units Involved in the Battle of the Java Sea, 27 February 1942

Allied Eastern Striking Force

CRUISERS

De Ruyter (Dutch); Flagship; 6450 tons; 7 x 5.9″ guns.
Java (Dutch); 6670 tons; 10 x 5.9″ guns.
Houston (American); 9050 tons; 9 x 8″ guns.
Exeter (British); 8390 tons; 6 x 8″ guns.
Perth (Australian); 7040 tons; 8 x 6″ guns.

DESTROYERS

Kortenaer (Dutch); 1310 tons; 4 x 4.7″ guns.
Witte de With (Dutch); 1316 tons; 4 x 4.7″ guns.
Electra (British); 1375 tons; 4 x 4.7″ guns.
Encounter (British); 1375 tons; 4 x 4.7″ guns.
Jupiter (British); 1690 tons; 6 x 4.7″ guns.
J. D. Edwards (American); 1190 tons; 4 x 4.7″ guns.
Alden (American); 1190 tons; 4 x 4.7″ guns.
Paul Jones (American); 1190 tons; 4 x 4.7″ guns.
Ford (American); 1190 tons; 4 x 4.7″ guns.

Japanese Force

CRUISERS

Nachi   (*Myoko* class); 13,380 tons; 10 x 7.87″ guns;
Haguro   (16 x 24″ torpedoes; 33¾ knots.

Naka   (*Sendai* class); 5195 tons; 7 x 5.5″ guns;
Jintsu   8 x 24 ″ torpedoes; 35¼ knots.

These older cruisers were acting as leaders of the destroyer flotillas.

DESTROYERS

4th Destroyer Flotilla of six ships.
2nd Destroyer Flotilla of eight ships.
The particular ships cannot be allocated with certainty, but were presumed to be:

Hatsutsuki   (*Akatsuki* class); 2090 tons; 6 x 5″ guns;
Ikazuchi   9 x 24″ torpedoes; 38 knots.
Inadzuma

Ooshio   (*Asashio* class); 1961 tons; 5 x 6″ guns;
Asashio   8 x 24″ torpedoes; 35 knots.
Asagumo

Yukikaze
Tokitskaze
Amatsukaze (*Kagero* class); 2033 tons; 6 x 5″ guns;
Kuroshio   8 x 24″ torpedoes; 35½ knots.
Oyashio
Natsushio
Hayashio

The name of one vessel is not accounted for.

APPENDIX 3

Japanese Torpedoes

Certain of the Japanese naval capabilities at the outbreak of hostilities were underestimated by the Allies. Among these was the torpedo which the Japanese had developed by 1933 to replace the orthodox, compressed-air torpedo. By the Second World War the Allies were still using the standard 21-inch torpedo or, for the Fleet Air Arm purposes, the old 18-inch which had to be dropped at a height of about 20 to 50 feet.

The Japanese had perfected a 24-inch, oxygen-propelled torpedo, the Type 93, which was known as the 'Long Lance' and was later developed into the Type 95, Mark II. It was 30 feet in length, with a total weight of 6000 lb, and between 1100 and 1210 lb of high explosive in the warhead. This compared favourably with the 800-lb warhead of the old standard 21-inch. The Japanese torpedo had a speed of 49 knots at 5760 yards and 36 knots at 43,500 yards.

When fitted to ships the torpedo mounting fully protected the personnel, and spare torpedoes were housed on a fore-and-aft line adjacent to the mountings. Reloading time was fifteen minutes.

Torpedoes of this design were used by the aircraft that attacked the *Repulse* and *Prince of Wales*, and they were reported to have been dropped from heights varying between 200 and 500 feet. There were no glider or tail attachments, and the torpedoes went straight to their targets, hitting at depths between 10 and 16 feet.

APPENDIX 4

Pamalla

Letter sent by Captain J. McCahon, Royal Marines, to the Japanese Senior Officer at Pamalla. This is the last of many such letters sent during the eight months at the camp:

To the Senior Officer
Imperial Japanese Navy   1st September, 1943

SIR,

I beg to repeat the state of health of the prisoners of war in this camp. Since the supply of quinine ceased 27th July the number of cases of malaria has rapidly increased, and will continue until we are all afflicted. 165 have suffered from it since we arrived. Of the 191 now in camp only 31 were not on the sick list during August. The medical state at 0900 hrs this morning was:

  1 desperate
  3 dangerous
  7 very serious
  14 serious
  33 are suffering from daily attacks (malaria)
  30 are unable to eat camp food and are now starving
  107 are now suffering from malaria.

As time goes by this will increase. Last week two men died through lack of quinine. Unless something is done immediately we must anticipate at least 10 deaths during the coming month and there is every possibility of the number being very much higher. I have asked repeatedly for supplies of fresh fruit, milk, eggs, coconut oil, chickens, pork, fresh meat of any kind and these have not been provided. Even papaya leaves, which have certain valuable qualities as a febrifuge or phoretic, have not been supplied recently. We have had none for the last three days. Salt, which is required for treatment of skin and cooking, is not supplied in sufficient quantities for the maintenance of health.

As it is beyond the resources available to remedy this state of affairs, I beg you very strongly to report your condition to the International Red Cross, Geneva, Switzerland, with a view to allowing them to deal with us or attend us here to save this useless and needless loss of life. At present nothing short of first-class medical facilities can save the lives of a number here, and the majority of the remainder will require a considerable period of convalescence and recuperation in a cold climate before they will be fit again. A number unfortunately will be semi-permanent invalids. Our value as combatants is now nil and will remain so for a considerable period. The International Red Cross has been founded to alleviate suffering and loss of life to people who unfortunately find themselves in our position. It was used by several nations during and after the 'Great War 1914–18', and failure to call its assistance now on our behalf would I feel be taking an extremely grave decision.

I have the honour to be, Sir,
Your obedient Servant,
J. McCahon,
Senior British Prisoner of War
Captain, R.M.

The following extract from the official report gives some of the cold facts about Pamalla:

On 15 January 1943 a draft of 200 (26 officers, 3 Merchant Navy officers and 171 ratings) were selected from the British prisoners of war at Macassar for a working party at Pamalla, which is situated on the west coast of the S.E. leg of Celebes, almost due west of Kendari, a few miles south of Kolacoa. The draft left Macassar on 16 January 1943, arriving at Pamalla the next day, and left Pamalla to return to Macassar 15 September 1943, arriving there on 16 September.

The state of the camp on return to Macassar was:-

16 dead.

13 dangerously ill. 2 of these died at Macassar in November from the effects of treatment suffered at Pamalla.

66 were unable to walk more than a short distance.

76 were able to walk not more than 2 miles without baggage.

28 were considered fit.

166 had suffered from malaria.

87 had had dysentery.

75% required treatment for ulcers.

APPENDIX 5

Nagasaki Camp: Morning Report of Room Chiefs

With some variations, the morning-report routine was as follows:

Koskei	Attention!
Dai go shitsu	Daily report, Room 5
Join	Number in room
Tiko	Number absent
Gengai	Number present
Bango	Number off (all hands around room to tally with *gengai*)
Tiko-wa	Absent are:
Myushitsu	In sick bay
Nyum	In hospital
Shushin	In bed
Suyi	Cooks
Eisseihai	Sick-berth attendants
Eiso	Number in cells
Gokei	Total of absentees

At the end of the above report made to the Sergeant of the guard, accompanied by the Orderly Officer in the background:

Ito maishi   *No particulars.*

The Nip parade would then pass on to the next room, and the room chief would then give the order, '*Yasume*. Stand at ease'. Then the room parade would fall out, but would have to wait until all rooms were inspected before the two cooks of the day could line up at the galley for the morning rations.

APPENDIX 6

PROCLAMATION
by
General[1] Sir Thomas Albert Blamey, GBE, KCB,
CMG, DSO, ED,
Commander-in-Chief Australian Military Forces

TO: *All the people* of BORNEO, and the remainder of the NETHERLANDS EAST INDIES EAST OF LOMBOK STRAITS, BRITISH NEW GUINEA, NEW BRITAIN, NEW IRELAND, SOLOMONS, BOUGAINVILLE and adjacent islands, OCEAN, NAURU and BISMARCK ISLANDS.

WHEREAS by an Instrument of Surrender, signed at TOKYO on the second day of September, 1945, by command and on behalf of the Emperor of Japan, The Japanese Government and the Japanese Imperial General Headquarters and accepted by the duly authorised Representatives of the United States, the Republic of China, the United Kingdom and the USSR, the *Unconditional* Surrender of the abovenamed Allied Powers of the Japanese Imperial General Headquarters and of all Japanese Armed Forces and all Armed Forces under Japanese control wheresoever situated, was proclaimed:

AND WHEREAS 'General Order No 1 – Naval and Military' has been issued by Japanese Imperial General Headquarters to all Commanders of the Japanese Armed Forces wheresoever situated order-

---

[1] Later Field Marshal. Died May 1951.

ing such Commanders to ensure that all Japanese Armed Forces and all Japanese Controlled Forces should immediately cease hostilities, lay down their arms, remain in their present locations and surrender unconditionally to Commanders acting on behalf of the above-mentioned Allied Powers:

AND WHEREAS I, General Sir Thomas Blamey, GBE, KCB, CMG, DSO, ED – Commander-in-Chief of the Australian Military Forces, have been duly designated to accept the surrender of all Japanese Armed Forces and all Japanese Controlled Forces in the abovemen-tioned Islands, Territories and Areas: TO YOU, all the above peoples, *and* especially to all *PRISONERS OF WAR* and other *citizens* of the *United Nations* now in the said *Islands, Territories* and *Areas* I send my greetings and congratulations upon your impending liberation by the Allied Military Forces.

I ORDER YOU TO OBEY *Proclamations, Orders* and *Instructions* issued by me or by the Australian Commander designated by me in respect of your Island, Territory or Area.

I FURTHER ORDER you to remain calm, to carry out peacefully your ordinary business or occupation, and to remain in your present place of abode there to await *Proclamations, Orders* and *Instructions* to be issued by me or my authorised Representatives.

Signed this second day of September 1945,

T. A. BLAMEY, General
Commander-in-Chief Australian Military Forces.

APPENDIX 7

HMS Exeter, 6th Battle Honour, Sunda Strait 1942

1 Arising from correspondence with the Chairman of the River Plate Veterans during 1980/81 the Admiralty Board has awarded the Battle Honour 'Sunda Strait 1942' to HMS *Exeter* commemorating her final action during the morning of 1 March 1942.

2 HMS *Exeter* sailed from Surabaja during the evening of 28 February 1942, in company with HMS *Encounter* and USS *Pope*. *Exeter* had recently been damaged in action, and with only two boilers in operation was capable of 16 knots, but while on passage during the night steam was raised in two more boilers, allowing her to work up to 23 knots. The force was ordered to proceed to Colombo via the Sunda Strait, along a track which was intended to avoid known enemy surface dispositions, and minimize the risk of aircraft detection. The three ships were sighted in the Java Sea and were intercepted at 0930 on 1 March, well to the east of the Sunda Strait where HMS *Perth* and USS *Houston* had encountered and been sunk by Japanese forces during the night. Four Japanese heavy cruisers opened fire at about 1000. The *Encounter* and *Pope* laid a smokescreen and the *Exeter*'s repair parties managed to flash up one more boiler and raise her speed to 26 knots, but her fire control system was defective, and the fall of shot had to be plotted and correction applied by Dumaresq. The Japanese, aided by air spotting, fired quickly and accurately but did not obtain a seriously damaging hit until approximately 1120, when an 8-inch shell struck the *Exeter*'s forward boiler room, starting a serious fire which forced the abandoning of the space. Steam power was soon lost and the ship was immobilized,

although all guns which could bear on the enemy continued to fire. At 1130, a Japanese destroyer torpedoed the cruiser from short range. A total of 14 torpedoes were fired and 20 minutes later the *Exeter* capsized and sank. The Captain, 44 officers and 607 ratings were rescued by the Japanese. HMS *Encounter* and the *Pope* were ordered to proceed independently when the *Exeter* was stopped, but both were later sunk, the British destroyer by gunfire, and the American by bombing and gunfire. *Encounter*'s ship's company were immediately rescued by the Japanese, the Commanding Officer, six officers and 143 ratings being picked up, but the *Pope* was lost some distance to the eastward, and the rescue was delayed by two or three days, when only a few survivors remained.

3 All survivors were taken to prison and not released until September 1945. No awards were made before 22 January 1946, when Captain O. L. Gordon MVO became a CB; the Cdr (E) became a member of the DSO; and three DSCs and eight DSMs were awarded; seventeen officers and ratings were also mentioned in despatches, one posthumously.

4 In recounting this action, the Admiralty Board has decided that the Battle Honour is justified in that this was 'an exceptional case where outstanding efforts were made against overwhelming odds'.

NOTE

A commemorative stained glass window featuring St Andrew exists in the Chapel of St Andrew within Exeter Cathedral. The dedication reads as follows:

> Dedicated in memory of the officers and men who gave their lives in the last two actions of HMS *Exeter* in the Java Sea on the 27th February and 1st March 1942 and those of her company who died in Captivity. And a thanks offering to Almighty God from those who surviving the dangers of the sea and the violence of the enemy by His Good Grace returned to their Native Lands.
>
> St Andrew. Cruiser Crest of HMS *Exeter*. Semper Fidelis.